THE BENEFICIARY

THE
Beneficiary

BRUCE ROBBINS

DUKE UNIVERSITY PRESS

DURHAM AND LONDON   2017

Printed in the United States of America on acid-free paper ∞
Designed by Heather Hensley
Typeset in Garamond Premier Pro by Copperline Books

Library of Congress Cataloging-in-Publication Data
Names: Robbins, Bruce, author.
Title: The beneficiary / Bruce Robbins.
Description: Durham : Duke University Press, 2017. |
Includes bibliographical references and index.
Identifiers: LCCN 2017025496 (print) | LCCN 2017042413 (ebook)
ISBN 9780822372172 (ebook)
ISBN 9780822370123 (hardcover : alk. paper)
ISBN 9780822370215 (pbk. : alk. paper)
Subjects: LCSH: Humanitarianism—Philosophy. | Social justice—
Philosophy. | Equality—Philosophy. Human rights—Philosophy. |
Cosmopolitanism—Philosophy.
Classification: LCC BJ1475.3 (ebook) | LCC BJ1475.3 .R633 2017 (print) |
DDC 172/.2—dc23
LC record available at https://lccn.loc.gov/2017025496

Cover art: COLOA Studio/Shutterstock.com

This book is dedicated to
the memory of my son,
Andreas Morris Robbins
(1989–2014).

There were no borders to his tenderness.

—

CONTENTS

ACKNOWLEDGMENTS

This is a short book, but it has taken a long time to write, and I have been the beneficiary of more friends and colleagues than I can possibly name here. For memorable moments of insight, interrogation, and incredulity, I am especially grateful to Amanda Anderson, Jonathan Arac, Paul Bove, Stefan Collini, Richard Dienst, Simon During, Ken Hirschkop, Ronald Judy, Dominick LaCapra, Tina Lupton, Edward Mendelson, David Palumbo-Liu, Martin Puchner, Nikil Saval, Helen Small, Gayatri Spivak, Nirvana Tanoukhi, Katie Trumpener, Jeffrey Williams, and Robert Young. No matter how hard the times, Laura Kipnis, John McClure, and Jim Livingston have just kept on offering me emotional and intellectual sustenance. The project has benefitted more than it deserves from the signature creativity and intellectual generosity of Bonnie Honig; her friends will know what I mean. Given the impediments and distractions, I'm not sure this book would exist at all without the unearthly kindness and psychologically astute editorship of Ken Wissoker. I have never been able to find adequate words for what I get from cohabiting with Elsa Stamatopoulou.

Portions of several chapters have appeared in substantially different form in the following publications:

"All of Us Without Exception: Sartre, Rancière, and the Cause of the Other," in *The Meanings of Rights*, ed. Costas Douzinas and Conor Gearty (Cambridge: Cambridge University Press, 2014).

"Barbarians at the Gates," *n+1*, November 2015 (online).

"George Orwell, Cosmopolitanism, and Global Justice" in Bruce Robbins and Paulo Lemos Horta, eds., *Cosmopolitanisms*. New York: New York University Press, 2017.

"The Financial Sector as a Zone of Moral Confusion," *Occasion* 7 (2014): 1–6, http://arcade.stanford.edu/occasion/financial-sector-zone -moral-confusion.

"Hope," *Political Concepts*, January 2016 (online).

"The Logic of the Beneficiary," *n+1* 24 (2016): 13–24.

"On the Rentier," *PMLA* 127:4 (October 2012): 905–11.

INTRODUCTION

In a secret State Department memo of 1948, George F. Kennan wrote, "We have about 50% of the world's wealth, but only 6.3% of its population. . . . In this situation, we cannot fail to be the object of envy and resentment. Our real task in the coming period is to devise a pattern of relationships which will permit us to maintain this position of disparity."[1] It is remarkable that Kennan's statement had to be kept secret and, when it was ultimately leaked, was considered a scandal. How did it come to look like something that could not be publicly admitted? One might have expected that Americans would *want* America to enjoy as high a proportion of the world's wealth as possible.

The anticipated awkwardness might be merely practical, as it seems to be for Kennan. If the rising tide that lifts all boats turns out to be a misleading figure for the global future, as it has been for the past, envy and resentment are to be expected. In that case, passengers on a well-provisioned tourist ship (to adapt the metaphor) might well worry about going ashore among the stranded and undernourished natives. But the awkwardness may also be moral. It may be that a sizeable demographic has come to assume that no country, including their own, deserves to be disproportionately richer than other countries. The idea of such a moral norm is more than a little mysterious—where would it possibly have come from?—and seriously counterintuitive, given how much howling xenophobia currently buffets the nations of Europe as well as (especially since the election of Donald Trump in November 2016) the American public sphere. And yet its existence seems the most plausible explanation of why people would be embarrassed, whether by the "position of disparity" itself or by Kennan's frank recommendation that the United States do all in its power to maintain it.

I take this embarrassment as suggesting that there is more cosmopolitanism out there than one might have suspected, and cosmopolitanism in a stronger than usual sense. Being nice to people who come from elsewhere is, well, nice, but it would mean more if we could look critically at our own nation from a viewpoint that includes other viewpoints, judging it by a standard that acknowledges that the well-being of the rest of humanity is a norm for us, including its economic well-being. The fact that so many people were embarrassed seems to imply that this more demanding sense of cosmopolitanism is not just an abstract ideal but an actual, substantial, perhaps even measurable influence on collective feeling.

If so, one would like to know what history could account for such a norm and, morally speaking, what sense we should make of it. These are the two questions I pose in what follows. I will not pursue all the promising answers, which include various forms of egalitarianism—revolutionary and reformist—and religious as well as secular modes of thought. I will start with statistics like Kennan's, though statistics don't answer these questions either. The suggestion that the United States or the "developed" world enjoys a disproportionate share of the world's resources has been made innumerable times in innumerable numerical permutations. "The average rates at which people consume resources like oil and metals, and produce wastes like plastic and greenhouse gases," Jared Diamond writes, "are about 32 times higher in North America, Western Europe, Japan and Australia than they are in the developing world. . . . With 10 times the population of Kenya, the United States consumes 320 times more resources than Kenya does."[2] The official statistics on world hunger are comparable. When you are informed that, unpleasant as they are, these numbers have been systematically low-balled, it hardly matters.[3] You get the point. But your eyes are likely to glaze over. The statistics don't shape themselves spontaneously into a narratable history or a practicable moral. Like a picture that needs a caption, they cry out for some sort of story or argument. It is an excellent thing that they circulate, and circulate widely, but it was not by such numerical means that people arrived at the cosmopolitan wisdom they possess, such as it is, and it is not by producing more such statistics that we will arrive at the greater wisdom we need so as to negotiate a more suitable place for ourselves in a global order that, morally speaking, does not seem very orderly.

This book does not set itself up as a source of reliable moral guidance—in fact it offers precious little moral guidance except perhaps for the idea that charity is no solution and that, if you do want to make yourself feel better by means of philanthropic giving, you would do well to supplement it with some reasoned form of political engagement. What the book tries to do is to tell a story that the numbers themselves cannot provide. If you are wondering how people in the prosperous West began to feel uncomfortable about their "position of disparity" vis-à-vis the less prosperous Rest, one obvious place to look is the history of humanitarianism. *The Beneficiary* proposes a revisionist view of that history. Rather than focusing on the disparity itself, with its appeal to empathy and abstract fairness but also, perhaps, to national or civilizational pride, the book focuses on a somewhat more rare-fied feeling: that your fate is *causally linked*, however obscurely, with the fates of distant and sometimes suffering others.[4] The idea that I am causally responsible for someone's suffering appeals to something in me that is stronger than fairness or empathy. Causal responsibility is of course more than Kennan himself acknowledges, and it is also more than humanitarianism can afford to coax out of its donor base. It dictates the telling of a different story, though traces of that story can be detected in some of humanitarianism's best-known texts.

Consider what may be the most discussed passage in what would soon co-alesce into a humanitarian canon: the Chinese earthquake in Adam Smith's *The Theory of Moral Sentiments*. After hearing news of the death of hundreds of thousands in a terrible earthquake in China, a European gentleman of refined feeling would no doubt feel sympathy and reflect profoundly but,

Smith notoriously predicted, would also sleep as soundly that night as if he had heard no news at all. The same person would not sleep a wink, however, if told he would lose his own little finger the next day.

Smith's example seems irrefutable. Which of us is not fundamentally self-interested or selfish—Smith's preferred term is not "selfishness" but "self-love"—in the sense Smith so memorably isolates? There is much and ever-increasing insomnia in the world, but the sufferings of distant others are probably not among its primary causes.

Against self-love, Smith and the emergent humanitarianism of the period appealed to a disinterested sense of common humanity. But a disinterested sense of common humanity was not the only force pushing in the other direction. Even during Smith's lifetime, when the news of an earthquake in China would have taken months to get to Europe and it was thus impossible to imagine anyone but fellow Chinese helping Chinese earthquake victims in distress, the Europeans Smith was addressing were not in fact disinterested spectators of suffering in China. They were causally connected to China. Smith was a tea drinker. His habit of drinking tea in Scotland did not initially depend on the coerced importation of opium by Britain into China, where the tea was grown, but during his lifetime the imports and the coercion were steadily growing. The social consequences of the opium dumping were comparable to an earthquake (Smith elsewhere used the analogy to describe British colonial policy in Asia). In this sense, Smith's supposedly impartial spectator could be considered an interested party. He was a beneficiary of the suffering he thought he was merely observing from afar.

This is a kind of perception that has become familiar, often in postcolonial settings. Take for example a brief passage in Jamaica Kincaid's novel *Lucy* in which Lucy is taken to see "an old mansion in ruins, formerly the home of a man who had made a great deal of money in the part of the world that I was from, in the sugar industry. I did not know this man, but if he hadn't been already dead I would have wished him so" (129). The sentence says that the house came from the profits of the sugar industry, that the profits of the sugar industry came from slavery, and that we must learn to see slavery, sometimes, when we look at houses, impolite as that may seem. One might think such moments were impossible until very recently. As I will show, they have a long and interesting history. The material connections lurking behind humanitarian reflections were not invisible to Adam Smith's eighteenth century. This was the era when abolitionism arose and began its slow march toward victory. Abolitionists made use of campaigns for the boycott of sugar from plantations that exploited slave labor. The iconic argument was that when you sweetened your tea, you were doing so with the blood of the slaves who cultivated the sugar cane. Thus every cup of tea became a carrier of potential political awareness. (The genre is of course still flourishing, and not just in campaigns against sweatshop labor: "The average American is responsible, through his/her greenhouse gas emissions, for the suffering and/or deaths of one or two future people.")[5] The century in which humanitarianism emerged also bristled with consciousness of how commodities newly enjoyed at home depended on coercion, violence, or mere unpleasantness elsewhere.[6] Interesting as the detached, impartial spectator may be, equally interesting, surely, is the fact that it was born along with its opposite number, the beneficiary. Both have a history, but only one of those histories is well known.

The word "beneficiary" smacks of the courtroom. It's not a word I would go out of my way to choose as a self-description. I offer it here anyway despite or perhaps because of its gracelessness, which helps us see ourselves, as we deserve, in an estranged and uncomfortable way. According to the dictionary, a beneficiary is one who derives advantage, as when one receives an inheritance from a will or compensation from an insurance policy. Older meanings involved holding land by feudal right, holding an ecclesiastical living, or simply receiving gifts from someone. Intriguingly, none of these meanings suggests that what you receive as a beneficiary is in fair exchange for services rendered or indeed recompenses you in any way for anything. The older senses thus catch a nuance of amorality that's just right: you are rewarded by an impersonal structure, legal or bureaucratic, that doesn't need or want to know anything about you except that you happen to be in the right place at the right time. What you might deserve as a person has nothing to do with it.

When I use the word, I am almost always referring to the subcategory of the *well-intentioned* beneficiary: the relatively privileged person in the metropolitan center who contemplates her or his unequal relations with persons at the less-prosperous periphery and feels or fears that in some way their fates are linked. The beneficiary is the main character of this book.

Still, I do not promise a colorful or psychologically realistic portrait. The term is really only a placeholder, a way of personalizing a viewpoint on the world that is neither quite humanitarian nor quite political and that needs a new and better name. I am not really interested in exploring the subjectivity of such a person—for example, feelings of "liberal guilt," though in such an argument the subject of guilt can hardly be avoided. To make the beneficiary a kind of character is really only a way of recognizing that in becoming connected the world has also become divided—divided between haves and have-nots—and that its much-acclaimed interconnectedness has brought with it causal and therefore moral relationships whose meanings and even existence remain puzzling and obscure.

Who is a beneficiary? You are, probably. If you had not benefitted from some ambitious higher education, it seems unlikely that you would be dipping into a book with so earnest and unpromising a title as this one. The education that has prepared you to read this paragraph may not guarantee much in terms of job opportunities, income, or security, but on the global scale (the scale of global economic statistics with which I began) it makes you one of the privileged. I will not ask any intrusive questions about where the money for your education came from; there are rules of politeness surrounding questions about income, which will be touched on below. But I will assume that from the perspective of the planet as a whole, such an education remains a scarce commodity and a rare privilege. You are both well intentioned and, I would guess, relatively well informed. You have heard, for example, about the suicides at Foxconn and perhaps also about the anti-suicide nets that were subsequently installed.[7] You were glad to find out that after the rash of suicides and suicide attempts, wages were raised, at least somewhat. But you have an uneasy sense that the silicon chips inside all your suddenly indispensable devices are still manufactured in circumstances so harsh and toxic that for the workers who make them, suicide does not seem an unreasonable option. As a person of goodwill, you are not pleased to find yourself stuck in this self-conscious dependency on bad working conditions. When you say ruefully, to yourself or to others, that our beautiful iPhones and iPads wouldn't exist without low-paid and overworked Chinese workers, you are speaking the discourse of the beneficiary.

In its pure form, the discourse of the beneficiary refers to something between a recognition of global economic injustice and a denunciation of it. It does so in a range of tonalities, not all of them political, some perhaps more rueful than indignant, that share two characteristics: (1) they are addressed to beneficiaries of that injustice, not to its victims, and (2) they are spoken by a fellow beneficiary. (Rule #1 can sometimes be broken; to my knowledge rule #2 cannot.) Each of these defining elements escapes from direct political speech as we usually recognize it and indeed seems to frustrate political engagement. Imagine trying to organize a political movement or demonstration by pointing out an injustice and then appealing not to its victims but to those who *benefit* from that injustice. (Well, yes, the environmental movement does something like that, but *injustice*—the fact that some suffer more from climate change and others suffer less—has never been its central theme.) The discourse of the beneficiary excludes an immense number of possible statements that here and now might seem politically more urgent and more valuable. And yet it would be hard to say that the statements it enables are politically valueless. It would not be wasted breath if, say, a northern European were to repeat in northern Europe what Greek prime minister Alexis Tsipras said shortly before his election in 2015: "The deficits of the South are at the same time the surpluses of the North."[8] This is an example of the discourse of the beneficiary. If enough people were to say such things, the result could be a lifting of austerity policies that have damaged and destroyed a statistically significant number of lives. It's not an uncommon way of speaking, but to my knowledge it has never been named or analyzed.

As I was finishing this book, I discovered that the word "beneficiary" had been picked up and reflected on very usefully by Robert Meister in his 2011 volume *After Evil: A Politics of Human Rights*.[9] In situations of transitional justice such as truth and reconciliation commissions, Meister argues, there has been too much focus on victims and perpetrators and not enough on so-called bystanders. Many of these bystanders would be more accurately described, he says, as "structural beneficiaries," that is, "those who received material and social advantage from the old regime and whose continuing well-being in the new order could not have withstood the victory of unreconciled victims" (26). That victory would have meant a redistribution of material rewards. Redistribution is the real issue; discussions of impunity and disclosure are largely distractions from it. His is of course not just an argument about tyrannies that have recently fallen, or for that matter about the past. It also raises the standard by which we judge the regimes we now live under: "No evil can be truly past as long as its beneficiaries continue to profit from it" (30).

Meister is brilliant on the beneficiary's psychology, with its peculiar modes of unconsciousness and self-reproach, and equally brilliant in pushing his argument toward innovative and practical outcomes—notably, a legal rephrasing of claims for "reparations" not in terms of what victims are owed but in terms of what beneficiaries ought to be obliged to pay. My argument has no comparably precise target or payoff. In order to take that extra step, it would have to jump forward to matters on which I lack the necessary expertise, such as transnational political movements and nongovernmental organizations. In general I am a supporter, but here I will have nothing of significance to add. To my mind, it remains a minor miracle that the great powers ever ceded any sovereignty at all to the United Nations. The fact that the UN system has thus far not acted more effectively can be interpreted, with some generosity, as a local historical phenomenon, compounded of the pressures of the Cold War and the neoliberal hegemony that took over when the Cold War ended. To me, it is not an eternal or essential truth about the system. A democratic reform of the Security Council, for example, would make that form of collective transnational agency suddenly look much more plausible. But to say this is only the very beginning of a long conversation about how a more just redistribution of global resources might one day be achieved. Don't expect to find much of that conversation here.

If it's true, as Meister suggests, that "no evil can be truly past as long as its beneficiaries continue to profit from it," then some people will want to have nothing to do with the subject. They will feel, and with some justification, that if people alive today are to be held responsible for terrible deeds putatively committed by their very distant ancestors, the chain of causality is being stretched too thin and the result will be purity crusades that have no natural endpoint and that will be less likely to remedy injustices than to commit further ones. If the discourse of the beneficiary were understood to recommend fresh inquiry into whether the Jews killed Christ or to demand reparations for the descendants of those sacrificed by the Incas, I too would avoid it.[10] Important as they are to the logic of the beneficiary, questions of ethics in relation to the passage of time will not be central to this book.[11]

My subject here is common sense about economic equality at the global scale. I am still a bit surprised that this common sense has developed far enough to allow Meister and me, among others, to take it for granted. But I think there are many of us who do, most of us not individual perpetrators of atrocity. If in a sense all of us are sinners, I'm not sure that "perpetrator" is the most useful category in which to put us. One does not have to be a saint to recognize the claims of global justice, or even to do something in response to those claims, when people make them, as they do, by means of strikes, suicides, protests, and appeals. The fact that a certain selfishness or self-love is unlikely to disappear any time soon does not mean that economic equality is just a pipe dream or that "abolishing a part of yourself" (George Orwell's phrase) cannot possibly be in the cards. Rather than associating the beneficiary with what Meister calls "evil," I see a certain potential in the beneficiary's pained perception of a causal relationship between her or his advantages and someone else's suffering. The category also helps me see things we have been missing in writers like Orwell, Jamaica Kincaid, Wallace Shawn, Jean-Paul Sartre, Virginia Woolf, John Berger, and Naomi Klein.

Orwell is my best example of the beneficiary and the figure to whom I return most frequently. From my perspective, Orwell is less a figure of the Cold War, as he has so often been presented, than a creatively cosmopolitan voice grappling with dilemmas of global economic justice that the Cold War obscured and that did not come into their own until the antisweatshop movement that followed it—until Orwell had found his worthiest inheritor, I would argue, in Naomi Klein. "Under the capitalist system," Orwell wrote pungently in 1937, "in order that England may live in comparative comfort, a hundred million Indians must live on the verge of starvation—an evil state of affairs, but you acquiesce in it every time you step into a taxi or eat a plate of strawberries and cream."[12] Orwell makes the relation between prosperity here and hunger there not just a shameful incongruity—the sort of thing that might figure in a humanitarian appeal—but an illustration of implacable economic causality. And he brings it home by talking about what we eat.

This is not to say that writing of this sort counts unambiguously as political speech. Political speech is usually seen as addressing the victims of an injustice, who might be expected to rise up against it, and exhorting them to take action. As I've said, the discourse of the beneficiary addresses itself primarily, perhaps even exclusively, to those who benefit from the injustice, who therefore might naturally be expected *not* to rise up against it. Yet it assumes that those who benefit from it are nonetheless capable of rising up against it—for example, by campaigns for ethical consumption that try to enlist prosperous First World consumers on behalf of much less prosperous Third World producers. Humanitarianism's seemingly apolitical disinterestedness therefore comes back as a factor that a transnational politics must somehow integrate into itself.

Perhaps I give people like Orwell and Klein, who point the way to that integration, too much credit. I certainly don't rush to complain, as I might, that nonbeneficiaries are being excluded or spoken over when they take up a subsidiary place in Orwell's or Klein's acts of imagination, imagination that comes "from above" as well as from afar. "From below" remains the going mantra. But the process of global democratization, I would maintain, cannot afford to do without the input of those who are empowered (that is, who *are* beneficiaries) and yet who also dissent from and even denounce the system that empowers them. This is what I called, in *Perpetual War: Cosmopolitanism from the Viewpoint of Violence* (2012), the volume to which this is a sequel, the paradox of empowered dissent. By focusing here on the beneficiary, I am picking up this paradox again, but this time trying to make sense of it as a peculiarly transnational phenomenon, characteristic of a discourse whose ambition is to cross the boundaries of the nation-state and find or invent a politics in a zone where many observers judge politics properly speaking to be nonexistent or even inconceivable.

Taking its cue from Larissa MacFarquhar's extraordinary book *Strangers Drowning* (2015), chapter 1, "The Starving Child," enters into an argument with the utilitarian philosopher Peter Singer, whose "effective altruism" inspired a number of MacFarquhar's do-gooders. Singer offers a child drowning in a shallow pond as a model of the moral obligation incumbent on the distant, well-fed observer of the hungry. His inspiration came from the 1971 famine in Bangladesh. Paying attention to the historical circumstances of that famine, I argue, points toward a better though also a more strenuous model of moral obligation than Singer's and thus also to an alternative to the humanitarian paradigm generally.

Chapter 2, "You Acquiesce In It: George Orwell on the System," reflects on Orwell's idea of what that system is and on the ethical consequences of inhabiting it. If he had not been so sure that we do inhabit a "system,"

Orwell might not have been able to moralize about the consequences that follow from our ways of life for distant others. Systems dilute individual responsibility, but they also create it. Are we sure we live in one, or on one? There is of course controversy over whether the structures, networks, or operations of power (the list of possible nouns might be extended) can be properly summed up in the synthetic or totalizing concept of system. Chapter 2 brings theorists of global inequality such as Immanuel Wallerstein and Branko Milanović into a debate which is also a history. If the beneficiary did not spring into sudden existence with the post–World War II phase of globalization or the austerity program imposed by European financial institutions on Greece, it's because system too, I argue, goes back further in time. George Eliot's investment in Indian railways helps illustrate the growing ethical force of knowingly inhabiting a global system. We are accustomed to thinking that gross simplifications between "us" and "them" must be denounced, as Edward Said denounced "Orientalism." But what if it is just such a gross simplification that the system imposes? In that case, would fine-grained detail and nuance really be the necessary correctives? The tormented use of the pronoun "you" that Orwell shares with Jamaica Kincaid is one piece of evidence, I suggest, that we remain trapped in an economic Orientalism. But it is also evidence of the perceptions this entrapment has the power to generate.

Chapter 3, "A Short History of Commodity Recognition," links Orwell's version of common sense to an unlikely source: global capitalism itself, as described in its radiant multinational sublimity by enthusiasts from Adam Smith to Thomas Friedman. How did capitalism's miraculous interconnectedness get associated with moral scandal? My answer begins with mercantilist misogyny, which blames women for luxurious consumption and, in a classic dialectical twist, thereby empowers them to link their everyday lives with political realities far away. The chapter takes the commodity recognition scene forward to Virginia Woolf and then back to Adam Smith, whose Chinese earthquake, under close inspection, comes to look like something other than the primal scene of humanitarianism it has been taken to be.

Chapter 4, "The Nation-State as Agent of Cosmopolitanism," adds a crucial stage to the historical argument of the previous chapter. In *Upward Mobility and the Common Good* (2007) I talked about the presuppositions that had to arise in order for the welfare state to come into being.[13] That argument turns out to be crucial here as well. You cannot see anything as wrong unless and until you can see or at least sense that it can be otherwise. The greatest obstacle to moral critique is the idea that, as Margaret Thatcher insisted, "there is no alternative." The welfare state proved that an alternative does exist. Jacques Rancière, in a critique of Sartre and French solidarity with Algerian national liberation, suggests that there is no genuine politics outside the territory of the nation-state. I answer with a double argument: on the one hand, yes, there can be politics outside national borders, but on the other hand, Rancière is right to play up the crucial role of the state. Only the rise of the modern nation-state and in particular the welfare state made it possible for a moral critique of global economic inequality to achieve anything like its present form. My example, developed at some length, comes from the period when Orwell worked for the British Ministry of Information during World War II.

Chapter 5, "Naomi Klein's Love Story," takes off from Larissa MacFarquhar's profile of Klein in the *New Yorker*, a piece in which she seems to defend Klein in advance against being dismissed as one of the do-gooders who would later appear in *Strangers Drowning*. Following Klein's career from *No Logo* (2000) to *This Changes Everything* (2015) and teasing out from it themes of disembodiment and desire, the chapter reflects on Klein's investment in infrastructure (which is not a consumer commodity) as well as the coincidence that leads her, like Orwell, to the historical moment of rationing during World War II. It argues that Klein's take on climate change points her readers toward what might be called, a bit provocatively, global justice for selfish people. And it concludes by showing how issues of economic redistribution on the global scale, literally unspeakable in terms of anyone's domestic political agenda, hide out under "other business" like remittances and refugees.

Chapter 6, "Life Will Win," takes up the idea, also borrowed from MacFarquhar, that what the application of ethics to global economic inequality is up against is finally nothing less than "life" itself. Imagining a dialogue between Naomi Klein and antiutilitarian philosophers such as Bernard Williams, especially those who appeal (as Williams does) to Nietzsche, I suggest that life is not on only one side of the issue. It gives me a certain satisfaction to draw toward the conclusion on such a flagrantly overambitious topic by discussing the meaning of life.

The conclusion, "You Can't Handle the Truth," reads moments from Aaron Sorkin's script for the film *A Few Good Men* and Ari Shavit's account of a 1948 massacre of Palestinians in *My Promised Land*, both of them about recognizing civilian debts to military violence, in order to distinguish the discourse of the beneficiary (as it is interpreted throughout the book) from the more familiar and intuitive scenario in which people feel themselves the beneficiaries of acts committed in a more or less distant past, as in discussions of "white privilege." The book ends by suggesting how various and intriguing the instances of beneficiary thinking are that I did not have space or energy to draw into this argument, and what my collection of unexpected global insights might mean for a more strenuous, more demanding, and more popular cosmopolitanism.

Readers will perhaps consider this whole enterprise a bit quixotic, given the surge of "America first" nationalism that helped propel Donald Trump into the White House. The bigger news of the election campaign, it seems to me, including Bernie Sanders's role in it, is the recognition on the part of large numbers of voters that globalization has not been good to them. In a sense, as the mainstream economists did not fail to point out, it *has* been good to them. If you compare their lives with those of workers on the shop floor of Bangladeshi shoe factories or Chinese chip makers, most Americans would have to count as beneficiaries of globalization. (No one is asking how all this looks to the Chinese and Bangladeshi workers.) But that is not how it feels. Globalization has come to feel obscurely unfair. And this feeling, now widespread in the metropolitan core, seems destined to devour the nationalism that is its current manifestation and to move on to the systemic relations of core and periphery that can make better sense of it.

Chapter 1

THE STARVING CHILD

After he read Singer's article, everything
Aaron bought, even the smallest, cheapest
thing, felt to him like food snatched from
someone dying. Nobody would buy a soda if
there was a starving child standing next to the
vending machine, he thought; well, for him
now there was always a starving child
standing next to the vending machine.

It seems worth noting that the starving child next to the vending machine,
whom I borrow from Larissa MacFarquhar's book *Strangers Drowning*, is
not an actual child. Aaron does not observe someone starving. The child
next to the vending machine is an idea he summons up from far away after
reading the philosopher Peter Singer.

I say this not to engage in philosophical quibbling but because some
readers will find Aaron's social vision a bit nearsighted. After all, he is not
noticing the homeless people around him, some of them hungry and some
of them children, who have been known to make use of vending machines.
Most Americans don't have to fantasize to conjure up malnutrition. Hunger
and poverty are very present realities in America. On this subject the figures
available from an NGO such as Feeding America are unambiguous. If he's in
search of economic injustice, Aaron doesn't have to look overseas or resort
to leaps of imagination. Observation will do.

Yet on second thought, Aaron is not getting things entirely wrong. Being so malnourished as to risk dying of it—starvation in the strict sense—is in fact rare in the United States. (It's rarer still in many other countries, not all of them "developed." A country can be much less prosperous than the United States but do much better than the United States in ensuring that everyone has at least a minimum to eat.) The charitable appeals circulated by Feeding America speak of hunger and of "food insecurity," but they don't brandish the thermonuclear term "starvation." Feeding America knows its business. Talk of starvation would be overkill.

So let us assume that Aaron is not mistaken about these two fundamental facts, whatever else he may or may not be in error about: there *is* starvation, and it *is* far away. At the scale of the planet, I will assume that is in fact the proper starting point. "We"—more on what I mean by "we" below—are not starving. Other people are. And if that's the way it is, then however bemused MacFarquhar may be by the do-gooder, she is correct not to dismiss do-gooders as merely naive or delusional or obnoxiously eager to flaunt their moral superiority. They may be condescending and (given how hard it is to live up to their principles) likely to be at least somewhat hypocritical, but, she concludes, "they are the best of us" (167–68).

Living every day with eyes fixed on global economic inequality, like Aaron, does not make for tranquility of mind. If it is a spiritual exercise, it is arguably overambitious, like sleeping in your coffin. It could be seen as a pathology or a curse. The sympathetic reader may therefore be tempted to show Aaron a way out of his unnecessary self-punishment. In a sense that's the point of this book, though before I get to that point I will have to give more time to Aaron and those like him than you may think they deserve.

You may want to inform him that images of starving children far away have been thrown in people's faces before, and not always with impeccable motives or crystal-clear logic. Boomers raised by parents who had been through the Great Depression were often told to eat everything on their plates not just because I said so but because children were starving in Africa or Asia or another place their parents probably didn't know much about. This didn't do the Africans or Asians any obvious good. Yes, the older generation probably did know something about not having enough to eat. (Historian James Vernon estimates that until recently parental references to the hungry 1930s were roughly equal in quantity to references to starvation in the Third World.)[1] It was perhaps safer for parents to channel their often-harrowing experiences through the imagined situation of distant foreigners. In any event, the causality implied by this dietary arm-twisting could only be sketchy. Its sketchiness is even more salient if you compare images of starvation then and now. Yesterday's starving child seemed to say that you should gobble up what you are lucky enough to have in front of you. The child next to the vending machine seems to say exactly the opposite: that you should walk away from the vending machine, consuming nothing at all. Suddenly starvation elsewhere is no longer a reason to consume but on the contrary an argument against consumerism. By itself, history informs us, the mere existence of starvation doesn't say anything very specific.

Will it help Aaron to know that representations of distant suffering have a history, as it happens, a history rich in leaps of the imagination like his own? Will he feel any less burdened by his relative good fortune? Right now, I imagine him saying, it is clear that something must and can be done. Compare the value to me of the flagrantly superfluous luxuries I am in the habit of purchasing, on the one hand, with the value to the hungry of the food, clothing, and shelter that might be purchased with the same money, on the other. Who would not feel inclined to change her or his habits? Who would not want to start transferring that money to those who really, really need it? That is the reasoning recommended by Peter Singer, the philosopher who inspired several of the figures MacFarquhar profiles, including Aaron, and whose example of a child drowning in a shallow pond gave MacFarquhar her title. Money spent on luxurious consumption, Singer argues, should be spent on meeting the basic needs of the distant poor. So forget the diet soda and give the money—give all the money you don't absolutely need—to a well-chosen charity. It is this argument that Aaron finds "irrefutable."[2]

Moral philosophers have certainly tried to refute it. "If all Americans or Europeans stopped buying consumer goods," Anthony Appiah responds in *Cosmopolitanism: Ethics in a World of Strangers*, "the result would almost certainly be a collapse of the global economy" (168). This would mean a huge drop in government revenue, hence also of the development assistance that Singer wants to expand. It would mean the even more severe impoverishment of those regions of the world whose poverty inspired Singer's thinking in the first place. The actual consequences of everyone adopting his principle don't seem foremost in Singer's mind. Like "Clean your plate!," his position isn't the obvious basis for a responsible platform or policy.

At the same time, this response feels a bit evasive. It stops short of thinking what might emerge from the ruins. It may or may not count as a refutation of Singer, but can it possibly refute Aaron? What Aaron is offering up is less a philosophical proposition than a feeling of outrage. Aaron can't stomach either the fact of global inequality or the confident imperviousness of our everyday moral values, based as they are on immediate local obligations, to the thought of more distant obligations. To say that his feelings don't immediately translate themselves into practical proposals is not to say that he is wrong to hold them and to keep looking for some form they might yet take. Commissioning a feasibility study seems the wrong way to go. These materials have to be held onto, lived with, allowed to simmer for as long as it takes. However awkwardly phrased, concern for global justice has to be given its due space.

One way to give it space is by reconsidering the history of humanitarianism. In a sense, Singer starts where humanitarianism starts. With you. How lucky you are not to be starving! This is of course not what humanitarianism tells its addressees, but it is how humanitarianism silently divides the world: some of you are fortunate and well fed, and those who are have responsibilities to those (over there) who are not. As Luc Boltanski writes in *Distant Suffering*, this is humanitarianism's primal scene. Here are the lucky; there are the unlucky. They have no kinship or solidarity in common. Nothing connects them except their common humanity. The paradigm is the Good Samaritan, he who helps a suffering stranger who shares with him neither a common interest nor a common identity.[3]

I will come back to this binary division of the world. It may seem unacceptable in the same way that any large generalization about individual human beings is unacceptable. It is of course also vulnerable to the more specific objection with which I began: what about the poor here at home? In *Austerity Ecology and the Collapse-Porn Addicts: A Defence of Growth, Progress, Industry, and Stuff*, Leigh Phillips raises just this point in a discussion of Naomi Klein. Klein's recent book on climate change, *This Changes Everything* (2015), circles back unexpectedly to the most influential theme of her early antisweatshop best seller *No Logo* (2000): the fact that affluent consumption in the West looks especially bad when seen from a global point of view. This makes Phillips crazy. "It was the assumption of equally grandiose levels of wealth in that little word 'we' in the demand that 'we all should consume less' that bothered me so much," Phillips comments. "The idea that 'we' in the West, every last one of us, were living a life of Riley, of carefree luxury and prosperity. I certainly didn't feel that I or many of my friends in similar situations were overconsuming at all" (8).[4] Others will no doubt be tempted to say the same, whether thinking of their own limited buying power or of the still less privileged around them. But Klein is not Peter Singer. She is not talking about "carefree luxury," or indeed about luxury at all as judged by American standards. Her standards are global ones. How poor are America's poor *relative to the poor in the rest of the world*? According to William MacAskill in *Doing Good Better: How Effective Altruism Can Help You Make a Difference*, someone living below the US poverty line, earning $11,000 per year, is in the top 15 percent of world income distribution. Someone earning $28,000 per year, the median individual income in the United States, is globally speaking in the top 5 percent. Someone earning $52,000 or more is in the top 1 percent (15–17).

In light of these figures, it seems defensible for Klein to use her "we." In fact it seems not merely defensible but obligatory. What would justify not remembering the divide between "us" and "them" at the global scale? This "us" and "them" is roughly analogous to what Edward Said denounces with his concept of Orientalism. In a surprising agreement with humanitarianism, it invites us to recognize what we may think of as an economic Orientalism— not as a matter of discourse but as a matter of fact. Much has been said against the actual effects and even the motives of humanitarianism. For me, however, humanitarianism's fiercely simplifying assumption of a structural inequality between global rich and global poor counts as a virtue. How could it not, given the general inability of everyday politics (including the politics of humanitarianism's critics) even to acknowledge, let alone do anything about, this planetary scandal?

As for other aspects of humanitarianism, I will have my own objections, many of them (predictably) political ones. But my chief objection can also be described as ethical. Ethically speaking, I will argue, the problem with humanitarianism is that it is not demanding enough.

This will sound counterintuitive. As practiced by a philosopher like Singer, humanitarianism is routinely described as overly demanding, even insanely so. Consider the essay that inspired Aaron to see a starving child next to every vending machine. Singer's "Famine, Affluence, and Morality" (1972) has been credited with initiating the movement called "effective altruism." It has even been set to music. But the essay is best known for the brief but unforgettable example with which it illustrates its fundamental principle: "If I am walking past a shallow pond and see a child drowning in it, I ought to wade in and pull the child out. This will mean getting my clothes muddy, but this is insignificant, while the death of the child would presumably be a very bad thing." This Good Samaritan–like scenario brings rescuer and rescued more or less face to face. It does not make unreasonable demands on the rescuer. That is one key to its seductiveness: the pond is shallow. The rescuer's life is not at risk. But Singer immediately extends the example so as to demand much, much more. Distance, he says, is irrelevant. Your obligations to distant and invisible children are the same as to the child in the shallow pond. And because the number of distant and invisible children who are in danger of death is effectively infinite, your obligations do not stop with the dry cleaning bill for one suit of muddy clothes. In fact, there is no obvious stopping place for those obligations until you have surrendered everything you possess beyond the bare minimum necessary to sustain your life.

Singer is surely right that if everyone in the prosperous countries acted upon this principle, "our world would be fundamentally changed" (107). (*How* it would be changed is another question.) It is just as sure that this is not going to happen. True, his outlandish proposal has more going for it than might appear. Psychologically speaking, there is a well-documented pleasure in the prospect of divesting from the self. That pleasure is difficult to quantify and may not end up weighing heavily against the various forms of hedonism that remain in the ascendant, but it is not negligible. Why would it be? It's a predictable effect of the asceticism that Max Weber long ago diagnosed in delayed gratification. Delayed gratification is necessary, Weber argued, to capitalism's early stages. In this later stage of capitalism, the ascetic impulse has arguably and paradoxically migrated from the realm of production—the work ethic—to the realm of consumption. The enthusiasm that has gathered recently around locavore cuisine and Fair Trade, such as the success of the antisweatshop movement before the great derailment of September 11, 2001, is otherwise inexplicable. The ethical consumer is cultivating and (re)fashioning the self. That can be fun.

And yet of course it remains true that Singer is asking for too much.

Many commentators have noticed that there is a kind of nihilism in Singer's argument: a refusal to recognize any value whatsoever in the ordinary objects, activities, and commitments that he asks people to abandon in order to save the starving. As MacFarquhar observes, Singer's ethical stringency undermines everyday ethical judgments: "If sacrificing your life for a stranger is as much a duty as not lying or stealing; if buying a pair of shoes is as bad as failing to rescue a child drowning in a pond; then it can seem that not lying or not stealing is no more required than sacrificing your life for a stranger" (*Strangers Drowning*, 68).[5] Antiutilitarian philosophers such as Bernard Williams, trying to protect as much as possible of the unreasoned givenness of life as we know it, suggest that Singer and his allies have carried rational calculation further than it can be allowed to go if we are to hold on to what makes us ourselves. Appiah is deliberately provocative on this issue; he demands the right, in full knowledge that somewhere children are starving, to enjoy a night at the opera. But the same point can be made without referring to anyone but the suffering themselves. Once their initial hunger has been appeased, wouldn't the same moral obligation fall on them as well? Shouldn't they be asked to sacrifice everything they have beyond the bare minimum in order to satisfy the unappeased hunger of others, whether near or far? Shouldn't they too be forbidden from enjoying any goods or services that are not essential to their survival on the grounds that someone, somewhere is still in need? There is no relief from the moral pressure Singer puts on human life. Under those conditions, the hungry might not want to be rescued at all.

So why do I insist that Singer's humanitarianism is not demanding too much, but too little? Because his model remains the Good Samaritan. Consider the 1971 famine in Bengal, which provoked Singer to write "Famine, Affluence, and Morality." In 1971 Singer looks at the news and sees Bengalis who don't have enough to eat. He notes that there has been what he calls a "civil war," but he is not really interested in why the Bengalis don't have enough to eat—whether the causes are, say, natural or human. Had he looked a bit deeper, he would have found that many of the causes were not only human but also political. And not only political, but political in a way that involved the past conduct and present interests of the people to whom he was appealing for charitable donations. Perhaps he was deliberately avoiding the investigative pathways that have led to distinctions between deserving and undeserving poor. But in so doing he also avoided and obscured the links between "us" and "them."

The "civil war" and famine in Bengal came about in the midst of what we would now call an invasion and a genocide: the invasion of East Pakistan (now Bangladesh) by West Pakistan, to which the United States supplied military aid and diplomatic cover before, during, and after the massacres. Recent scholarship dealing with US foreign policy during that period, and in particular the influence of Henry Kissinger, has rediscovered the aptly named "Blood telegram," signed by the US consul general in Dhaka, Archer Blood, and (in Christopher Hitchens's words) "denouncing the complicity of the United States government in genocide."[6] Greg Grandin, who sees Kissinger less as a foreign-policy realist than as a philosopher of "imperial existentialism" (*Kissinger's Shadow*, 13), nevertheless puts the story in realist terms: "Nixon compared the slaughter to the Holocaust, indicating that he realized the immorality of remaining quiet. Kissinger told him not to worry. Kissinger wanted to appease Pakistan's ally, China. And Pakistan itself was an important Cold War friend" (117–18).[7] "In the aftermath of the 1965 Indo-Pakistani War," Katherine Maher writes, "the word *famine* itself became a tool for setting policy priorities—a lexical weapon that the administrations of both Indira Gandhi and Lyndon B. Johnson wielded in a masterstroke of politics. The strategic withholding of US aid [from India] helped touch off a severe drought in some Indian states; citizens suffered mass unemployment, inflation, and displacement, while the cities saw strikes and riots."[8]

If even Richard Nixon realized the immorality of remaining quiet about the 1971 genocide, what do we say about Peter Singer, who is silent about the policy decisions and the massive violence against civilians and instead speaks only about hunger, an effect, abstracted from its causes, that can demand only humanitarian empathy?

Anyone concerned at that time about global justice should have demanded political action and accountability, just as we should be demanding political action now where similar situations threaten to arise and persist.

My point is not just that the famine had causes and that humanitarians ig-nore those causes—a familiar and perhaps tiresome critique of humanitar-ianism in the name of politics. It's true that treating only the effects allows the same causes to produce more of the same effects the next day or week or month. (If you rehydrate children who will be dehydrated again the next day, you are doing a good thing, but you are not really "rescuing" them in the sense—Singer's sense—that you would rescue a drowning child.) The idea that politics addresses deeper and more intractable causes of suffering that must, however, be addressed is a legitimate objection, but I want to say something more. Singer, like most humanitarians, can see only one line of causality linking the fortunate and the unfortunate: if you don't act, he says, you are at least partly responsible for the outcome that you failed to pre-vent. His focus is on sins of omission. Sins of commission are not a simple or symmetrical add-on, but they must in fact be added. Granted, they are at least as hard to recognize, measure, and evaluate. Perhaps they are even harder. The responsibility of the American electorate for a president and a secretary of state who chose to be actively complicit in a genocide about which they had been fully informed by their consul general and other staff members—yes, this responsibility is complex and oblique. But it is also real and unavoidable. The people Singer is exhorting to donate their superfluous funds are not merely causally linked to the starving by omission, in the sense that they are capable of alleviating the hunger. As the constituency behind their elected officials, at least, they are among the causes of the suffering. This means that the paradigm of the Good Samaritan, who is supposedly connected to the suffering victim by nothing but common humanity, does not cover the case.[9] And it means that the listener bears a heavier moral re-sponsibility. We were not merely spectators-who-could-do-something. It's not just that deeper causes exist. It's that those deeper causes involve things we have done, via our representatives, and we are now doing. They involve our own collective interests, our own collective conduct.

Collective responsibility is of course a vexed subject. Human rights pur-ists, their attention monopolized by the individual's confrontations with the state, will deny that any such thing exists. The quest to assign responsibility properly could also lead to an infinite regress in which we search for the causes of the causes of the causes, and so on. That is probably not the best way to spend the very limited time we are going to devote to the cause of global economic justice. Against the deep background of all these complications, humanitarianism's choice of surface reading—here are the hungry, let's feed them—makes a certain intuitive sense. But there are causes in the middle ground, so to speak, that it would be morally irresponsible to ignore.

Another example. It's no surprise that humanitarianism, dependent as it is on funding from the wealthy, has shown little curiosity about how the wealthy acquired the money they can then give away. But some consideration of that chain of causes is clearly in order. Singer's most recent book, *The Most Good You Can Do: How Effective Altruism Is Changing Ideas about Living Ethically*, begins with a young man who, inspired by Singer's ideas, takes a job in an arbitrage firm on Wall Street in order to have more money to give away and thus do the most possible good with his life. Based on the good he does by his charitable giving, Singer presents him as a shining exemplar of the effective altruist. This route is well traveled. MacFarquhar devotes a section of her book to a couple that model their careers around the same proposition. She does not ask, however, just as Singer doesn't ask, how much damage to the world might be caused by the money-making activities on Wall Street that are intended to fuel their subsequent charity. The calculation would no doubt be far from simple. But these are math people. If they set their talented minds to it, they could at least make an educated guess. Why don't they try? The idea does not seem to have occurred to them that, as one suspects, they may be doing much more harm by their financial activities than they could possibly undo by their philanthropy. They may have gone from distributing fish to teaching people to fish, and maybe even handing out fishing poles. But what if they are also causing the fish shortage?[10]

The inability of the global poor to pay for the food they need has a variety of causes, David Rieff writes in *The Reproach of Hunger: Food, Justice, and Money in the Twenty-First Century*. But prominent among them is "the virtual takeover of the world's commodities markets by speculators whose entry radically increased the volatility of these markets, causing wild price swings in the cost of food staples" (xv). To this rich theme must be added Michael Massing's argument, published in the *New York Review of Books* on January 16, 2016, on "How to Cover the One Percent": "As the concentration of wealth in America has grown, so has the scale of philanthropy. Today, that activity is one of the principal ways in which the superrich not only 'give back' but also exert influence." Their money goes untaxed, their influence is unelected and largely unregulated. As Massing shows, their philanthropy is subversive of democracy even when it is at least nominally intended to benefit the impoverished.

A hypothetical Humanitarianism 2.0 would have to take into account these tighter chains of causality connecting the fortunate with the unfortunate. What would it look like? The pages that follow will not assume that humanitarianism, however renewed, remains a viable or unavoidable vehicle for the concern with global justice. But in pursuit of this question, I will necessarily go back through some of humanitarianism's history. I want to show that concern with the causal linkages between the lucky and the unlucky in fact *has* a history and that the prospect of an organized concern for global justice that goes beyond the humanitarian imaginary is therefore not merely hypothetical or new.

To rephrase: the premise of this argument is that the existence of stronger causal links, however neglected by humanitarianism's spokespeople and historians, offers evidence that concern for global justice is in fact anchored in ordinary moral intuitions. One of the strongest arguments against Singer's blueprint for global economic redistribution is that it ignores ordinary moral intuitions. These intuitions no doubt keep life imperfect, as of course it is, but also make it less imperfect than it would be otherwise. Those of us who are not trained in moral philosophy will perhaps be irritated by the moral philosophers' blithe universalizing about such intuitions. The discipline asks: This is how you feel, is it not? You would not throw the fat man in front of the trolley in order to save five others, is that not so? And it carries on as if the question could be settled by how you said you felt.[11] The historical approach adopted here—more on this below—will assume on the contrary that the responses of people in different times, places, and social categories are likely to differ significantly. Their intuitions may instruct ours. If our intuitions orient us toward quiescence, there may be social and structural reasons for that. Intuitions are historically contingent, produced in and by history. However, like the moral philosophers, I too will put a great deal of weight on the ordinariness of these contingent intuitions. The evidence out of which I will build my case comes less from great thinkers than from a history of everyday intuitions, many of them literary. That includes intuitions that seem most resistant to global justice.

Take, for example, moral intuitions about Wall Street and the financial sector. Arbitrage, the career choice of Singer's ethical altruist, is a form of trading in financial instruments, such as stocks, bonds, currencies, and derivatives. It aims to exploit different prices in different markets in order to make a risk-free profit. (Look the term up on Wikipedia, taking care not to skip the section at the end on the fall of Long-Term Capital Management in 1998 and the role of the Federal Reserve in the bailout that followed, which was necessary, so it was said, to save the entire economic system from collapse. Risk-free, indeed.) The fact that to Singer none of this seems worth mentioning, coupled with the much larger fact that so little was done to punish or rein in the financial sector after the disaster of 2008, suggests that moral intuitions on this subject remain severely underdeveloped. Historically speaking, however, it is worth noting that complaints about the specific underdevelopment of ethico-financial intuitions go back at least as far as George Orwell. Orwell was not afraid to use morally loaded terms such as "rentier," "parasite," and "worthless idler." He did so in the name of what he called decency. And because he pinned his hopes to decency, he noticed that decency did not seem to work well against economic injustice, in particular the sorts of injustice associated with the financial sector, which were becoming more characteristic of his own society and have of course become even more characteristic of our own: "Foreign oppression is a much more obvious, understandable evil than economic oppression. Thus in England we tamely admit to being robbed in order to keep half a million worthless idlers in luxury, but we would fight to the last man sooner than be ruled by Chinamen; similarly, people who live on unearned dividends without a single qualm of conscience, see clearly enough that it is wrong to go and lord it in a foreign country where you are not wanted."[12]

"People who live on unearned dividends" are causally connected to those who don't, the people from whom dividends—that is, corporate profits—are extracted. This is a strong linkage. It is not often mentioned in the mainstream media even today, so one might naturally conclude that it is only a far-left fringe that has ever paid any attention to it. But that would be a mistake. In fact there is a rich history of the *consciousness* of this causal connection. Orwell is an important example. John A. Hobson's *Imperialism: A Study* (1902) is another. But consider the still earlier example of George Eliot. Eliot had investments in Indian public works, including transportation.

Thanks to the invention of new financial instruments (yes, they had them too), in the 1850s and 1860s large numbers of middle-class Englishmen were for the first time able to participate in overseas investment. In 1860, while receiving the first profits from her novel *The Mill on the Floss*, Eliot was investing two thousand pounds, a lot of money at the time, in "East Indies" railway stock. She was reassured that her return of 5 percent was "guaranteed." What the innocent-sounding word "guaranteed" meant was that if the Indian railway didn't make enough profit to pay the 5 percent, the money would still be paid; it would be raised by Indian taxes. In other words, the money would be taken forcibly from the Indians. And that's exactly how things went. The railway did not turn out to be profitable. But this did not stop the English investors from being paid. By 1869, something like fifteen million pounds had been disbursed to them under the guarantee system. Eliot's comfortable return on her investment was money taken from the pockets of India's inhabitants—it would not be overly melodramatic to say it was food taken from their mouths. In an 1879 letter, Eliot acknowledged that she saw the causality here when she wrote that the disastrous failure of the Second Anglo-Afghan War would be "a black day of Indian finance, which means alas a great deal of hardship to poor Hindus" (Henry, 78).

Most of our moral intuitions favor those close to us. To the extent that those close to us are doing relatively well within the system—which is not to be taken for granted, of course—our moral intuitions therefore protect the economic status quo. "Whatever my basic obligations are to the poor far away," Appiah says, "they cannot be enough, I believe, to trump my concerns for my family, my friends, my country" (*Cosmopolitanism*, 165). But why assume it's trumping or nothing? Giving up such concerns is certainly too much to ask. But it is also too much to ask for an entirely painless redistribution of the world's resources in which a leveling of goods, services, and life chances in favor of the global poor would happen and yet my family, friends, and country would sacrifice nothing at all. If I don't want to concede that I and those around me will have to pay any price whatsoever for global economic justice, I can either give up entirely on global justice by intensifying personal responsibility (I can say they are poor because of their culture, because they have too many children, because their states are corrupt) or I can buy the snake oil that the proponents of capitalist globalization have been peddling for a long time: leave the market alone, and it will eventually produce economic justice all by itself. The latter gives global capitalism too much credit. The former assigns too much significance to individual agency.

And yet global economic justice is now something that can at least be conceptualized as a goal. Indeed (as I will be arguing), it has become markedly easier to conceptualize. And capitalism deserves some of the credit. As James Vernon puts it in his book *Hunger: A Modern History*, "The market and laws of contractual exchange established that one was both invisibly connected to strangers and accountable for the remote consequences of one's own acts" (18). Vernon is paraphrasing an argument made at greater length by Thomas L. Haskell, a historian of abolitionism. The abolition of slavery is often considered humanitarianism's highest moment and the best evidence that moral crusades can overcome economic self-interest and have a genuine impact on history. Trying to explain it, Haskell argues that capitalism's "more telling influence on the origins of humanitarianism" came not through the class interests of the (often Quaker, free-market) abolitionists but through "changes in the market wrought in *perception* or *cognitive style*." Specifically, the development of global markets meant "a change in the perception of causal connection and consequently a shift in the conventions of moral responsibility" ("Capitalism," 238).

Like Singer, and for that matter nearly all humanitarians, Haskell understands these "altered perceptions of causation in human affairs" (239) as an increased confidence in the ordinary person's ability to act on remote events. This new confidence was real, and it had moral consequences. More human behavior opened up to critique. For you can object only to that which you can imagine being otherwise. If you can't imagine it otherwise, you will not see it as wrong, hence open to being righted. As Haskell put it, "We cannot regard ourselves as causally involved in another's suffering unless we see a way to stop it" (255).

On this point Haskell is agreeing with Bernard Williams, who argued that the ancient Greeks could not see slavery as wrong not because their sense of justice was premodern but because they could see no way to live without slaves. But here they diverge. As social arrangements and material technologies change, Haskell responds, so do moral intuitions. History in the era of the capitalist market has reduced what is taken to be the domain of necessity and has expanded the zone of plausible action. For Haskell, unlike for Williams, this change is decisive. The ancient Greeks did not see slavery as wrong any more than a majority now sees eating meat as wrong.[13] The fact that we do see slavery as wrong is a moral improvement. Like most humanitarians, Haskell sees the rise of humanitarianism as lending support to a view of modernity as progress. Progress seems a bit of a stretch even to Haskell himself. "Since capitalism supplied only a precondition," he notes, "no one need be surprised that the subsequent history of capitalist societies has not been greatly distinguished by humanitarian achievements" (276). With one important qualification, however, his progressivism can perhaps be defended. The qualification is that it has become more possible to see capitalism as a system causally linking victims and beneficiaries.

For the past two decades, in part because of the dark shadow of military interventions in humanity's name, the prevailing tone of humanitarianism's historians has been dark and cynical. "This book is about aid and charity," Michael Maren writes in *The Road to Hell: The Ravaging Effects of Foreign Aid and International Charity*—"aid and charity as an industry, as religion, as a self-serving system that sacrifices its own practitioners and intended beneficiaries in order that it may survive and grow" (11). "Humanitarianism does not prevent famine," Alex de Waal writes in his Foucauldian *Famine Crimes: Politics and the Disaster Relief Industry in Africa*. "To be precise," he says, "the intractability of famine is the price that is paid for the ascendancy of humanitarianism" (5). Even more measured statements tend to be infused with disillusionment, skepticism, and pessimism. Fiona Terry's point is in her title: *Condemned to Repeat? The Paradox of Humanitarian Action*. "Where is the evidence," David Rieff asks in *A Bed for the Night: Humanitarianism in Crisis*, "apart from the creation of new legal norms and the assertion and reassertion of the idea that the human rights culture is beginning to have a real impact on wars and famines and failed states, for the claims of the optimists who speak, like Michael Ignatieff, of a 'revolution of moral concern'? Is there not in fact more evidence to support the opposite conclusion?" (10). Pessimism remains the keynote of Rieff's latest book, *The Reproach of Hunger* (2015). In a review of Gary J. Bass's *Freedom's Battle: The Origins of Humanitarian Intervention* (2008), Samuel Moyn uses Bass's own nineteenth-century case studies (for example, Gladstone's campaign against the "Bulgarian atrocities") to show that "the plight of the suffering couldn't be separated from overarching imperial rivalries and awakening national sentiments." "Humanitarianism," he writes, "while universal in its rhetoric, has always turned out to be a specific political project in practice," which is to say shot through with racism, imperialism, hierarchies of power, "a creature of great-power politics, with all that entails."[14] Even a dedicated insider like Didier Fassin declares that its vices are intrinsic to it: "Humanitarianism is founded on an inequality of lives and hierarchies of humanity."[15]

These are knowledgeable observers. There is nothing here I would dispute. If my story is less grim, it's partly because it is less tied to the hope of meeting immediate demands for action and partly because I never shared the high expectations for humanitarianism that recent history has so bitterly disappointed. Subtract those hopes and expectations, and you have elements of what I would call progress.

"Hunger," Vernon writes, "it was eventually recognized, was not the fault of the hungry" (*Hunger*, 3). This is the defining moment in what he calls "The Humanitarian Discovery of Hunger." Until midway through the nineteenth century, hunger had been seen "as a good and necessary thing; it taught the lazy and indigent the moral discipline of labor" (2). Thus "starvation was unnewsworthy and the hungry evoked little sympathy" (17). It is only when the hungry could be redescribed as "innocent victims of forces and events beyond their control" (19) that hunger could be discovered as an object of humanitarian efforts. It seems odd that there should be any hesitation about classifying this step as an example—in fact quite an important example—of what must be called progress. Yet to say this is to suggest that a "no fault" view of hunger is satisfactory, and perhaps even goes as far in the right direction as it is possible to go. This is by no means obvious. Who is to say that those "forces and events beyond their control" are beyond *anyone's* control? Who is to say whether, if the hungry are not at fault, it follows that *no one* is at fault? Haskell's example of an earthquake in Mexico, beckoning him (in this case, unsuccessfully) to come to the aid of the victims, of course implies a no-fault view of suffering. That is also true of Adam Smith's more famous example of an earthquake in China in *The Theory of Moral Sentiments*, a landmark in the history of humanitarian theory. (The availability of the earthquake to indicate suffering that is not traceable to human action may of course diminish if there are further revelations about the responsibility of oil companies for the increased frequency of earthquakes in the Midwest.[16]) But if there is fault for hunger, whose fault is it? And if a finger can be pointed, will the finger pointing still find a place within what is called humanitarianism? What difference will it make to the possibility of organizing feelings against global poverty and in favor of global economic justice? These questions point toward the possibility of a narrative in which humanitarianism would transcend its limits.

Didier Fassin is right that humanitarianism is founded on the inequality of lives—specifically, the inequality between the lives of the compassionate and the lives of the suffering. But that is also the truth about what I have been calling economic Orientalism: the world *is* so divided, not primarily in terms of discourse or affect but in terms of access to material resources. To say that humanitarianism is founded on global inequality is therefore to assert only that (unlike everyday politics) it has very properly defined itself around the economic injustice that for our planet is arguably most definitive. It is not to say, with the most cynical, that it is devoted to *maintaining* this inequality.[17] At best, it alleviates and remediates while also naturalizing the fundamental divide. It will indeed have to become something else in order to become economically anti-Orientalist. It will have to see its audience as causally linked to the suffering to which it is invited to respond—linked not merely as potential rescuers but also as beneficiaries of the system that produces that suffering. At present, this seems too much for humanitarianism to take on. Haskell, for example, can see that capitalism has expanded the possibilities for doing remote harm as well as remote good. But he cannot see capitalism as itself a cause of the harm that humanitarianism will then be asked to remedy. Luckily, he makes this recognition easier for others.

Chapter 2

YOU ACQUIESCE IN IT

George Orwell on the System

Humanitarianism, which is preoccupied by suffering at a distance, does not tend to blame capitalism for that suffering. The left, which does blame capitalism, has not tended focus as much on suffering at a distance. "Workers of the world, unite! You have nothing to lose but your chains!" Here Marx and Engels are of course denouncing what will come to be called capitalism. But for them capitalism's victims are not far away; they are all around, close enough to be addressed directly. In these famous lines the workers are a "you," but elsewhere in *The Communist Manifesto* and in Marxism generally indignant speakers and suffering victims are joined in a seamless "we." With some exceptions, the left allows for no geographical divide between the fortunate and the unfortunate. And the fact that geography is not decisive has rhetorical advantages. Left speech is not ordinarily obstructed by a nagging consciousness that the speakers might belong among the fortunate, not the unfortunate, and in that sense might be part of the problem, and might therefore have to be addressed differently.

Now consider a statement that may not be in quite the class of "Workers of the world, unite!" but that certainly deserves to be better known than it is. "Under the capitalist system," George Orwell wrote in 1937, "in order that England may live in comparative comfort, a hundred million Indians must live on the verge of starvation—an evil state of affairs, but you acquiesce in it every time you step into a taxi or eat a plate of strawberries and cream."[1]

Orwell was very much a part of the thriving Left culture of the 1930s. He had been commissioned by Victor Gollancz, publisher of the Left Book Club, to report on social conditions among the unemployed of the industrial north. Many of his contacts on that trip were supplied by the National Unemployed Workers' Movement. His description of the underground lives of the miners in *The Road to Wigan Pier* became a classic of political ethnography. In the second half of the book, however, he wrote instead about himself, his own path to socialism, and the costly mistakes of self-representation he felt socialism in Britain had been making. The Communist Party objected; Gollancz admitted he found those sections of the book "repugnant." But he did not refuse to publish them. It is in those later sections that Orwell lifts his eyes from the newsworthy deprivation and squalor around him and suddenly speaks instead about inequality at the scale of the world.

Like MacFarquhar's Aaron, Orwell is inattentive, at this moment at least, to the suffering right in front of him. He also commits the sin of which Leigh Phillips accuses Naomi Klein: he speaks of his fellow countrymen in general as if they were all living in "comparative comfort." This is especially awkward given that he has shown no miners taking taxis or eating strawberries and cream. He also implies that if the English in general are to continue living in the style to which they are accustomed, a hundred million Indians *must* continue to live in conditions of extreme want. Like the "you acquiesce in it," this "must" is pretty aggressive. It makes the relation between prosperity here and hunger there something more than a shameful incongruity, as with Peter Singer and his fellow humanitarians. Orwell points to a seemingly unavoidable economic causality. They are poor because we are rich. We are rich because they are poor.

This is the logic of the system as Orwell sees it—unbearable, but also, here and now, inescapable. That's what it means to say that you inhabit a system. For Orwell, the inequality between England as a whole and the inhabitants of its colonies is not incidental to class struggle at home (or class struggle in the colonies) but the single most definitive fact of his historical moment, trumping all other inequalities. Yes, the gap separating rich and poor in England is flagrant and unacceptable; Orwell spends many pages describing the lives of the poor in vivid and sometimes excruciating detail. But however compelling to the senses, domestic inequality is outweighed and overruled by the distant, undescribed inequality between the world's rich regions and its poor regions. What is known locally as the working class, Orwell insists, is really only a small fraction of those who perform the functions of a working class and who suffer accordingly. The largest portion of the British working class, made up as it is of foreigners who live far away and out of sight, remains unknown and undescribed. Six years later, in the darkest days of World War II, Orwell is still allowing himself to be distracted from present urgencies by the same peremptory, absolute state of affairs. "The overwhelming bulk of the British proletariat doesn't live in Britain but in Asia and Africa," he writes. "This is the system which we all live on."[2]

"This is the system which we all live on." This proposition doesn't have the same ring as the much-quoted coinages of *Animal Farm* and *1984*. Unlike those Cold War classics, the second half of *The Road to Wigan Pier* has not made a place for itself in the high school curriculum. But in the era of Occupy and the still resonating Bernie Sanders campaign, perhaps its pedagogical day is coming. There would be much for students in the class to discuss.

Orwell's proposition about "the system" has immediate consequences for who we think we are. Including the slogans of Occupy itself. If we took Orwell seriously, for example, we might feel we have to hesitate before declaring that we are the 99 percent. Some of us no doubt already experience difficulty when we are invited to repeat these rousing words. But if we do not believe in our hearts that we are the 99 percent, we disbelieve it in a strange, half-hearted way. We know, of course, that the percentages are not precise and were never really intended to be. Occupy's slogan did not arise because someone did the calculations and estimated that 99 percent was more accurate than 66 percent or 92 percent or 85 percent. It arose because the target it aims at is widely felt to deserve real indignation, especially since the financial crisis of 2008. And we tolerate the slogan because it's in the nature of slogans to simplify, often extravagantly. To agree with Orwell about the system that we all live on, however, would mean that we would have to suspend this half-hearted disbelief. It would mean that the 99 percent slogan is misleading *even as a slogan*—even as a guide, in other words, to the strong, simple emotions to which we are ready to sacrifice our very limited free time. Our time and our emotions would have to be split. For Orwell, the guide to our political emotions cannot be exclusively those who benefit most from the system, such as the bankers and insurance company directors and financiers. The financiers and insurance company directors and bankers may run the system and profit egregiously from it, but in the global perspective, the global perspective that for Orwell trumps all others, we too, as taxi-taking and strawberry-eating inhabitants of the metropolis, are the system's beneficiaries. The target has to include ourselves.

Saying that we are all beneficiaries, like saying that we are the 99 percent, is another slogan. It works at a similar scale of gross, emotional simplification. It also comes uncomfortably close to reversing the other, more proven battle cry. Globally speaking, it says, we are closer to being the 1 percent than the 99 percent. And you acquiesce in it. How does *that* feel? For the moment at least, I'm not trying to make it feel better. Talk like this allows emotion of some sort to run high. When large and intimate terms like "you" and "we" are thrown around like this, it's a sign that the rules of politeness that discourage generalizing about collectivities have been waived. In order to give talk like this a respectful hearing, you have to be prepared to stay in your seat even when you suspect you are in the presence of a rant. You may well be.

When I entertain Orwell's hypothesis that we are all beneficiaries, which "we" do I personally have in mind? To begin with, I think of the people I work with and the profession I work in, which will probably include a fair proportion of those kind enough to be reading this page. I know that non-tenure-track faculty now make up something like 70 percent of those employed in American higher education. I know that their positions are insecure and their working conditions and home lives are therefore much more difficult than they need to be. It remains arguable, however, if by no means uncontroversial, that the majority of this profession would have to count as middle class even within the United States, let alone in the global perspective. And those for whom the quaint American usage "middle class" really signifies what in Europe would mean "working class"? Their numbers are appreciable, given that even relatively generous graduate stipends put many of their recipients below the poverty line. But even most of *those* would have to count, from Orwell's viewpoint, as beneficiaries of the system. Some of us, to repeat, would be called working class even in America. Some of us are people of color. Some of us are here only because colonialism was there. All of these things can be acknowledged without having to disavow the fundamental proposition: we are beneficiaries of the global capitalist system, and most of the people we address when we write and teach are also beneficiaries of the global capitalist system. We are not merely inside it; that is easy enough to say. We are beneficiaries of it. That is harder. But it ought to be something we can admit to ourselves and factor into what we say and do.

And if we did factor it in? The first idea that comes to mind is exacerbated and unproductive guilt—responsibility for the suffering of others that finds no satisfactory outlet in action that might lessen that suffering. The second is a boost in self-importance. Combine the two, and you get a mixture that threatens to be toxic, especially given the recent history of military humanitarianism and the proliferation of transnational do-gooders, many of them uninformed and all of them unelected. Is it anything more than a strategy for self-exoneration? The answer to this question may turn out to be the most polemical aspect of this book. Thinking of ourselves as beneficiaries would mean treating with more than the usual respect our potential to make a difference. That would be an alternative to the cocktail of irony, self-conscious marginality, and ethical hyperscrupulousness that we tend to choose for ourselves without even consulting the menu. It's other people, we tell ourselves, who do all the great harm in this world, and also other people who suffer most of that harm. Those who suffer most are the ones who will one day have to step forward and say no to it. We hope they will. In the meantime, we will go about our humble business, irrelevant as it may be. One virtue of listening to Orwell is that, rather than merely experiencing self-loathing, one is obliged to think of self-loathing as a collective and structured phenomenon with a place in the world and, for all we know, perhaps even a destiny.

The fact that Orwell's proposition is so hard to live with does not mean it's empirically incorrect. One could even imagine it as evidence of a sort that Orwell is not incorrect at all. You can glimpse some of the same kind of trouble, and incidentally glimpse also how much of this beneficiary discourse there is out there, by looking at Jamaica Kincaid's nonfiction book *A Small Place* (1988). Kincaid addresses a potential tourist, arriving in Antigua and looking out the window at the beautiful beach: "You see yourself taking a walk on that beach. . . . You see yourself eating some delicious, locally grown food. You see yourself, you see yourself . . ." Like the "you" in Orwell's "you acquiesce in it," this is an aggressive "you." Why is it so aggressive? Because, I think, Kincaid is not really writing about tourists but about the relations between Antigua and the metropolis, where the tourists come from but also where she herself resides. Rather than looking at the landscape the tourist has come so far to see, she looks *through* the landscape to the chains of causality that have made it what it is. This, she says sarcastically, is what you the tourist must not do: "You must not wonder what exactly happened to the contents of your lavatory when you flushed it. You must not wonder where your bathwater went when you pulled out the stopper. You must not wonder what happened when you brushed your teeth. Oh, it might all end up in the water you are thinking of taking a swim in; the contents of your lavatory might, just might, graze gently against your ankle as you wade carefree in the water, for you see, in Antigua, there is no proper sewage disposal system."

"You" get punished by swimming into your own shit. Were it not for Kincaid, this is probably something you would have found unimaginable. But what do you get punished *for*? It's not merely for being (perhaps) a white-skinned tourist in a dark-skinned people's country. It's not merely because your country has a sewage disposal system and Antigua doesn't. It's for the lines of causality that connect the lack of a sewage disposal system in Antigua with a better sanitized life back in the United States: "When you sit down to eat your delicious meal, it's better that you don't know that most of what you are eating came off a plane from Miami. And before it got on a plane in Miami, who knows where it came from? A good guess is that it came from a place like Antigua first, where it was grown dirt-cheap, went to Miami, and came back. There is a world of something in this, but I can't go into it right now" (13–14). The hypothetical encounter of the swimmer with a floating turd completes a circle that begins and ends with the swimmer—food goes into the swimmer's body, shit comes out. The shit must go somewhere, just as the food must come from somewhere. You who eat do not know yourself unless you also know where your food came from as well as where your shit goes. What Kincaid is saying to "you," as I read her, is that your most intimate bodily identity is constituted by your relations with distant places, and you do not have the right to remain ignorant of those relations even if they are ordinarily invisible to you, and even if they are very hard to hold in the mind—hard to hold in the mind even for Kincaid herself. In one sense she is from Antigua. In another, perhaps stronger, sense, she is from the United States. Like her readers, she is herself a beneficiary. And that is why she says, "There is a world of something in this, but I can't go into it right now"—why she is unable to denounce without also denouncing herself. In spite of her anger, she is confessing to a deep if involuntary fellowship with the "you" she is punishing.

In the same spirit, consider Wallace Shawn's *The Fever*. Shawn gives the system he tries to denounce a traditional name: the fetishism of commodities. Like Orwell, he presents the act of looking through commodities to see the social relations hidden away behind them as literally unbearable, as if it delivered a sense of the world that the human eye or the human heart is simply not constructed to sustain:

> A naked woman leans over a fence. A man buys a magazine and stares at her picture. The destinies of these two are linked. The man has paid the woman to take off her clothes, to lean over the fence. The photograph contains its history—the moment the woman unbuttoned her shirt, how she felt, what the photographer said. The price of the magazine is a code that describes the relationships between all these people—the woman, the man, the publisher, the photographer—who commanded, who obeyed. The cup of coffee contains the history of the peasants who picked the beans, how some of them fainted in the heat of the sun, some were beaten, some were kicked.
>
> For two days I could see the fetishism of commodities everywhere around me. It was a strange feeling. Then on the third day I lost it, it was gone, I couldn't see it anymore.

As it happens, Shawn gets back his ability to see the fetishism of the commodity. But not before concluding that his life is unjustifiable: "The life I live is irredeemably corrupt. It has no justification" (63).[3] Yes, this is how it feels to be a beneficiary. Your hands are dirty.

A social scientist's notion of dirty hands at the global scale is one way of describing Immanuel Wallerstein's theory of capitalism as a world system.[4] World-systems theory posits that, for roughly the last five hundred years, the metropolitan core has been regularly and systematically siphoning off a sizeable portion of the wealth produced at and by the periphery. As a result, the metropolis has been able to redistribute a portion of this portion to its own less- or underprivileged, thereby softening the system's worst effects at home, blunting potential antagonisms, keeping the peace. To belong to the working class at the core, therefore, does not mean the same thing as to belong to the working class at the periphery. For Wallerstein, this is a general rule about all class identities. The class identity you possess where you live is not determined by the reigning social hierarchy of that place alone; rather, it is always subtly or not so subtly affected by the geopolitical relations linking your place of residence to other, distant places. In world-systems theory, class is relative—relative to your location in the global system.[5]

Consider an extreme case: people "on the bottom rung" of the ladder such as the illegal Mexican worker interviewed for a *New York Times* series on class in America.[6] He often works ten hours a day, six days a week in a New York restaurant. He shares a tiny room with nine other Mexicans. He does not live a privileged life. Still, he has a cell phone and a DVD player and, more important, he sends money back to family members in Mexico. Remittances of this kind make a significant difference to the people at home and are actively encouraged by their governments. Often, for example in El Salvador, they are one of the country's principal sources of revenue.[7] In the Caribbean they are wooed as investment capital and carry potential claims of identity and political influence.[8] This is true as well for the Philippines, where Naomi Klein did much of the research for *No Logo*. Some observers are eager to celebrate migration and remittances as "the answer to global poverty," as Jason DeParle writes in his study of the issue in the Philippines. This means, he comments, "obscuring the personal price that migrants and their families pay. It could be used to gloss over, and even justify, the exploitation of workers."[9] It would be obscene to see remittances as the answer to global poverty. But it would be almost equally obscene to pretend that transfers like this are not happening, that they could not possibly happen because the supposed senders of money home are in fact starving, or reduced to the absolute minimum necessary to sustain life. What looks like a bare minimum in one place can elsewhere mean a small but significant surplus. Remittances are evidence of what is sometimes called the international division of labor, which divides the "developed" and "developing" worlds. Even gross and intolerable poverty on the prosperous side of the international division of labor is not, globally speaking, mere subsistence. It allows for the accumulation of some surplus, or what will look and behave like a surplus once it gets to the other side of the line, where poverty is still more extreme. And what is true for Mexican workers living ten to a room in New York is truer still for those of us with more living space and fewer obligations to distant relatives.

It will of course be said that statements such as Orwell's reveal nothing more interesting than "bourgeois guilt." My premise here is that bourgeois guilt is not uninteresting.[10] How could it actually be uninteresting when it generates so much of what is labeled progressive? In any case, what you get from Wallerstein is a revision of what it means to be "bourgeois." Technically, according to Wallerstein, the term is imprecise. To say that this is the (world) system we all live on is to say that, for better or worse, those who are beneficiaries include a great many people in the metropolis who could by no means be properly described as bourgeois. It is of course not unprecedented to address inequality at a global scale. As I said, "Workers of the world, unite!" does exactly that. But the divide between rich and poor that Marx and Engels assume is not geographical. Nor do they assume, as Orwell does, a gulf of inequality separating *even workers* in the global North from the workers as well as the bourgeoisie in the global South. If the assumptions of world-systems theory and dependency theory, which Orwell anticipates, sometimes seem to oversimplify the vectors of responsibility at the planetary scale, they also create complications within the class system at the national or local scale. In the Third World, elites are not simply elites. In the First World, workers are not simply workers.

This is of course revisionism, and it has sometimes been angrily rejected as such. But those who reject it do not have better explanations for persistent inequality at the global scale. If they did, the proposition that "the overwhelming bulk of the British proletariat doesn't live in Britain but in Asia and Africa" would have long ago ceased to sound so plausible.

Or does it sound so plausible for reasons that are less empirical than moral? Rather than conceding that Wallerstein offers social-scientific support to the moral fervor of Orwell's "this is the system which we all live on," you might object that Orwell brings to the surface of world-systems theory a hidden and less creditable commitment to moralism. When Wallerstein describes the condition of the Third World masses as absolute immiseration (as distinguished from mere relative inequality), it's as if he and Orwell are playing in the same moral poker game. Wallerstein sees Orwell and raises him. Wallerstein's insistence on the absoluteness of Third World suffering looks like what more dialectical Marxists would call "Third Worldism"— putting the Third World first, whether in agency or in exploitation, and keeping it there no matter what, if necessary in defiance of the evidence. To say that whatever happens, the same victim is always paramount and is always suffering to the same, unbearable degree—this suggests that Wallerstein has made up his mind in advance about the First World's primal and irremediable guilt, as if he has decided to be uninterested in any empirical validation and deaf to any whispers of historical change. This looks like moralizing. One may well want to be dealt out.

The moralizing, or the appearance of moralizing, is not a subject to be dismissed lightly. Perhaps Orwell's peculiar vision of global power relations is both as troubling and as effective as it is only because it is also or even primarily a moral vision. The Judeo-Christian assumption of an infinite, unrepayable debt still floats like an alluring ghost through the souls of many of the secular, seeking an object to which it can be reattached. Orwell might be understood as taking that indebtedness and transferring it from God to the poor of the Third World. This move has the advantage of making the world seem morally meaningful. It also has disadvantages. It makes our moral choices seem too simple, and it severely limits how much fresh information can be taken in either about or from the poor of the Third World.

This worry cannot be dismissed. For better or worse, however, the fresh information that has been coming in does not flatly contradict Orwell's planetary vision of how things are. According to World Bank economist Branko Milanović, there is ample empirical evidence that the geopolitical division between have and have-not countries not only persists but (as Orwell said) outweighs the division between haves and have-nots within any given country. Milanović writes, "Now, in contrast to the 19th century, most differences in income can be attributed to someone's country of citizenship rather than their position within their own society."[11] Thus to achieve "even simple equality within states"—already a utopian goal—"would make very little difference to global inequality" (16). In his latest book, *Global Inequality: A New Approach for the Age of Globalization* (2016), Milanović recognizes the existence of economic trends working to reduce global inequality, especially in Asia. "But," he concludes, "we are not there yet. Our world today is still a world in which the place where we were born or where we live matters enormously, determining perhaps as much as two-thirds of our lifetime income" (5). "The bottom line is that for global inequality to go down, the world needs fast growth in other places besides China. That growth seems most likely to occur in Asia; it is doubtful that it will occur in Africa" (213). Milanović does not suggest that confidence in economic trends would be well placed.

If that's the situation, then political action is necessary, but action within any one country will not adequately address the problem, nor will action that remains confined by the national limits that have hitherto shaped most if not all of what we mean by politics. To make a difference to global inequality, you will need beneficiaries to begin to see themselves as such, which means seeing themselves in global perspective and acting accordingly. You cannot simply wait for the nonbeneficiaries to see that they are clinging to the unclean end of the stick. As Wallerstein says, it is hard for even the most revolutionary political movements on the periphery to have any effect on the system itself, that is, on the terms of exchange between periphery and metropolitan core. It seems both careless and complacent, therefore, to put one's faith in the prospect that significant change in the world's distribution of resources can ultimately come only from the pressure of those who are not included in the beneficiary's "we."

As the Empire recedes and China and India rise, the urge to argue with Orwell about the facts has expressed itself in other revisionisms. Niall Ferguson and others argue that Empire brought the world the blessings of modern communications, humanitarianism, parliamentary democracy, and of course capitalism. This is true, though the blessings have been mixed. To be filled with gratitude for them, as Ferguson is, you would have to ignore some facts that Orwell himself was in no position to ignore. One of his favorite subjects on his BBC broadcasts to India was food rationing. While he was broadcasting, there was a famine in Bengal. To institute rationing in India would have meant not cutting back on Indian consumption but, on the contrary, offering the Indian population the guarantee of at least some food. It didn't happen. In December 1942, after months of dithering, British administrators in India finally realized that something had to be done and called for immediate shipments of grain. The request was refused. If the government were to meet this request, Lizzie Collingham notes in her book on food during World War II, *The Taste of War*, "Shipping and supplies would have to be withdrawn from either British soldiers fighting the Germans or British civilians making do on corned beef. . . . Churchill was not inclined to be generous with India at Britain's expense. He is said to have claimed that Indians had brought these problems on themselves by breeding like rabbits and must pay the price of their own improvidence" (145). In the beginning of 1943, the prime minister ordered a 60 percent cut in both civilian and military shipping in the Indian Ocean. "India was ordered to live on its stocks and with this instruction Churchill exported shortages within the empire's food system to India" (145). Estimates of the Indian dead run from 1.5 to 4 million people.

You could also admit that bad things happened during the Empire and still reply, with other proponents of global capitalism, that they are uncharacteristic of globalization as such. The zero-sum logic of Orwell's 1937 outburst may have been borne out under colonial rule and in wartime—India is ordered by its colonial masters to ship food to Britain, and therefore Indians starve—but to keep applying it after World War II and the era of national liberation were over is to indulge, some would say, in crude, economically naive propaganda. Some disparity between rich and poor is necessary, yes, but only in the sense that it nurtures incentive. And relative disparities are one thing; absolute deprivation is another. Absolutely speaking, all boats have been rising. Perhaps it is true that socially unpleasant and even dangerous levels of disparity remain, but if so they should be seen as the inevitable result of a trade-off with economic efficiency—a trade-off that we have every reason to accept, given the increase in the world's average standard of living. If you want evidence that the prosperity of the North does not depend on maintaining the South in a state of poverty, look no farther than the economic rise of the Four Asian Tigers, Hong Kong, Singapore, South Korea and Taiwan, followed by China and India. China's economic rise has been so spectacular that it is seen as being well on its way to becoming the new global hegemon. If so, Orwell's message in a bottle would seem to have passed its expiration date.

To this the response might be either statistical or impressionistic. How much has changed since the era of colonialism? How different is the situation of George Eliot in the 1860s and 1870s, knowing that her guaranteed 5 percent return on her Indian railway stocks was being taken out of the mouths of the Indians, and the austerity policies imposed on Greece by the European financial establishment? Again, the banks were bailed out, the investors paid back. Again, it has been the locals who are obliged to do the paying. Their standard of living collapsed and their unemployment rate soared. They have not been heating their homes in winter. They have been looking for their dinner in dumpsters. And things have been like this for years.[12]

As for the statistics, they are there for the googling. In a June 2013 comparison of the standard of living in China and the United States, the *Guardian* lists China's GDP per capita as $9,100 and the United States' GDP per capita as $48,900, more than 5 times higher. Other figures are of course also relevant, including China's trade surplus and the US trade deficit, but in terms of the standard of living of those presently alive in both countries (and it is of the present that we are speaking, though how can we do so without factoring in both the future and the past?) much more relevant is China's surplus of deaths attributed to air and water pollution. Then there is access to basic resources such as medical care. Hard as it is for an American to mention that issue without pausing to note the terrible inequities of access to medical care within the United States, those inequities pale in transnational comparison. An example is the widely publicized violence in China against doctors and other hospital staff who refuse treatment to patients in dire need.

This point extends well beyond the world's emergent superpower. Let us concentrate solely on India, once Orwell's paradigm and now another supposed poster child for global capitalism's power to redistribute resources more equitably around the world. "Even accepting the government's official poverty line," Siddhartha Deb writes, "with an absurd ideal budget for the poor that 'includes princely sums of . . . forty rupees per month for health care' (an amount that 'might buy something like the equivalent of an aspirin a day'), 'a full 30 per cent of the population in 2009–10, or more than 350 million people,' live below it. A more realistic poverty level, on the other hand, would include nearly 80 percent of the population." Deb is quoting from Amartya Sen and Jean Drèze. For Sen and Drèze, the pertinent social indicators reveal an India that has not benefited much from globalization's much-touted economic miracle. "'Nutrient intakes (calorie, protein, micronutrients—almost anything except fat) have decreased' in 'the last twenty years,' while children and adult women 'are more undernourished in India (and South Asia) than almost anywhere else in the world.' India is rated 'as the most polluted among 132 countries for which comparable data are available,' while 'one fifth of all Indian men in the age group of 15–24 years, and one fourth of all women in the same age group, were unable to read and write in 2006.'"

This is not far from the apocalyptically famished India that Orwell conjured up in 1937. There has been change, of course. But there has also been the persistence of profound inequality. This is why, for many of us, whether we are located in the global metropolis or not, an inability to ignore the stark and unyielding global disparity in resources and life chances continues to define what Orwell called decency, and this even if China is indeed more powerful (on the whole not a bad thing) and if the average standard of living in the world has indeed risen (as it has). But decency never turns out to be quite as common as Orwell hoped. Let us rephrase, therefore: an inability to ignore this global disparity continues to define what it means to belong to the left. Perhaps unsurprisingly, this is the answer Gilles Deleuze gave when asked, what does it mean to be on the left? "Those who are not on the left and who live in the comparative wealth of a relatively privileged first world country," he responded, "perceive problems of inequality and injustice from their own perspective. Sensing that their position is untenable and under threat, they ask 'what can we do to make this situation last?' By contrast, those on the left perceive the situation from the perspective of the horizon, the point farthest from their center of privilege. These people 'know that it cannot last, that it's not possible, [the fact that] these millions of people are starving to death, it just can't last, it might go on a hundred years, one never knows, but there's no point kidding oneself about this absolute injustice.' Those on the left know that such problems must be dealt with, that the problem is not to find ways to maintain the privileges of Europe but that of 'finding arrangements, finding world-wide assemblages' which address these problems."

The finding of such worldwide assemblages and arrangements is, indeed, a problem. What party makes them its first order of business or even puts them on its agenda? There is something mysterious here. On the one hand, this task seems to define the essence of the left. On the other hand, it doesn't look like it belongs to real, ongoing left-wing politics at all.

A sense of mystery also hangs over the steps leading to that sense of basic, unshirkable obligation. Like Orwell, Deleuze sets the "comparative wealth of a relatively privileged first world country" against "millions of people starving to death." What he does not do is add, with Orwell, that the comparative wealth *depends on* the millions being reduced to starvation. You can agree about the suffering and the injustice and you can therefore count yourself a leftist of the very committed sort Deleuze describes while also balking at the further proposition that the disparity between rich countries and poor countries is the result of a systemic and fundamental contradiction—in other words, the proposition that we are rich only because they are poor. Even Branko Milanović, who has done more than any other economist to publicize global inequality, writes in the first paragraph of *Worlds Apart* (2005), "I did not deal with causality" (vii). Statements such as Orwell's clearly would not have the same moral force if causality were not something they insisted on.

"This is the system which we all live on." To say live *on* is a lot stronger than to say live *in*. Is it too strong to be persuasive? Is it inaccurate? Does Orwell's morally weighty message burden us all unfairly, laying on more complicity and more responsibility than "you" as an individual most likely deserve, whoever you are? The collective project of undoing global inequality might not demand that we all individualize and personalize our implication in it. We might decide that it is not productive, politically or ethically, let alone practically or psychologically, to allow the self-blaming to go quite so far. One way to reject the onerous implication that we live "on" a system would be to reject the idea that "system" is the right word for whatever it is we are part of.

If by "system" we mean something like the solar system, then of course no such thing exists on earth, at least in the domain of economics. Wallerstein has been criticized as a "neo-Smithian" for presuming, like Adam Smith, that the working of the market can be analogous to the frictionless, self-organizing movement of planets around the sun. But even Wallerstein's understanding of "system" has room in it for seemingly extraneous yet necessary acts of coercion. Without coercion, system as he sees it could not have been established. (Marx made the same point when he described what he called "primitive accumulation.") Nor, more importantly, could the system continue to hold together without further acts of coercion.[13] Whereas orthodox Marxism sees no capitalism without "free," which is to say wage, labor, for Wallerstein capitalism includes slavery. Slavery of course cannot be maintained without the habitual application of physical violence. So Wallerstein's is not a system in the sense that impersonal mechanisms of exchange operate smoothly and independently without need for human intervention. Yet "system" is very much his word.

In his critique of Edward Said's *Orientalism*, Aijaz Ahmad asks why, for Said, "the West has *needed* to constitute the Orient as its Other in order to constitute itself and its own subject position." Why is it, in Said's view, that the West "*must* inferiorize the Other?"[14] Among those from whom Said borrowed this implacable logic, the first on Ahmad's list is Jean-Paul Sartre.

Whatever category Orwell belongs to, Sartre clearly belongs to the same one. Consider a passage from his preface to Frantz Fanon's *The Wretched of the Earth*, published in 1961:

> You know well enough that we are exploiters. You know too that we have laid our hands on first the gold and the metals, then the petroleum of the "new continents," and that we have brought them back to the old countries. This was not without excellent results, as witness our palaces, our cathedrals, and our great industrial cities; and then when there was a threat of a slump, the colonial markets were there to soften the blow or to divert it. Crammed with riches, Europe accorded the human status *de jure* to its inhabitants. With us, to be a man is to be an accomplice of colonialism, since all of us without exception profited by colonial exploitation. (25)

Sartre is denouncing global exploitation. His denunciation is addressed to the beneficiaries of that exploitation—in this case, Sartre's fellow Europeans. And it is spoken by someone who acknowledges, if only obliquely, that he too is a beneficiary. Some will wish Sartre had decided to red pencil the phrase "all of us without exception." Sartre vacillates awkwardly between heavy sarcasm ("excellent results") and self-indictment ("With us, to be a man"). But as with Orwell, the questionable excess of this "all of us" seems best understood not as a problematic trait of personality or individual style but rather as evidence of a shared structural contradiction: the contradictory situation of someone denouncing a system that he finds intolerable but to which he nevertheless continues to belong, from which he continues to derive certain benefits and privileges, from which he may have no possibility of making a clean break—and which he can only denounce to others who also continue to belong to it. I will call talk like this the discourse of the beneficiary.

Sartre was a hero of Europe's anticolonial left. One reason why is that, as we have seen, he put a great deal of stress on the necessary role played by the colonies in Europe's self-constitution. For Ahmad this is a mistake. Ahmad thinks Hegel's dialectical parable of Lord and Bondsman is a misleading model for the West's relation to the Rest. In *Being and Nothingness*, *Anti-Semite and Jew*, and elsewhere, Sartre offered an influential rewriting of Hegel's parable. He made the dominating gaze at an inferiorized Other into something like a requirement for the achievement of selfhood. You could either dominate or be dominated, objectify or be objectified; there was no other option. In Sartre's version of Hegel's life-and-death struggle of rival consciousness, as Genevieve Lloyd summarizes it, each "strives to be the one that retains freedom, turning the other into an object. It is impossible for both lookers to be reciprocally free, recognizing one another's 'being-for-self.' Thus the Sartrean antagonists struggle for the role of looker."[15] For Ahmad, this story leads directly to the error of what he calls "Third Worldism," a sort of regional identity politics. To which he replies, "We live not in three worlds but in one" (*In Theory*, 103).

One can agree with Ahmad about Sartre's interpretation of Hegel and its influence on Said, as I do, and still see value in the sense of necessity that Sartre projects onto Europe's mistreatment of non-Europe—that is, his deploying of the discourse of the beneficiary, which depends on the beneficiary's place in a global system. The concept of exploitation no longer seems as firm as it once did, but what the discourse of the beneficiary assumes is the existence of a system, not a perfectly zero-sum model of exploitation within it.[16] Ahmad does not reject the notion of system as such. Capitalism is indeed a system, for Ahmad, but "the different parts of the capitalist system are to be known not in terms of a binary opposition but as a contradictory unity—with differences, yes, but also with profound overlaps" (*In Theory*, 103). Differences, yes: but what kind? If we are talking about when a given region was integrated into the system, what slot it was integrated into, and how its possibilities of development or escape are constrained by where it fits into the system, then practically speaking, it's almost as if those differences *were* ontological, as the Orientalists falsely believed. How much would it matter if, say, we decided that they pertained to a structure of inequality between global North and global South that was not inherent on the one hand, but on the other hand had remained in place, roughly speaking, for four or five hundred years?

In short, how much of a difference would it make, ethically and politically speaking, to replace the word "system" with "history"? Not all that much. To benefit from a system that extracts and produces commodities far away is also to be the beneficiary of a certain history. But it would be premature to allow one term to replace the other. After all, it is capitalism's greatest theorists and enthusiasts who themselves tell us that capitalism is indeed, and in a strong sense, a system. That helps explain where Orwell's zero-sum vision came from. The question is especially puzzling considering that it could not have come straight out of left culture, committed as that culture was to the activism of the downtrodden to whom it was reaching out.

Chapter 3

A SHORT HISTORY OF
COMMODITY RECOGNITION

In talking out of turn about hunger in South Asia, Orwell was speaking from experience, capitalizing on his five years as an increasingly disaffected military policeman in Burma. But he was also feeling the very topical pressure created by the rise of fascism. Like many others, he recognized the need for an international alliance against Hitler and Mussolini comparable to the organized internationalism that had helped get him to Spain to fight against Franco. As he saw with unusual clarity, the prospect of worldwide antifascist solidarity was endangered both by the colonialism of the Allies and, just as important, by the economic disparity between what had not yet come to be called the First and Third Worlds. In his essay "Not Counting Niggers," he refused "to lie about" the disparity in income between England and India, a disparity so great that, Orwell asserts, an Indian's leg is commonly thinner than an Englishman's arm. "One mightn't think it when one looks round the back streets of Sheffield, but the average British income is to the Indian as twelve to one. How can one get anti-Fascist and anti-capitalist solidarity in such circumstances? . . . Indians refuse to believe that any class-struggle exists in Europe. In their eyes the underpaid, downtrodden English worker is himself an exploiter."[1] Orwell does not say the Indians are wrong. Nor does he want to say that they are right, and one understands his hesitation. Yet that is what he suggests, repeatedly if not loudly or wholeheartedly: at the global scale, even underpaid and downtrodden English workers *are* exploiters. The project of establishing international solidarity will have to admit that fact if it intends to get anywhere.[2]

Why did this matter so much to him? Christopher Hitchens writes in *Why Orwell Matters*, "Orwell may or may not have felt guilty about the source of his family's income—an image that recurs in his famous portrait of England itself as a family with a conspiracy of silence about its finances—but he undoubtedly came to see the exploitation of the colonies as the dirty secret of the whole enlightened British establishment." Hitchens is referring here to the origins of the Blair family fortune (long gone by the time Eric Blair/George Orwell was born) in Jamaican sugar, hence in slavery, as well as his father's role as a minor functionary in the opium trade.[3] Hitchens is one of many critics who have raised the theme of guilt in Orwell and—the difference needs to be underlined—who have explicitly placed this self-blame at a cosmopolitan scale, identifying it as a psychic relation that does not stop with the domestic working class but gives unaccustomed emphasis to distant foreigners, especially but not exclusively the subjects of the Empire. The question is whether this guilt was merely a personal eccentricity, responsible for "adventures in class-crossing" that his exasperated friends and colleagues took (in Louis Menand's words) "as reproaches directed at their own bourgeois addiction to comfort and decorum. Which they were."[4]

Commodity Recognition Scenes

Quirky as Orwell's personality may have been, there was nothing outlandish about his habit of paying ethical attention to the place of sugar and opium in his life. The notion that the commodities around us are the bearers of an interesting history is not unfamiliar. After all, the recognition that the objects we consume display the labor of others, much of it coming from distant places, and that in a sense we are beneficiaries of that labor belongs to capitalism's basic sales pitch. As for example when the *New York Times* columnist and best-selling author Thomas Friedman, writing in *The World Is Flat*, lists the nations and corporations that the components of his Dell laptop come from:

> Here are the key suppliers for my Inspiron 600m notebook: The Intel microprocessor came from an Intel factory either in the Philippines, Costa Rica, Malaysia, or China. The memory came from a Korean-owned factory in Korea (Samsung), a Taiwanese-owned factory in Taiwan (Nanya), a German-owned factory in Germany (Infineon), or a Japanese-owned factory in Japan (Elpida). My graphics card was shipped from either a Taiwanese-owned factory in China (MSI) or a Chinese-run factory in China (Foxconn). The cooling fan came from a Taiwanese-owned factory in Taiwan (CCI or Auras). The motherboard came from either a Korean-owned factory in Shanghai (Samsung), a Taiwanese-owned factory in Shanghai (Quanta), or a Taiwanese-owned factory in Taiwan (Compal or Wistron). (416)

This is not the end of the quote; the sentences go on in exactly the same "came from" format listing another eleven components in thirty more lines of text. Friedman concludes with a musical metaphor: "This supply chain symphony—from my order over the phone to production to delivery to my house—is one of the wonders of the flat world" (417). It is something like music that Friedman himself produces with his syntactically regular list making and its prolonged effect of rhythmic repetition, each repetition varied or syncopated with the name of one or two fresh new corporations. The idea that so much distance, so much linguistic and cultural diversity could climax in the delivery of a useful object to your door does come to seem a wonder, even a thing of beauty. The system delivers the goods. What a system it is! How lucky I feel to be its beneficiary.

The obvious ancestor of Friedman's supply chain symphony is Adam Smith. Consider as a commodity recognition scene the famous passage at the end of the opening chapter of *The Wealth of Nations* in which Smith lists all the occupations that have been involved in making the simple woolen coat of one simple laborer. First comes the shepherd, then the sorter of the wool, the wool comber or carder, the dyer, the scribbler, the spinner, and so on. Like Friedman's laptop passage, this one too goes on and on and on, making its rhetorical effect in part by a seemingly endless accumulation of elements. I spare you Smith's full list, as I did with Friedman's. But this is not just politeness. In trying not to test your patience, I'm also dampening the intended effect. Smith is in the business of generating sublimity. As he piles on kind after kind of specialized work that the division of labor divides and hides, the coat becomes dazzlingly, immeasurably precious. Like infinity in a grain of sand, one humble commodity reveals a dumbfoundingly complex organization of diverse and far-flung human efforts. Smith spells this effect out in his conclusion: "Observe the accommodation of the most common artificer or day-laborer in a civilized and thriving country, and you will perceive that the number of people of whose industry a part, though but a small part, has been employed in procuring him this accommodation, exceeds all computation" (12).

Sublimity is what we are accustomed to find on those occasions (they are not so terribly rare) when we stop and, rather than merely making use of the commodity, we pay it real attention and recognize something else about it or about where it comes from. As we are invited to do by the genre of the commodity history, a suddenly ubiquitous species of popular nonfiction featuring over-the-top titles such as *Corn and Capitalism: How a Botanical Bastard Grew to Global Dominance*; *Tobacco: A Cultural History of How an Exotic Plant Seduced Civilization*; *The Potato: How the Humble Spud Rescued the Western World*; *The World of Caffeine: The Science and Culture of the World's Most Popular Drug*; *Cod: A Biography of the Fish that Changed the World*; and *Mauve: How One Man Invented a Color That Changed the World*. Such titles suggest that all of these commodities, even the humblest, have the power to get continents discovered, dynasties toppled, mountains moved. We take them for granted, but we shouldn't: all of them have changed the world. Which is to say that we, the consumers who demand and receive them and invest them with our desire, have changed the world. The consumer shares with the commodity a sublime, almost divine power.

It's the system's power, but it is also, in a strong sense, our own power. One of the genre's heroic story lines might be described as commodity democratization. You begin with an exotic commodity such as chocolate or coffee or tobacco that, when first imported into Europe, was restricted to courtly or aristocratic circles either by its price and scarcity or because it was blocked in its circulation by other antiquated and elitist vestiges of traditional society. Then you tell the story of how this protagonist, usually an underdog though also touched with a mysterious hint of natural distinction, managed to spread across the social spectrum, dropping dramatically in price as taxes and prohibitions were lifted and becoming triumphantly accessible to the eager masses. In a history of chocolate, for example, the trajectory leads from the first chapter title, "The Tree of the Food of the Gods," to the last chapter title, "Chocolate for the Masses." The villains of this narrative, numerous and colorful though also bumbling and ineffectual, are the kings, priests, moralists, and would-be experts who declaimed quaintly against the new products, whether in the name of loyalty to national tradition (beer or wine against coffee or tea) or fiscal greed or perhaps warning of dire effects on public health and apocalyptic scenarios of moral chaos to follow. With rare national exceptions, these enemies of the consumer are always vanquished. Their interference is never effectual for long. The commodity always arrives at its proper, mass destination. The consumer gets what she or he wants.

The propaganda here, if that is the right word, is liberal in the older sense of the word: it is both procapitalist and antistatist. What a marvelous system this must be, you are told again and again, that has brought to your doorstep or breakfast table all these exotic and pleasurable things you never would have known existed, things once reserved for the lords of mankind, yet also things without which you would not, you suddenly realize, be yourself. With so much resistance to overcome from superstitious, self-interested, and intrusive authorities, you must be grateful that the commodity, or the system for which it stands, had within it a power to overleap all obstacles of law, dogma, and distance. You must be grateful that as consumer you both benefit from that power and share in it.

There is nothing shocking, then, in the fact that we have learned—to the extent that we have—to think of ourselves as intimately and causally connected to distant strangers by a global system. We have had at least two and a half centuries to get used to it. What we may not be prepared for is the feeling that there might be something scandalous or even just fishy about all this interdependence. *The Wealth of Nations* features no scenes of a coal miner coughing up blood or a housewife trying to unplug a blocked drain in winter or a laborer raging like Lear on the heath in an economic storm, wearing only rags and wishing that simple woolen coat were there for him to put on.[5] Close readers of Smith and Friedman could no doubt discover glimmers of recognition of victimhood, of exploitation or suffering, something at the site of production that at least calls for a second look, but no such recognition is visible to the naked eye.[6] What one is curious to know, then, is the path by which we got to Orwell on miners: "All of us really owe the comparative decency of our lives to poor drudges underground, blackened to the eyes, with their throats full of coal dust, driving their shovels forward with arms and belly muscles of steel." How and when and why did belonging to a smoothly functioning system come to be seen, to the extent that it has, as a debt owed to "poor drudges," which is to say a moral problem? How far we remain from resolving or even thinking through that problem is clear from the words "poor" and "drudges." And yet it is a big step from Smith and Friedman to Orwell or Shawn. How could we, or even a portion of us, have taken that step? How did it become possible to perceive dependence on the labor of others, on the one hand, and inequality in the circumstances of life, on the other hand—neither of them initially felt to be scandalous in itself—as combining to constitute a scandal?

There is clearly a history here, but it's not one that's featured in the standard textbooks. And it doesn't rise from self-evident achievement to still higher achievement. It is an uneven, syncopated history composed of ideological embarrassments and unintended consequences.

By "commodity recognition scenes" I mean a sort of mild epiphany in which some familiar consumer good is suddenly recognized as coming from a distant place of origin and from the labor of the distant inhabitants— potentially, at least, their coerced or otherwise unpleasant labor. In one sense, scenes like these go back as far as Periclean Athens, which already could not feed itself but depended for its supply of grain on trade with the so-called barbarians living around the Black Sea. "We can afford such pleasures," Pericles said, "because imports come in, through our empire, from everywhere on earth, making others' property belong to us as much as does our own."[7] But the first such scenes I have been able to discover in which labor specifically becomes visible as a problem or potential problem belong to a tradition in which a male moralist points the finger at a woman in the act of consuming a luxury. One early modern example would be when Jonathan Swift's Gulliver observes that "this whole globe of earth must be three times gone round, before one of our better female yahoos could get her breakfast, or a cup to put it in." There is no pain here, but there is an appreciation of work demanded from afar and accomplished. Swift notices that in order for the first meal of the day to be consumed, much distance had to be covered, much time and energy had to be expended, and expended by creatures belonging to a different category from those who were doing the consuming. Of course he fails to notice that what's true for a female yahoo drinking her morning tea out of a porcelain cup is equally true for yahoos who are male. Males and females drink the same tea out of the same cups. Labor seems to stand out as a problem only when it can be attributed to the desires of females. Commodity recognition scenes in the strict sense emerge by virtue of misogyny.[8]

There is a long line of such antiluxury observations, many and perhaps most of them actively engaged in blaming women. In F. Scott Fitzgerald's *Tender Is the Night* (1934), for example, we are shown Nicole on a buying spree: "She bought colored beads, folding beach cushions, artificial flowers, honey, a guest bed, bags, scarfs, love birds, miniatures for a doll's house and three yards of some new cloth the color of prawns." The list goes on. Then we are given another sort of list:

> Nicole was the product of much ingenuity and toil. For her sake trains began their run at Chicago and traversed the round belly of the continent to California; chicle factories fumed and link belts grew link by link in factories; men mixed toothpaste in vats and drew mouthwash out of copper hogsheads; girls canned tomatoes quickly in August or worked rudely at the Five-and-Tens on Christmas Eve; half-breed Indians toiled on Brazilian coffee plantations and dreamers were muscled out of patent rights in new tractors—these were some of the people who gave a tithe to Nicole, and as the whole system swayed and thundered onward it lent a feverish bloom to such processes of hers as wholesale buying, like the flush of a fireman's face holding his post before a spreading blaze. (55)

It is good to receive all this information about "the whole system." Here, if not in Smith, the world economy seems to have some unpleasantness inherent in it. At a minimum, it has girls "rudely" forced to work on Christmas Eve, Indians toiling on coffee plantations, and dreamy inventors "muscled" out of their rights. Thus the system can be abruptly compared to the destructiveness of a fire out of control. It is also good to be informed about

Nicole's personal connectedness to this system. But Fitzgerald seems to forget that this same information about rudeness and ill treatment would apply equally well to people who are not on buying sprees but merely purchasing modest daily necessities. And it would also apply to people who are not women. It should not only be Nicole's female face that is illuminated like a fireman's in front of a spreading fire. Again, it's as if the system's downside could not get itself noticed at all unless for one reason or another it could be seen as gender specific. Only the female beneficiary, it seems, is a scandal.

For a history of the moralizing of the commodity, this is an unpromising start. And yet it *is* a start. After all, I would argue, a misogynous recognition of distant labor is better than no recognition of distant labor. Once the recognition is out there, it becomes at least theoretically possible for the misogyny to be subtracted, leaving behind a perception that is valuable in itself and could be turned to other uses. The same female hyperresponsibility used by men to blame women, Elizabeth Kowaleski-Wallace observes, could for example "be used by a woman writer to rally other women for a liberal cause" (*Consuming Subjects*, 43). And in the eighteenth century, this is just what happened. Blamed for their luxurious consumption, a large number of women drew the logical conclusion that what they consumed was a political matter, and that it was a political matter precisely because it did connect their households to the distant labor of others. Much of the distant labor, they went on to realize, was performed by slaves. Thus women such as Elizabeth Heyrick and Lucy Townsend took the lead in the sugar boycotts that accompanied the abolitionist campaigns of the 1790s, aimed at slave-grown sugar. As Adam Hochschild says in *Bury the Chains*, his history of British abolitionism, "The boycott was largely put into effect by those who bought and cooked the family food: women" (195). At a time when women did not belong to the tiny proportion of the population that could vote and when sugar had become the nation's largest import, the oil of the day, the refusal of sugar was both attention-grabbing symbolism and a mode of extraparliamentary politics that offered some real leverage to the unfranchised. Whether a voter or not, who could be totally immune to a message declaring that the conditions of Caribbean labor lay right there before you, as close as your teacup? A pamphlet by the Quaker William Fox popularized the equation of a pound of sugar with two ounces of a slave's flesh. "At their most vehement," Charlotte Sussman notes, "abolitionists proclaimed that 'every person who habitually consumes one article of West Indian produce is guilty of the crime of murder'" (*Consuming Anxieties*, 43).

Saying no to morally contaminated produce was of course a display of "virtuous personal sacrifice," and therefore liable to be dismissed as offensively self-righteous. But it also had the capacity to become, in Hochschild's words, "a sharper political tool" (*Bury the Chains*, 327). The word "boycott" entered the English language only in 1880, when Irish tenant farmers in a time of bad harvests resisted eviction by ostracizing the agent of an absentee landlord—that is, by withdrawing their labor. The practice of course antedated the term: what else was the Boston Tea Party but the spectacularly successful performance of a boycott? Since then, the tactic has proved its political sharpness on any number of occasions. Gandhi's independence-movement boycott of British goods and the Montgomery bus boycott in the civil rights era are two of many. A century after the Irish farmers put the word in circulation, the boycott of apartheid in South Africa in the 1980s was characteristic of the new period in being both international and centered less on abstention from work than on abstention from buying. That would also seem to hold for the growing and increasingly effective twenty-first-century boycotts of Israel. The antisweatshop movement of the 1990s, which hit a bump after September 11, 2001, seems back on track a decade and a half later thanks to its new confluence with sensitivity to climate change, the locavore trend, and environmentalism in general, all of which place a high value on tracing the causal chains leading to and from commodities.

The case for the significance of commodity recognition can be made, then, in strictly political terms. But what interests me more here is a history that is more moral and cultural (in other words, that underlies or facilitates the politics) and that is also messier—messy enough to call for some close reading.

As I have been suggesting, the story of how the commodity gradually becomes available for politicizing, if not yet a political issue in its own right, cannot be understood without factoring in unappetizing materials such as misogyny. But even if one manages to see these ideological materials dialectically—that is, as bad things from which good things can potentially come—this story is still full of setbacks and vacancies as well as unexpected points of light. From the point of view of commodity recognition, the abolition of slavery, for example, was a disaster. When the emancipation bill passed in 1833, the reasoning behind the sugar boycott suddenly collapsed. The former slaves might be bent double on the same plantation, sweating in the same sun, and even being whipped by the same overseers, but once they were legally free men who were paid wages for their labor, sugar by and large no longer looked tainted. Discussing a piece in the 1850 Christmas issue of *Household Words* that listed the "foreign commodities—raisins, currants, nutmeg, raw sugar, and ginger" that went into making the quintessentially English dish, Christmas pudding, the historian Lara Kriegel notes that by that time sugar was no longer a token of the sufferings of producers. On the contrary, it had become "a vindication of abolitionism, proof that with freedom from chattel slavery came diligence and toil" (*Grand Designs*, 230). Sugar still represented labor, but now it represented free, proper, diligent labor, labor that did not seem to be a scandal.

As Kriegel observes, the article in *Household Words* anticipated Marx's wish, expressed seventeen years later in his exposition of commodity fetishism, "that goods could 'speak' and thereby express the labor spent in their production" (232). "As they appeared before him, the animated commodities discussed with Oldknow the labor and trade practices of the nations they represented. The patriarch assessed his spectral guests against the English ideals of hard work, diligent labor, and free trade. He applauded the Genius of the Currant, a 'little free trader' who pronounced the virtues of intercourse among nations. Oldknow chided the ploughman, who uttered a plea for 'protection'" (230). Contrary to the prevailing view, labor did not have to be kept "hidden or invisible" (233), for it was simply not understood as a sign of injustice. Nineteenth-century England understood labor as a neutral norm that allowed the efforts and the merit of all nations to be compared. If the comparison tended to favor the English, well, that was not their fault. People were responsible for themselves. The industrious Northerner got what he deserved, and so did "the slothful Cingalese craftsman" (233). Poverty could of course be recognized, but not, globally speaking, as an undeserved fate. It was certainly not presented as an effect of a global economic system that operates single-mindedly for the greater profit of England.

In short, today's dominant common sense was already in place. Poverty is widespread and terrible, but its causes are unenlightened culture, overpopulation, and political corruption. It's something that its victims do to themselves. We note it with regret but also with detachment.

In spite of the forcefulness of free market ideology, however, commodity recognition did not simply disappear. Thomas Hood's "The Song of the Shirt" (1843) put much-repeated words to what was clearly a mainstream, bipartisan perception: "It is not linen you're wearing out / But human creatures' lives." In the course of arguing against cosmopolitanism ("I am not bound to feel for a Chinaman as I feel for my fellow-countryman"), George Eliot makes concessions that register the unexpected moral weight that commodities continue to possess for her. She is bound, she writes, "not to demoralize [the Chinaman] with opium, not to compel him to my will by destroying or plundering the fruits of his labor." This is a harsh commentary on the Empire's normal operating procedure. It remained possible to arrive at such commentary by way of opium, tea, and other commodities.

In the first chapter of Eliot's *Middlemarch*, Dorothea inspects some emeralds she has inherited, trying to decide whether to keep them or not. It's widely seen as a wonderful moment, but little attention has been paid to the specific form her moral scrupulousness takes. Dorothea looks through the jewels to the labor behind them: "Yet what miserable men find such things, and work at them, and sell them!" We are of course permitted to think of our scrupulous, luxury-shunning heroine as somewhat confused. Dorothea considers the labor behind the emeralds, but she does so only after declaring that if she wore the emeralds she would look like she was "pirouetting." And she does not give them up, though ultimately she will give up much more of her inheritance. The point may be that where the system of commodities is concerned, moral consistency, which the refuser or boycotter may be seeking more ardently than political effectiveness itself, is even less accessible than political effectiveness. Shouldn't those who boycotted sugar also in good conscience have boycotted cotton, which is not a luxury and is not associated with pirouetting? Shouldn't Dorothea focus on what is miserable about the labor rather than what is miserable about the men who perform the labor? "Miserable" might mean economically deprived, or morally deficient, or simply unhappy. Dorothea seems to be trying to suggest that it's the hard labor of dealing with the jewels that makes them miserable in one or more of these senses. But that reading is undercut when she equates finding and working at the jewels, which seem strenuous occupations, perhaps underpaid and perhaps bad for the health, with merely selling them, which might get a raised eyebrow from the gentry but presumably is no worse in these respects than selling anything else. If Eliot wanted to refer to eight-year-old Indian children risking an early silicosis death from grinding agate, she has taken the long way round.[9] Still, she has gotten somewhere.

When Dorothea contemplates the emeralds, she considers herself to be in the presence of a luxury, not a necessity. The distinction is not self-evident. Immanuel Wallerstein insisted that as long as international trade involved only luxuries, as in the premodern period, it did not constitute a world system. A world system properly speaking came into being only with the large-scale exchange of staples, which is to say necessities. For it is only when necessities are traded that distant others enter into relationship with the whole society that uses them and the users enter into relationship with the whole society of the producers. That is what a system is. In his book *The Social Life of Things: Commodities in Cultural Perspective* (1986), Arjun Appadurai reverses Wallerstein's argument. Demand is the domain of subjectivity, not of objective need. There are no objective necessities. Hence there is no system. For Appadurai, demand must be separated off once and for all from the misleadingly authoritative concept of "needs" (29). Thus luxury can no longer be defined by contrast with necessity. Who is to say what is necessary, and to whom? So-called luxuries are better thought of as "goods whose principal use is rhetorical and social, goods that are simply incarnated signs. The necessity to which they respond is fundamentally political" (38). As Appadurai's title indicates, this is indeed a "cultural" perspective on the commodity. The effects of bestowing priority on culture show in the fact that whatever "political" means, it has to make do without two categories that usually seem essential both to political analysis and to the luxury/necessity distinction. First, Appadurai's politics no longer feels impelled to distinguish the rich from the poor. Second, it no longer assumes that global capitalism forms a system that constrains the desires of its inhabitants. Appadurai's brilliant and influential essay "Disjuncture and Difference in the Global Cultural Economy" can be understood, accordingly, as an effort to liberate culture from economics—that is the crucial "disjuncture" he proposes—by ruling out any system that would claim to coordinate the various "'scapes," thereby subordinating any one 'scape to any other. I note in passing that Appadurai's vision of the global cultural economy is a fast-working antidote to the throbbing moral migraine that Orwell seemed to want to turn into an epidemic.

To many in the humanities, Appadurai's cultural understanding of the commodity will seem very congenial. If there is no higher authority that can trump culture, as Appadurai suggests and as humanists tend to agree, then desire has been emancipated once and for all from moral and political oversight. Dorothea can stop looking nervously over her shoulder. She can receive in full the beauty of the emeralds without worrying about any putative misery that might have been involved in procuring them. Why penetrate beneath their surface brilliance? Is her worry really anything other than reflex obedience to some misogynous norm that she has long ago internalized?

Yes, it is. As Appadurai suggests, there are indeed things about the commodity that one will not notice as long as one is forever looking through it to the hidden realm of production beyond. But to forget production entirely would not be an improvement. Isn't Dorothea right, finally, to worry about where her emeralds come from? The moral of the novel's ending is certainly not that Dorothea should stop worrying and learn to love her inheritance. Spoiler alert: what the novel teaches her is to give that inheritance up.

Dorothea worries, at least in part, because jewels are luxuries. Her worry is thus evidence of sorts in favor of Wallerstein's distinction between luxuries and necessities. It's by following necessities that we can know anything at all about the worrisome way in which the majority of human beings are living.[10] How the majority of human beings are living is what matters to Dorothea, and it is what ought to matter. System exists if there is general constraint on ordinary people's lives. The rich are different from you and me; they are much freer. To decide whether or not the world is a system by consulting the freedom of the rich, a freedom that is literally extraordinary, is to give oneself over to what we used to call false consciousness.

It's by following luxuries, however, that we can know what it is we could live without. Blaming women for luxurious acts of consumption is not just misogyny. By asserting, however unconvincingly, that there exists a category of beings, namely men, who whether they actually make use of them or not supposedly do not need these commodities, we get to the real point: that the commodities are not in fact needed. It's a perverse way of getting to the point, but the point had to be made. What was needed was of course in the process of changing. According to the pathbreaking commodity historian Wolfgang Schivelbusch, the history of *Genussmittel*, or "articles of pleasure," which "include all spices and condiments as well as stimulants, intoxicants, and narcotics such as tobacco, tea, coffee, alcohol, and opium," is the development of "new needs" (*Tastes of Paradise*, xiii). The expression is an oxymoron. If the need for these objects is new, then we used to be able to live without them. And if we didn't need them then, then do we really need them now? Perhaps they are not really needs at all. The consuming self is thus reminded or informed that it was born free and that it has the power to break its chains, which were only recently forged.

Virginia Woolf on the Docks

In 1931, a few years before Orwell went north to survey the condition of the miners, Virginia Woolf made a visit to the London Docks. Watching the ships loading and unloading, she found herself contemplating the vast system of world trade on display and did some hesitant "this is the system which we all live on" thinking of her own. The system, she decided, was her personal responsibility as a consumer. It all depended on her.

> The only thing, one comes to feel, that can change the routine of the docks is a change in ourselves. Suppose, for example, that we gave up drinking claret, or took to using rubber instead of wool for our blankets, the whole machinery of production and distribution would rock and reel and seek about to adapt itself afresh. It is we—our tastes, our fashions, our needs—that make the cranes dip and swing, that call the ships from the sea. Our body is their master. We demand shoes, furs, bags, stoves, oil, rice puddings, candles; and they are brought to us. (*London Scene*, 14–15)

Woolf could be talking about herself alone but doing it tongue in cheek, thereby acknowledging that to claim so much personal responsibility can only be a playful fantasy. Or she could be using journalism's royal "we" so as to make a less playful, more defensible claim for the agency of women consumers as a group (the sketch was initially published in *Good Housekeeping*). It's hard to decide. It's also hard to decide how critical of the system Woolf is being. The commodities Woolf chooses are a promiscuous mix of luxuries (fur) with necessities (stoves, candles), as if she had not decided how much distance to take from the tradition of misogynistic satire that blames women for indulgence in luxury. The task of making a change in the system appears abruptly, without preamble or explanation. Woolf clearly thinks something can be changed but not necessarily that something *needs* to be changed. She is certainly not engaging in a full-throated denunciation of global capitalism. No distant suffering is to be glimpsed. The labor that produces these commodities goes unmentioned; Woolf does not ask how much or how little of what they produce the producers are permitted to consume.

> One feels an important, a complex, a necessary animal as one stands on the quayside watching the cranes hoist this barrel, that crate, that other bale from the holds of the ships that have come to anchor. Because one chooses to light a cigarette, all those barrels of Virginia tobacco are swung onshore. Flocks upon flocks of Australian sheep have submitted to the shears because we demand woollen overcoats in winter. As for the umbrella that we swing idly to and fro, a mammoth who roared through the swamps fifty thousand years ago has yielded up its tusk to make the handle. (15)

Woolf imagines a "change in ourselves," but she does not say why a change is necessary. In fact you might say she steals her own thunder by preempting any and all likely answers to that question. Does the system have to change because, say, trade results in the destruction of nature or the exploitation of distant countries? According to Woolf's illustrations, not at all. "Suppose, for example, that we gave up drinking claret, or took to using rubber instead of wool for our blankets . . ." If Woolf were looking for an example of exploitation, even an allegorical one, she would not have chosen wool. Wool grows back, and in the meantime the sheep seem to get on quite well without it. If Woolf wanted to refer to rubber, whose cultivation had been associated with recent and well-publicized horrors in the Belgian Congo, she might have let it represent a problem rather than, of all things, a solution to a problem. Her commodities seem chosen so as to avoid any hint of theft, deprivation, abuse, or injustice. Why else would she speak of the umbrella handle made from the tusk of a "mammoth who roared through the swamps fifty thousand years ago"? The mammoth will no longer be needing that tusk.

Those from whom something has been taken that they do need—the people whose time and energy and perhaps health, freedom, and even life went into tapping the rubber trees, shearing the sheep, growing the tobacco, and so on—are strangely invisible. But if they are not suffering, what exactly is wrong with this picture? The closest Woolf comes to offering grounds for her understated antipathy to world trade is waste. The ugliness of waste might be taken to stand in for all the unintended and undesirable consequences of what we could call—though Woolf doesn't—capitalism or consumerism. "As we go steaming up the river to London we meet its refuse coming down. Barges heaped with old buckets, razor blades, fish tails, newspapers and ashes—whatever we leave on our plates and throw into our dust bins—are discharging their cargoes upon the most desolate land in the world" (8–9). "The dumps get higher and higher, and thicker and thicker, their sides more precipitous with tin cans, their pinnacles more angular with ashes year by year" (9). A great liner bound for India "makes her way through rubbish barges, and sewage barges, and dredgers out to sea" (9). Here the rubbish and the sewage look like evidence about world trade chosen to irritate prosperous metropolitan readers, readers who feel themselves to be metaphorical ocean liners making their way among lesser vessels, which is to say merely moving through "the most desolate land in the world." These lines do not seem addressed to those doomed to inhabit this desolate landscape. The argument about world trade is not aimed at someone whose health or material self-interest might be damaged by world trade, but at someone whose aesthetic sensitivities might be offended by it.

And yet even this polemical projection of waste seems to fall short of real offensiveness. After taking her distance from the "severely utilitarian" temper of the docks, which tests everything for its "mercantile value" (11), Woolf suddenly finds aesthetic pleasure in the midst of utilitarianism, pleasure in the overcoming of wastefulness:

> Trade is ingenious and indefatigable beyond the bounds of imagination. None of all the multitudinous products and waste products of the earth but has been tested and found some possible use for. The bales of wool that are being swung from the hold of an Australian ship are girt, to save space, with iron hoops; but the hoops do not litter the floor; they are sent to Germany and made into safety razors. The wool itself exudes a coarse greasiness. This grease, which is harmful to blankets, serves, when extracted, to make face cream. Even the burrs that stick in the wool of certain breeds of sheep have their use, for they prove that the sheep un-

doubtedly were fed on certain rich pastures. Not a burr, not a tuft of wool, not an iron hoop is unaccounted for. And the aptness of everything to its purpose, the forethought and readiness which have provided for every process, come, as if by the back door, to provide that element of beauty which nobody in the Docks has ever given half a second of thought to. (12–13)

Here the unrestrained profit motive seems to lead not to the unintended and inevitable production of waste, but on the contrary to an ecological system so perfect that nothing at all is wasted. Place is found for matter out of place, and out of nowhere comes "the element of beauty."

An appreciation of the system's beauty is not what a critic of world capitalism might have most fervently desired from Woolf. Here she sounds much closer than one might expect to Thomas Friedman or Adam Smith. Woolf may be disoriented, or diplomatically pretending to be. But when she puts more emphasis on her own power to change the system than on the victimization of others, a victimization that would supply the moral grounds for such a change, she may not after all be entirely mistaken either about the system or about her relation to it. Like the suffering the system causes, the power to change it is a pertinent moral fact about the system.

Consider how her "our body is their master" differs from what Amanda Anderson usefully calls "aggrandized agency." For certain feminist critics, Anderson argues, most women are embedded in "unreflective forms of power." But "strange exceptions occur, wherein certain historical subjects are exempted from networks of power, and consequently accorded what I will characterize as 'aggrandized agency,' which is marked by both critical lucidity and political potency" ("Temptations of Aggrandized Agency," 47). For Woolf, women consumers do not seem to belong to these strange exceptions. They are not exempted from networks of power. What Woolf sees on the docks is, precisely, how women are embedded in networks of power. In some ways, therefore, her readers resemble Anderson's ordinary, unenlightened, unaggrandized or agency-less women. They are connected to power without thereby achieving either political potency or lucidity. Indeed, the lack of lucidity may be taken as a result of being plugged in; that's of course a standard interpretation of political muddleheadedness. But the woman consumer in Woolf cannot be described as simply unenlightened or unheroic. Her agency is "aggrandized," if not exactly in Anderson's sense. On the one hand, power is accompanied by confusion—confusion about how responsible one is, confusion about the ethical nature of the system one beholds. On the other hand, the connection to power is real, and with it comes an as yet unrealized and indeed unspecified possibility of achieving a degree of lucidity and political potency. If Woolf is making a mistake, it is not a simple mistake. If she is indulging a fantasy, it is a not merely an escapist fantasy.

The discourse of the beneficiary is not utopian. It denounces the system on the grounds that things could be otherwise. In other words, it assumes the existence of a power to change things. Without power, it cannot judge. Its moral judgments are thus historically relative, almost shockingly so. At one extreme, it would hold that things cannot even be seen as wrong unless the capacity to change them already exists and is seen to exist. This is roughly the point that, as I mentioned above, Thomas Haskell makes about slavery: people could not realize slavery was wrong in the strongest, most morally actionable sense until they had also realized it was something they could dispose of, something they could live without. "As long as we truly perceive an evil as inaccessible to manipulation—as an unavoidable or 'necessary' evil—our feelings of sympathy, no matter how great, will not produce that sense of operative responsibility that leads to action aimed at avoiding or alleviating the evil in question" ("Capitalism," 255). From this perspective, Woolf's playful fantasy of power over international trade belongs to the history of humanitarianism as Haskell and others have interpreted it. And so does Adam Smith.

Adam Smith's Earthquake

Writing in 1760, Adam Smith added to the second edition of his *Theory of Moral Sentiments* a much-cited passage, clearly inspired by the recent Lisbon earthquake, that demonstrates how little the average educated European will care about disasters that happen very far away, even when such disasters result in enormous suffering:

> Let us suppose that the great empire of China, with all its myriads of inhabitants, was suddenly swallowed up by an earthquake, and let us consider how a man of humanity in Europe, who had no sort of connexion

with that part of the world, would be affected upon receiving intelligence of this dreadful calamity. He would, I imagine, first of all, express very strongly his sorrow for the misfortune of that unhappy people, he would make many melancholy reflections upon the precariousness of human life, and the vanity of all the labours of man, which could thus be annihilated in a moment. He would too, perhaps, if he was a man of speculation, enter into many reasonings concerning the effects which this disaster might produce upon the commerce of Europe, and the trade and business of the world in general. And when all this fine philosophy was over, he would pursue his business or his pleasure, take his repose or his diversion, with the same ease and tranquility, as if no such accident had happened. The most frivolous disaster which could befall himself would occasion a more real disturbance. If he was to lose his little finger to-morrow, he would not sleep to-night; but, provided he never saw them, he will snore with the most profound security over the ruin of a hundred millions of his brethren, and the destruction of that immense multitude seems plainly an object less interesting to him, than this paltry misfortune of his own.[11]

Few who have read this passage have been able to forget the little finger. The little finger has seemed intuitive, incontrovertible proof that, as one might expect capitalism's greatest champion to argue, individual self-interest or self-love is humanity's natural, irresistible inclination, and that the same can therefore be said about the free market system.

This is not the argument Smith wanted to make. He has an answer to the "little finger" problem. He immediately posits the existence within us of an impartial observer whose approval we crave and who could never approve of us valuing our little fingers over the lives of hundreds of millions of our brethren. Thus are we saved from excess of self-love. Smith organizes this demonstration around a strange and equally haunting hypothetical:

To prevent, therefore, this paltry misfortune to himself, would a man of humanity be willing to sacrifice the lives of a hundred millions of his brethren, provided he had never seen them? Human nature startles with horror at the thought, and the world in its depravity and corruption, never produced such a villain as could be capable of entertaining it. But what makes this difference? . . . It is not the soft power of humanity, it is not that feeble spark of benevolence which Nature has lighted up in the human heart, that is thus capable of counteracting the strongest impulses of self-love. It is a stronger power, a more forcible motive, which exerts itself upon such occasions. It is reason, principle, conscience, the inhabitant of the breast, the great judge and arbiter of our conduct. (136–37)

Our supposed desire for the approval of a personified "stronger power" is of course a restatement of Christian orthodoxy. Smith's "reason," that "great judge and arbiter" that saves us from self-love, is a barely secularized representative of divinity. It's a banal gesture, and a weak one; it has certainly not caught on in anything like the same way as the little finger has. Even an admirer of Smith's free market model like Jagdish Bhagwati simply forgets that Smith indeed followed the little finger with "the inhabitant of the breast" and therefore accuses him of Eurocentric inhumanity.[12]

However, Smith is also reimagining the causal power of the individual in relation to the system. And he too is doing so in a way that does not paralyze moral thinking, but on the contrary enhances its possibilities. There is a certain literariness in imagining the horror that would be inspired by a Gothic villain capable of refusing the trade-off. But there is an even larger flight of imagination here. To ask whether a man of humanity would be "willing to sacrifice" millions of fellow humans to prevent the loss of his little finger is to bring into imaginative existence the logical alternative in which that sacrifice would be rejected and the little finger would be lopped off. In that case, so the reasoning goes, the earthquake could be prevented. It's less a hypothetical than an incipient fantasy: the fantasy of an exchange in which, by accepting the loss of his little finger, the "man of humanity" would not just be willing to prevent the earthquake but also able to do so, and thus able to save hundreds of millions of lives. The man of humanity can face Smith's ethical conundrum only if he can conceive of himself as capable of performing what amounts to a miracle. In other words, Smith's scenario allows the distant spectator to imagine possessing, however briefly and conjecturally, powers traditionally reserved for God. Smith did not believe in superhuman agency—the record is clear on this—but the passage invites and even demands some identification with the superhuman agency Smith doesn't believe in.[13]

Or so one might think. But perhaps that agency is not superhuman at all. In stopping to specify that his "man of humanity" had "no connexion" with China, Smith makes it clear that other Europeans did have such a connection. The passage refers to the earthquake's probable effects on "the commerce of Europe." The question of whether the imaginative hypothetical might be informed by a real connection is also posed by Eric Hayot in *The Hypothetical Mandarin*. Didn't it matter that Smith transferred the earthquake from Lisbon to China, which was both more distant and "the first contemporaneous civilizational other" (9) for modern Europe? While increasing the geographical distance so as to create a still more perfect disinterestedness, as the new humanitarianism would demand, Smith never seems quite able or willing to banish interest, effect, causal linkage. What the passage lays out is not quite the figure of the disinterested observer contemplating the misfortunes of people far away, completely disconnected from his own well-being, a figure that has given Smith an important place both in the history of aesthetics and in the history of humanitarianism. It is a figure, rather, that tarnishes humanitarian's purity.

Literature is often seen as a democratic instrument capable of overcoming distance, an optical instrument for correcting moral myopia. As it is commonly read, the Smith passage makes this technology seem unlikely to succeed, the forces arrayed against it being so vividly brought to mind. Self-love seems too strong, and the extra distance Smith added in moving the earthquake to China of course makes things worse. How could a European care in the strong sense about something so far away that the very news of it would take months to arrive? In what looks like an effort to give more weight to the little finger than to the earthquake, Smith also surreptitiously presses down on the scale by giving them different temporal locations vis-à-vis the reader. The point about the threat to your little finger is not just that it is near rather than far. It is also upcoming, imminently awaited. The earthquake is not only elsewhere; it is also in the past. It's not just the earthquake but the past as such that cannot produce an equivalent for the sleepless countdown to an immediately impending amputation. Anticipation concentrates the mind more than memory does, especially when anticipation combines with the uncertainty of outcome (uncertainty of outcome is the crucial absence from the genre of the philosophical example) that always hovers over an event that has not yet happened. Any loss that might be preventable, however minor, is worth a special kind of worry. Anything that it is too late to prevent, however catastrophic, falls into a different psychological category.

All this is true, and yet Smith's fantasy also produces one unexpected and valuable effect. The fantasy of possessing supernatural powers, a fantasy that is both disguised and embodied in the hypothetical, supplies a necessary precondition for the empathetic function of literature. The passage does not of course pretend to represent Chinese subjectivity, thus inducing us to care about the good of other people whose lives are distant from our own. But it builds a bridge of a different kind. It creates a causal connection. And in so doing, it creates the possibility for a moral connection. It does so where Smith himself did not seem to believe such a connection actually existed. According to Haskell, whom I have already cited, moral relations depend on causal relations: people will not care about distant others if there is nothing the others do that can or does affect our destiny and nothing we do that can or does affect theirs. This is why ethics must be historicized: people are unable to see a situation as wrong unless the social and technical means have developed to change that situation. Taking off from the historical examples of abolitionism and vegetarianism, Haskell argues, as I've note above, that what people have been capable of seeing as wrong has depended on their ability to imagine that things might be otherwise. This is the situation addressed by Smith's hypothetical. The superpower fantasy, an underappreciated aspect not just of the Smith passage but of the philosophical example generally, undercuts the spectatorial disinterestedness that Smith himself foregrounds and thus brings into existence the possibility of moral relationship.

In so doing, moreover, Smith's flight of imagination also makes visible an objective chain of causality that in fact already existed but had not yet been widely recognized as such. As far as distant non-Europeans were concerned, Europe was not merely a conditional source of humanitarian assistance. As Orwell was to declare two centuries later, it was an actually existing source of historical harm. Orwell knew because of his family's entanglement in the dirty, conjoined histories of sugar, opium, and tea. And Smith knew it too.

We know that Smith drank tea. (Two personal anecdotes about him have to do with his absentmindedness when doing so.) We know that the tea he drank came from China. Smith also would have known it, and not just because he had a professional knowledge of global trade. During his lifetime, the growth of the tea trade was arguably the single most visible fact about world trade as such. "In the early eighteenth century some 200,000 pounds of tea were imported into Britain each year, and by 1757 this figure reached a staggering sum of three million pounds, by which point it had become the dominant commodity of trade." Smith would have known that British demand for Chinese tea was perceived by Britain to be draining its silver reserves and that the solution increasingly proposed was that the tea be paid for instead by the sale of opium, which the Chinese government tried and failed to ban. We do not know Smith's opinion of the impact of the opium, coercively imported by the British East India Company, on the people of China. (As noted, Orwell's family were eventually among those who benefitted directly.) The worst effects probably became visible only after Smith's death, when the Opium Wars brought the logic of the global system to light. But we do know something about Smith's opinion of the effect that the East India Company's rule was having on the people of India, where the opium was grown. Commenting on an act of 1773 intended to regulate the East India Company, Smith remarked that it was a bad sign that individuals working for the company were so eager to leave India as soon as possible: "It is a very singular government in which every member of the administration wishes to get out of the country, and consequently to have done with the government, as soon as he can, and to whose interest, the day after he has left it and carried his whole fortune with him, it is perfectly indifferent though the whole country was swallowed up by an earthquake."

A non-European country swallowed up by an earthquake: this is exactly the scenario imagined in the "little finger" passage. Here European indifference to this distant earthquake and its consequences for the non-Europeans again takes the form of a hypothetical. But here it is associated with the callousness of colonial exploitation. It's not quite an admission, though Smith's prediction was in fact that the effects of the East India Company on India would be "completely destructive." It's merely a sign that he is thinking— naturally enough, in the wake of that earlier Bengal famine and the corruption inquiry—that the earthquake is an acceptable analogy for the effect one country can have on the economy and way of life of another. We are only a short step away from considering the China earthquake as the metaphorical price that China pays for the tea Smith himself is drinking. Smith has of course made no use of actual supernatural powers either to prevent or to cause China's suffering. The powers he invokes in his hypothetical merely make manifest the objective social relations that join China to Scotland. And their logic reanimates his famous passage. I could prevent the equivalent of an earthquake, the passage almost says, and I could do so by sacrificing something as relatively trivial as a little finger, perhaps the one crooked outside the tea cup. After all, this scenario requires only that we look through the humble everyday commodity to what lies on the other side of it. And it is enough to trouble one's sleep.

Chapter 4

THE NATION-STATE AS AGENT
OF COSMOPOLITANISM

The philosopher Jacques Rancière, commenting on Sartre's preface to Fanon in an essay called "The Cause of the Other," is skeptical as to whether statements such as Sartre's deserve to count as "political." Sartre's preface, Rancière writes, "was paradoxical, for it presented us a book that was not addressed to us [that is, us Europeans]. The war of liberation of the colonized is theirs, Sartre told us. This book is addressed to them. They have nothing to do with us, and especially not with our protestations of 'beautiful soul' humanism. These are the last form of colonial falsehood that the war smashes in pieces, [a falsehood] to which the war opposes its truth. The truth of war was thus posed as the denunciation of ethics." As we saw earlier ("Crammed with riches, Europe accorded the human status de jure to its inhabitants"), Sartre is indeed scathingly critical of the well-meaning humanist and his merely ethical condemnation of the state's bad behavior. He writes, "Chatter, chatter: liberty, equality, fraternity, love, honor, patriotism, and what have you. All this did not prevent us from making antiracial speeches about dirty niggers, dirty Jews, and dirty Arabs. High-minded people, liberal or just soft-hearted, protest that they were shocked by such inconsistency; but they were either mistaken or dishonest, for with us there is nothing more consistent than a racist humanism since the European has only been able to become a man through creating slaves and monsters" (*The Wretched of the Earth*, 26). And yet because Sartre is of course addressing European readers even when he says (wrongly) that Fanon's book is indifferent to them, the result, Rancière argues, is simply more ethics. "The paradox of this anti-ethical affirmation," Rancière goes on, "is that by excluding 'the cause of the other,' it in fact defined a relation to the war that was purely ethical and purely individual" (*Aux bords du politique*, 208–9, my translation). In other words, the discourse of the beneficiary (we have all profited by colonial exploitation) is finally not political at all but merely ethical.

The fact that for many readers Sartre's discourse continues to work, at least in some fashion and to some degree, would seem to lend it an interesting political potential even if we agreed with Rancière that it doesn't count as fully or satisfactorily political. Rancière does not see the potential. He examines French writing in support of the Algerian cause, trying to make the case that solidarity in such a cause can count as political. Sartre is wrong, Rancière says, in offering a (Hegelian) celebration of war as "the negation of the negation" (Rancière, *Aux bords du politique*, 204), hence as a definitive break with colonial identity and the conquest of a new, universal humanity or citizenship. But the more interesting question, for Rancière, is not what war means to the Algerians; it's what antiwar politics means to the French. Is an antiwar politics, a politics that objects to war making against another people in one's own name, really a politics at all? "How could the cause of the Algerians become our cause," Rancière asks, "other than on a moral level?" (*Aux bords du politique*, 208). His answer is that it could and did become a matter of French politics, but only because the infamous repression of October 17, 1961—when many Algerians who had come out in the streets were savagely beaten, drowned, and killed by other means—happened in Paris. A complete news blackout was imposed by the French government, which sought to make its multitude of victims invisible. "For us," Rancière writes, "this meant that something had been done in our name here at home [chez nous]" (210). Rancière clearly means for the emphasis to fall less on what has been done in our name than on the fact that it was done "here at home." Other things had also been done in our name, but they were done elsewhere. Things done elsewhere did not become political for us no matter how bad they were, even if they were done in the name of all Frenchmen. Presumably the same would have been true, say, of the French war in Indochina.

What immediately follows in Rancière's text is a contrast between the effect of the police violence in Paris and the effect of images from Rwanda and Bosnia in the period when he was writing, the 1990s. These images "at best produce indignation" (211), Rancière says, but they do not produce politics, for "fear and pity are not political affects" (211). It is strange that Rancière is not willing to consider the possibility that what France was doing in Algeria might have produced a politics in France, even a politics of "not in our name." For Rancière, "not in our name" is not strong enough. If it doesn't happen on our streets, it's not politics. Nothing matters except what goes on "in French public space" (210). That's why Rancière insists that the key element is not the war in Algeria, conducted by the military, but the twin facts that military operations in Algeria were labeled police actions and that the atrocities in the streets of Paris were indeed committed by the police. Police, polis: what is central to the cause of the other is a "disidentification in relation to the French state" (212), that is, a rupture within French citizenship. The cause of the other does not seem to involve an identification with the Algerians themselves or any other exceeding, escaping, or negating of French national belonging.

"As it happens," Rancière goes on, "there was no identification with the combatants [the Algerians], whose reasons were not ours. . . . But there was inclusion within a political subjectification—in a disidentification—[an inclusion] of that identity that was impossible to take on [*assumer*]" (213). As I read this rather complicated sentence, he is saying that the cause of the other always involves "an impossible identification" (213). His example, one page later, is the slogan "We are all German Jews" (214), an identification that does not aim to confirm or produce any real social grouping. Impossible identification is valuable because what it produces is a difference at the interior of citizenship (219), an internal alterity. It is not valuable for what it does in itself; it has no capacity to generate a new transnational political subject. Without the restrictiveness of (a given, already-existing) citizenship, which is to say the structure of an already-existing state, Rancière clearly fears that the cause of the other will slip "from politics to ethics, absorbed into duty toward those who suffer and coming finally to be accompanied by the geostrategic policing of the great powers" (218–19). Like other human rights cynics, he warns us off with the specter of ethics becoming military intervention by the state in humanitarianism's name.

Still, Rancière does finally want to argue that "the cause of the other" can count as a politics. Though he neglects the cause of the other when the injustice to the other does not happen on French soil, though (for all his well-known commitment to the theme of equality) he omits the themes of economic exploitation and inequality that loom large in Sartre's preface, though his overriding concern is with "the struggle against war" (208) and he does not explore the possibility that war can serve the economic self-interest of some (perhaps including some of the poor) as well as injure or limit the self-interest of those who fight it or pay for it—in spite of all this, the key point is that he does not allow politics to be defined by self-interest. He rejects the definition of politics as a community's self-interested self-preservation (*conservation de soi*). Political subjectivity, as he presents it, is never identical with group self-interest: it is only by embracing "the cause of the other" that the worker or proletarian separates off from a group identity fighting for its interests against other groups and becomes a figure for citizenship.

For Rancière, in other words, disinterestedness, which seemed a reason why action taken elsewhere would not count as politics and which would thus distinguish politics from humanism or humanitarianism or simply an ethical concern for the other, is actually an unavoidable part of what makes a cause genuinely political. Disinterestedness is part of politics in the restricted sense that Rancière insists on: politics at the level of the nation-state. "All of us without exception," the distinctively self-lacerating and seemingly counterproductive note Sartre strikes in his preface to Fanon, turns out to mark an unexpected and helpful stage in the progress from politics at the level of the nation-state to concern for global economic justice.

Adam Smith's commitment to the free market helped make him a critic of Britain's conduct in colonies such as India. Conversely, a commitment to your own nation at the expense of other nations could make you a critic of the free market. It could motivate you to notice imported commodities, to follow out the local consequences of importing them, and to inquire into the circumstances (perhaps shameful?) under which they were produced. Along with misogyny, in other words, another factor favoring commodity recognition is nationalism.

Like misogyny, nationalism is not what one might have expected at this point in the argument. Saying nasty things about foreign goods and/or about the foreigners who made them does not seem a likely path toward cosmopolitanism in a significant sense of the term. It certainly does not offer what you would describe as a spotless pedigree. One might prefer to trace today's concern for global equality back to a nobler line of conceptual ancestors. Like misogyny, however, nationalism is very real and very easy to document, and its incontestable substance gives a certain heft to the history of commodity recognition, which might otherwise seem more well intentioned than well grounded.

Historical successes in mobilizing nationalism against a foreign commodity are common enough. The Boston Tea Party of 1773, three years before the publication of Smith's *Wealth of Nations*, is often taken as the first in a long series of boycotts, targeted import refusals, and "Buy American" campaigns aimed at fending off perceived threats to American interests and American identity. As Dana Frank observes in *Buy American!*, her invaluable history of these campaigns, their content has often been unashamedly racist. Their organizers were often sordid opportunists out to make a buck by exploiting patriotism. The analysis behind them almost always misunderstood the actual economic logic at work. And yet thanks to such nationalist campaigns, the habit was preserved and encouraged looking through commodities to recognize something on the other side—something that wasn't right.

Aside from supplying evidence that commodity critique has been happening and indeed has been becoming a perceptual habit, the key thing nationalism does for this story is to provide it with an agent—an agent powerful enough to stand up to consumer demand and, over the past seventy-five years or so, to redistribute at least some of society's wealth. As I have suggested, critique rises to another stage—some would say it only truly becomes itself—when it acquires the confidence that things can in fact be otherwise. Proof that where the circulation of commodities and wealth is concerned things really could be otherwise came from the nation-state, and more particularly from the welfare state.

The welfare state is of course an unlikely agent of economic cosmopolitanism. It doesn't try to abolish inequality, but only to moderate its worst effects, and it aims only at the domestic population, choosing on the whole not to acknowledge the existence of economic suffering outside the nation's borders even if, as sometimes happens, that nation is at least partly responsible for causing the suffering. Yet it's not clear that economic cosmopolitanism could have come into being in any other way.

The welfare state emerged, under national-democratic pressure, in order to rescue or protect fellow citizens from suffering that the market itself clearly would not prevent and that many had begun to see the market as having caused. It was only in the middle of the twentieth century, Norman Barry writes in *Welfare*, that the idea became more or less established that the state should be responsible for assuring the well-being of its citizens (viii). In order for this to happen, there had to be a shift in the prevalent theory of responsibility. In the nineteenth century, unemployment was still largely seen as a matter of individual character, just as the proliferation of beggars in Country X or Country Y was seen as reflecting the character of those individual nations. "The welfare problems that arose were not normally thought to be caused by the markets; the identification of a welfare problem as an inevitable outcome of laissez-faire was made later by social philosophers with a rather different ethical social and economic value-system" (29). The shift happened, of course, at the domestic scale:

> The decisive break came with the reversal of the explanation of the process of social causation, and the consequent effect this had on the idea of personal responsibility that had been a feature of nineteenth-century thought. The emergence of the case for the welfare state began with the argument that, instead of public welfare being the cause of dependence, loss of autonomy and of capacity for individual responsibility for action, the opposite was the case. The advocates of the welfare state were able to argue that the individual had little or no control over his destiny in the context of impersonal market forces: the market system was unpredictable, so that the Victorian ideal of self-sufficiency was not achievable for some groups. (34)

Though the agency enlisted to defend fellow citizens was the nation-state and the solidarity elicited to do this job was correspondingly limited, the conclusion drawn about the market was necessarily a broader one: that the market cannot be depended on to produce social justice. Generated within the framework of nationalism, this moral then (like misogynous commodity recognition) becomes available for more comprehensive conclusions. The system *you* can't rely on is also the system that *no one* can rely on—a system that might, therefore, be producing the sort of innocent victims on the international level that are already painfully visible on the domestic level. "It's not your fault": this is the wisdom the welfare state had to fight very hard to achieve, and of course is now obliged to try to sustain.[1] For all its fragility, however, it exists. The neo-Victorians are right, therefore, to say that individual moral responsibility has been undermined. (They are right again that society can't do without some quotient of it—how else do you say what needs to be said about the financiers?) Where the champions of individual responsibility are wrong is in thinking the world would be better off if responsibility were restored to the punitive status quo ante. You should *not* blame yourself for outcomes that were so largely and brutally determined by forces outside your control.[2] And in realizing this, you put yourself in a position to learn that you share this condition not only with much of your nation but with much of the rest of the world.

The jump from smaller to larger scales of solidarity, which often looks terrifying and even suicidal, is in fact how contemporary ideas of welfare themselves developed. This is the argument of Stefanie Börner's book *Belonging, Solidarity, and Expansion in Social Policy*. In the nineteenth century, Börner shows, mutual benefit societies, local or occupational, were often the main and even the only institutions that stood between people and disaster in hard times. They were the closest thing to what we would now call insurance. The proposal to replace such societies with national health insurance schemes therefore ran into stiff resistance. I don't know these strangers, far away, the way I know my neighbors and fellow guild members. Why should I trust that impersonal institutions will help me in my time of need? Yet the resistance was overcome. It proved historically possible to expand solidarity to a much vaster scale. The result became European social democracy. And if solidarity could be expanded in this way, then in theory it should be possible to do so again at a still larger, transnational scale. Arguments that such schemes demand prior solidarity and that such solidarity doesn't and cannot exist are clearly untenable, Börner says. In the earlier case solidarity didn't preexist the new institutional arrangements. It seems on the contrary that it is the trustworthy functioning of the institutional arrangements that creates the solidarity at least as much as the other way around. The transnational scale that interests Börner is the European Union. As the news has been demonstrating, nation-to-nation solidarity within the EU is by no means to be counted on. But that does not mean it can be dismissed as a mere fantasy. And thus it is not too soon to be more geographically expansive with Börner's argument, applying it as well to those who are not citizens of the EU.

In the name of what exists, then, I return to the unsuitable history that gradually builds toward demands for global economic justice. It's the rise of the welfare state that enabled people to recognize for the first time not only the justice of redistributing social resources so as to protect the victims of the market, but also the feasibility of doing so. From the moment when the welfare state became a more or less effective agent of redistribution, capable of offering a safety net for the most vulnerable, from the moment when it was seen as capable to at least some degree of compensating for the inadequacies of the market and insulating many from its injustices within the borders of the nation, its example was also available for use at a scale beyond the nation. And much of the anti- or counterglobalization movement has drawn exactly this conclusion, calling for capitalism's regulation just as the antisweatshop movement has continued the work of the antisugar boycott.

The standard reading of George Orwell's career suggests that he moved from socialist internationalism in the 1930s to patriotism in the 1940s. In the run-up to World War II, he was radically cosmopolitan enough to question, briefly, the value of fighting on the side of the British Empire, even against an enemy like the Nazis. But he reversed himself, becoming a vocal patriot and, as if to leave no doubts on the subject, vociferously berating other intellectuals for their supposed lack of patriotism. After the war, this turn against cosmopolitanism became part of the larger, depressing story of the Cold War binary and its chilling effect on intellectual life. To put it this way is in some ways to understate the case. Even as a cosmopolitan, Orwell had been a cultural conservative. One of his favorite political touchstones, as I've said, was decency. He relied on his faith in the decency of the ordinary citizen in order to make his case against imperialism: "No modern man, in his heart of hearts, believes that it is right to invade a foreign country and hold the population down by force." On the other hand, he did not see decency as effective against the financial sector: "Foreign oppression is a much more obvious, understandable evil than economic oppression. Thus in England we tamely admit to being robbed in order to keep half a million worthless idlers in luxury, but we would fight to the last man sooner than be ruled by Chinamen; similarly, people who live on unearned dividends without a single qualm of conscience, see clearly enough that it is wrong to go and lord it in a foreign country where you are not wanted" (126). Here national identity is destiny. The claims of nationhood are what you reject in Chinamen who might want to rule you, and what you affirm in yourself when you don't want to be so ruled. Unfortunately, they are also what you affirm when you demand your tea and your sugar, your taxis and your strawberries and cream even though one hundred million Indians are living on the edge of starvation. If nationality is human nature at its most unchangeable, then prospects for global economic equality seem dim.

In the "you acquiesce in it" passage, Orwell does not immediately go off in a more promising direction. That sentence is followed by what looks like an open invitation to backlash: "The alternative is to throw the Empire overboard and reduce England to a cold and unimportant little island where we should all have to work very hard and live mainly on herrings and potatoes. That is the very last thing that any left-winger wants" (140). The herring-and-potato diet seems pretty decisive. Does Orwell include himself among the "left-wingers" of the final sentence, who indignantly reject this diet and certainly do not wish England to become a cold and unimportant little island? It's not clear. It's equally unclear that he himself is committed to ending the injustice he so forcefully lays out. It seems likely that he is speaking as one of the taxi takers and strawberry-and-cream eaters, though there is room for doubt: for better or worse, Orwell's class politics were fueled in part by a vigorous personal asceticism. To assume that Orwell speaks not as an eager renunciate but as a fellow beneficiary, which would help explain why the passage is so at odds with itself, would not clarify other issues. If Orwell does not want England to give up its empire and go back to eating herrings and potatoes, then what does he want? If he too "acquiesces" in this "evil state of affairs" while continuing to insist on how evil it is, then where does he place himself, where does he belong? Assuming that he was to be successful in persuading a certain number of readers that this state of affairs is indeed evil, as he seems to be attempting to do, to what category would those readers who agree with him belong?

Let me put this more generally: what kind of membership is available to a European or Northerner who would take up the cause of ending inequality between global North and global South, a cause that is not in his or her self-interest but that also does not require face-to-face communication or collaboration with actual global Southerners, let alone the autonomous activity of those Southerners? If action creates membership just as membership creates action, what hypothetical action and what hypothetical membership does an indictment like Orwell's aim at? What might be done about the global injustice that Orwell describes, and who might do it?

The clause "you acquiesce in it" seems very tough on the (presumably English) reader. Does it have an impact that could be properly described as political? Does it lead anywhere? It would not appear designed to. Unlike tea or opium (commodities that we know he had on his mind because of his family's history), the taxi, the strawberries, and the cream are recognizably domestic products, or were at that time. This leaves the non-Indian reader a little farther from seeing, in the desired sudden flash of insight, what exactly India might have to do with his or her little luxuries. The choice of domestic over exotic goods can perhaps be read as symptomatic. Perhaps the strawberries and cream are there so that tea and especially opium (which made the tea trade possible) can be absent. In any case, their absence makes it easier to hide the mediations, the visible causal steps that would lead from comfort here to starvation there. Enumerating these steps would allow them to be retraced, thus indicating what we might be able to do about this situation— consumer boycotts, or whatever. By omitting them, Orwell gives us nothing to do, no possible deliverance from the universal culpability.

That's precisely the point of his next two sentences: neither he nor the British left can see any eligible option. By making the alternative so ineligible, Orwell makes the clash of interests between Indians and Englishmen seem total and inescapable. Extreme self-blame begets an equally extreme sense of necessity. There is no possible overlap of interests, no room for negotiation. Simply because we are who we are and they are who they are, our guilt too becomes total and inescapable. The logic, both paradoxical and utterly familiar, combines in one sentence ethical provocation and backlash against that ethical provocation. Thus the guilt disappears. If this exploitation is really as inevitable as you say it is, I reason, then I will refuse to feel guilty about it. After all, I have to get on with my life; that is, I have to try to change what can be changed and live with what can't. If this can't be changed, if there is really no alternative, then it's not my business any more. Poof— my guilt is gone. Naomi Klein, whose part in Orwell's posthumous story will become apparent below, is spot on in her analysis of the logic here: "Any movement that is primarily rooted in making people feel guilty about going to the mall," she writes in *No Logo*, "is a backlash waiting to happen" (429).

As I suggested above, the broader sharing of blame for global economic inequality might well be seen as a way of slipping out from under the burden of class guilt at home. If everyone without exception is an exploiter, then I feel a bit less of one myself. As a line of defense against the discourse of the beneficiary, this has proved appealing. Sartre and Orwell have both been accused of unproductive self-flagellation, and not without reason.[3] Whatever else it is, "We are the 99 percent" works as a stimulant to activism. Can one say the same of "all of us without exception" or "you acquiesce in it"?

Still, the passage leaves open the possibility, however faint, that Orwell might not consider himself that sort of left-winger—that he himself *might* be thinking about the advantages for England of throwing the Empire overboard and returning to a harder-working life style and a herring-and-potato diet. And this interpretation is encouraged by what follows. Orwell's eventual point, arrived at only after a lengthy detour about attitudes toward class, is that like the abolition of class distinctions, the abolition of the Empire (and the abolition of unearned income from overseas investments, which he characteristically adds) will mean, for the average middle-class person, "abolishing a part of yourself" (141). In some moods, he suggests that this is much too much to demand of anyone: "they are asking us to commit suicide" (148). In other moods, however, he suggests that abolishing a part of yourself will merely mean making some "uncomfortable changes" in one's habits (142). This might after all not be too much to ask. And if it isn't, then what he had not yet learned to call global economic equality would suddenly become a less utopian, a more conceivable and even feasible political project.

Was Orwell thinking seriously about such global questions? Neither his admirers nor his critics have tended to think so. And yet there is evidence that he was, and evidence of an eye-opening sort.

At the end of 1941 Orwell found himself an employee of the government. He worked for the BBC Eastern Service, writing and supervising pro-Allied radio broadcasts to India, himself supervised by the Ministry of Information. Critical discussions of this period in his life have tended to focus on whether, by making himself an instrument of government propaganda—something he never denied—he was contradicting his trademark ideal of individual truth telling. But to see the issue here as the individual and the individual's freedom of speech vis-à-vis the government is to adopt a liberal Cold War framework that was not at all Orwell's own, not during that period and perhaps not even as the Cold War loomed. In fighting fascism, Orwell was fighting for social justice. The government was part of that effort—no doubt the most effective agent, in wartime, but by no means the only one; it did not redefine the common goal as nothing more than patriotic self-defense. Hence for him there was no self-betrayal in cooperating with it, irritating as the cooperation might sometimes feel.

But the episode raises a more interesting point. In his effort to talk his Indian listeners into taking the side of their colonizers, Orwell obviously could not content himself with reciting the litany of Axis atrocities. In India, his listeners would be able to match them with atrocities committed by the British themselves. So atrocities alone could not be a winning move. What could push Indians into taking one side against the other? Orwell hoped for as long as he could that the government would promise India its independence.[4] But he also knew that the ultimate key was some move in the direction of social justice, at home and abroad. He had already said that solidarity would not work unless he could address the standard-of-living gap, which would always keep the Indians from recognizing the English as plausible allies. I have quoted his refusal to lie about the disparity in income between England and India, a disparity so great that, he asserts, an Indian's leg is commonly thinner than an Englishman's arm. If he was going to make his case, Orwell would have to find a way of speaking to the social justice point he had raised in *The Road to Wigan Pier* five years earlier. The comparative comfort of ordinary Englishmen depended on maintaining Indians in poverty. This was true not just of the taxi taking, strawberry-and-cream eating member of the middle class, but also of those well below them on the social ladder, the downtrodden and the underpaid, the people on the back streets of Sheffield. The English were all beneficiaries of a very bad system. Ideally, what Orwell would want to tell the Indians, then, would be that the English were prepared to live on less, and live on a colder and less important little island. But where could he find evidence of such a wild proposition? How could he even begin to address the subject?

Amazingly, that is exactly the subject he addresses, and on his first day on the job. His first weekly news broadcast for the BBC, on January 20, 1942, notifies his Indian audience that consumption in Britain has been restricted.

> Once war has started, every nation must choose between guns and but-
> ter . . . since England is an island and shipping is very precious, they [the
> working population] must make do with amusements that do not waste
> imported materials . . . the luxuries which have to be discarded are the
> more elaborate kinds of food and drink, fashionable clothes, cosmetics
> and scents—all of which either demand a great deal of labor or use up rare
> imported materials. . . . If you have two hours to spare, and if you spend it
> in walking, swimming, skating, or playing football, according to the time
> of year, you have not used up any material or made any call on the nation's
> labor power. On the other hand, if you use those two hours in sitting in
> front of the fire and eating chocolates, you are using up coal which has to
> be dug out of the ground and carried to you by road, and sugar and cocoa
> beans which have to be transported half across the world.[5]

Why should Orwell be telling this to his Indian audience? Why should they care? It seems almost inexplicable.

The next sentence makes it clear that, though bananas have disappeared and even sugar is "none too plentiful," Orwell genuinely approves of rationing: "In the case of a good many unnecessary luxuries, the government diverts expenditure in the right direction by simply cutting off supplies" (*Orwell: The War Broadcasts*, 72). I note in passing that luxuries are no longer gendered. In his second broadcast, on January 22, Orwell announces: "There is a great deal of evidence that food rationing has not so far done any harm to public health in Britain—rather the contrary, if anything. English people before the war usually ate too much sugar and drank too much tea" (74). It's not exactly a call for England to go on a herring-and-potato diet, but his enthusiasm does seem to exceed by a good margin what the Indians would naturally be interested in as well as what is strictly necessary in order to maintain wartime morale at home.

Three weeks later, on February 14, 1942, Orwell's approval of wartime rationing has gotten even more intense: "The ordinary people who have to put up with these restrictions do not grumble, and are even heard to say that they would welcome greater sacrifices, if these would set free more shipping for the war effort, since they have a clear understanding of the issue, and set much more store by their liberty than by the comforts they have been accustomed to in peacetime" (53). William John West, the editor of the BBC broadcasts, finds this evocation of an uncomplaining multitude almost unbearable. He comments in a note: "The resemblance between Orwell's writing here and the voice screeching about rationing over the telescreens in *Nineteen Eighty-Four* is striking. 'The ordinary people' who 'would welcome greater sacrifices' are very clearly the basis for Orwell's creation in that book, the 'Proles.'"[6]

The leap forward to *Nineteen Eighty-Four* may be inevitable, but it misses what has become a more significant point. Yes, Orwell came to feel revulsion for much of what he did for the Ministry of Information. But he also knew that in working there—in working for the state—he had served purposes he had believed in before the war, continued to believe in after the war, and freely announced when he did not have the government looking over his shoulder. In his "London Letter" in *Partisan Review* for August 29, 1942, Orwell sounds exactly the same note:

> The most sensational drop [under rationing] has been in the consumption of sugar and tea.... Two ounces of tea is a miserable ration by English standards ... the endlessly stewing teapot was one of the bases of English life in the era of the dole, and though I shall miss the tea myself I have no doubt we are better off without it. War and consequent abandonment of imports tend to reduce use to the natural diet of these islands, that is, oatmeal, herrings, milk, potatoes, green vegetables and apples, which is healthy if rather dull.... After the war Britain must necessarily become more of an agricultural country, because, however the war ends, many markets will have disappeared owing to industrialization in India, Australia, etc. In that case we shall have to return to a diet resembling that of our ancestors, and perhaps these war years are not a bad preparation. (519)

In talking up gustatorial austerity, in other words, Orwell was not simply helping the war effort or saying what his bosses wanted him to say. On the contrary, his broadcasts on rationing were among those that the government singled out for censorship. The following passage (from March 14, 1942) is one of many that were cut by the censors:

> The British people are disciplining themselves yet harder for the demands of total war. The penalties against those who operate the Black Market in food have been stiffened up, so that offenders can now get as much as fourteen years imprisonment. White flour is to be withdrawn from the market shortly, and only wheatmeal flour allowed. This alone will save half a million tons of shipping space every year. It is probable also that the use of petrol for mere pleasure or convenience will shortly be prohibited. No one complains of these restrictions—on the contrary, the general public are demanding that they be made even stricter, so that the selfish minority who behave as though Britain were not at war can be dealt with once and for all.[7] (64)

In the back of his mind, Orwell was clearly thinking both about antifascist solidarity in the present and about the prospects for global economic equality after the war was over. What other motive could he have had for harping on a subject that was of no obvious interest to his intended audience and that was irritating his bosses, who told him to back off?[8]

The government, though unenthusiastic about Orwell's choice of subject, had performed a service for him. It had given him a microphone, had authorized him to speak in its voice, and—most important—had demonstrated the malleability of national identity: that is, the malleability of "decent" human nature. Rationing showed that what English consumers wanted, or thought they wanted, did not have to be accepted as a law of the market. It could be successfully interfered with. Rationing was historical evidence of such interference, interference carried out moreover by more or less democratic decision making. In interfering with demand, the state was of course acting under pressure; it was the war that made regulation of the market both militarily desirable and politically possible. Yet it also made possible the full-fledged welfare state that would immediately follow, inspired in large part by the unusual democratization of the war effort. The collision of necessities resulted in a freedom that, however provisional, taught Orwell a very useful lesson: that the power existed that could effect some degree of economic redistribution. Under the proper circumstances, people were open to the prospect of being transformed, even partially abolished.

Let me say this in another way. For motives of his own, Orwell needed evidence of a will to curb British consumption. The war provided it in the form of a dramatic interruption in world capitalism and world interconnectedness, a prolonged moment in which the channels of world trade were largely closed down and tropical commodities such as tea, coffee, sugar, tobacco, and oil were suddenly in short supply. The state had taken on the unlikely task of defetishizing the commodity. The effect was not to send Britain back to a nearly self-sufficient precapitalist state, but it was proof of sorts—and proof was what Orwell wanted—that the British could after all be something other than what they were. National identity was not fate, even in such visceral matters as habits of eating and drinking. Abolishing a part of yourself had become state policy—policy that was clearly unpleasant and yet also, miraculously, popular. This was news worth telling the Indians about.

Orwell never quite spells out his logic, but it is clear enough, and it is far-reaching. If partial self-abolition had been policy, then it could become policy again. No one could legitimately assume that British consumption and Indian consumption were stuck forever at a ratio of twelve to one. Collective asceticism might win another place on the political agenda, this time motivated by something other than the Nazi threat—by the desire for ecological survival, for a slower rate of immigration, and perhaps also for global economic justice. The wartime state prefigured the totalitarianism of *Nineteen Eighty-Four*, but it was also a genuine effort of collective self-fashioning that prefigured other as yet unrealized possibilities, even if Orwell, who was already dying, never found the occasion to look beyond the newborn Cold War and think them through.[9]

The standard objection to partial self-abolition and other forms of renunciation or self-punishment is that they are too small. Moral or theological conversions by justice-tormented individuals could never become large enough in scale to have an appreciable impact on the real world. There could never be enough individuals who would convert. And even if there were, those who did pledge to abolish a part of themselves would never willingly abolish so much of what they possess and enjoy, so much of what makes them who they are. This is the main objection that Elizabeth Kolbert raises to Naomi Klein's *This Changes Everything*. In a review titled "Can Climate Change Cure Capitalism?," Kolbert turns in conclusion to the plan of Switzerland's so-called 2,000-Watt Society:

> The idea behind the plan is that everyone on the planet is entitled to generate (more or less) the same emissions, meaning everyone should use (more or less) the same amount of energy.... All you really need to know to understand the plan is that, if you're American, you currently live in a 12,000 watt society ... and if you're Bangladeshi, you live in a 300 watt society. Thus, for Americans, living on 2,000 watts would mean cutting consumption by more than four-fifths; for Bangladeshis, it would mean increasing it by almost a factor of seven. (16)

Kolbert does not argue with Klein about the justice of this redistribution of resources. She assumes, as a realist, that she need not enter into such questions because she can see in advance that it simply isn't going to happen. "To draw on Klein's paraphrasing Al Gore, here's my inconvenient truth: when you tell people what it would actually take to radically reduce carbon emissions, they turn away. They don't want to give up air travel or air conditioning or HDTV or trips to the mall or the family car or the myriad other things that go with consuming 5,000 or 8,000 or 12,000 watts" (16). As we shall see, Klein, like Orwell, found an answer to this objection in the memory of rationing during World War II.

The idea that national solidarity is not the antithesis of larger, more cosmopolitan solidarities but is on the contrary the material out of which larger solidarities must be constructed will not be surprising to anyone who has followed conversation about the "new" cosmopolitanisms over the last twenty or twenty-five years. What may be surprising, however, is the notion that hope for a more satisfying cosmopolitanism might come from national solidarity *during wartime*. And worse than that—from an extending of wartime to cover more of what we used to call peacetime. The single strongest thing Larissa MacFarquhar finds to say in defense of the realism of her do-gooders is that in time of war the do-gooders' enterprise looks much less unrealistic.[10] In *Strangers Drowning* she writes, "In wartime—or in a crisis so devastating that it resembles war, such as an earthquake or a hurricane—duty expands far beyond its peacetime boundaries. In wartime, it's thought dutiful rather than unnatural to leave your family for the sake of a cause. In wartime, the line between family and strangers grows faint, as the duty to one's own enlarges to encompass all the people who are on the same side" (9–10).

This is not a point about war itself, which of course demands a taking of sides. (It remains to be seen whether a moral equivalent of war could exist without a division into my side and yours.) It is a point about the proven malleability of the individual-as-consumer. As MacFarquhar says, collective conduct in wartime absolutely refutes the notion "that the reason do-gooders are so rare is that it's human nature to care only for your own" (10).

"Many people quickly realized that organized politics was a more effective vehicle for human progress," MacFarquhar notes, "than the full hearts of the leisured bourgeois" (108). Haunted as she is by the ethical choices her subjects have made and stuck to, she does not give much space to the notion that they might be saved by the realization that not everything is their individual responsibility. What they need as individuals in order to maintain their sanity happens also to be what worldly justice needs: institutions and collective action rather than individual consumer choices. On this point Naomi Klein is much clearer. Responding to Kolbert's review in the *New York Review of Books*, Klein writes, "Kolbert would prefer me to have written a book focused on individual consumer behavior: how much people can drive and turn on their TVs." There are dozens of books that do exactly that, Klein says, "that reduce the climate challenge to a question of individual consumer choices. My book is about the huge public policy shifts needed to make those low-carbon choices far easier and accessible to all."[11] At this stage in history, in other words, the changes necessary both to stop climate change and to redistribute the world's economic resources are unthinkable without the intervention of the same morally unsuitable agent that conducted World War II: the nation-state.

Chapter 5

NAOMI KLEIN'S LOVE STORY

Can global justice be a project for people who are not saints? What about the sinners, or those of us who might not even be bothered to think of ourselves as sinners? It makes more sense to start with what I will call self-centeredness. (I've used the word "selfishness" above, but that I now see was a provocation. Selfishness implies that *any* disregard for others is an *excessive* disregard for others. That is a strong version of utilitarianism. It's not what I believe.) For most people most of the time, conduct is determined by a moderate, managed self-centeredness, and it's hard to imagine that things could be otherwise. Centered in our habits and concerns as we have no choice but to be, most of us are almost certainly unwilling to surrender as much of what we possess and what we feel makes us ourselves as those extraordinary individuals profiled in Larissa MacFarquhar's *Strangers Drowning*. What do we have to say about the project of equalizing life chances on a global scale? What does that project have to say to us?

MacFarquhar may not yet have come up with the idea for *Strangers Drowning* in 2008, when she profiled Naomi Klein for the *New Yorker*, but it's clear from her very positive piece that she does not want to see Klein placed in what would become their company. "She was wearing dark jeans tucked into tall brown boots, a crisp white shirt, and a long black blazer. She was dressed for a fox hunt. She looked terrific" (MacFarquhar, "Outside Agitator," 62). "The most visible and influential figure on the American left" (62), MacFarquhar's Klein is also a reluctant activist who as a child was dragged to demonstrations by her progressive parents when she would have preferred to experiment with cosmetics in the bathroom. "She may have made up with her parents," MacFarquhar writes, "but in matters of style she stands firm against the activism of the old school . . . she is groomed as flaw-lessly as an anchorwoman" (64). Klein's care of the self goes hand in hand with self-irony, a refusal to inflate that self to unseemly proportions. "The only kind of protest she likes," MacFarquhar observes, is "theatrical enough to be entertaining and self-mocking enough to dilute the earnestness to a level that she can tolerate" (69–70). As MacFarquhar presents her, Klein's motto might be a slightly ironic line from her mother, the disability activist Bonnie Klein, that ventriloquizes the younger generation's angle on political life: "What's wrong with having a good time?" (64).

"What's wrong with having a good time?" is not a question one would have imagined Klein asking, at least if one took the word of her critics. As noted above, Leigh Phillips and Elizabeth Kolbert accuse Klein of a puri-tanical, self-flagellating anticonsumerism that irritates its target audience and has no chance of succeeding in the real world. For Phillips and Kolbert, the real world is populated by people who, justifiably or not, will cling for as long as possible to the not-so-trivial luxuries, such as air conditioning and air travel, that make their lives easier and more interesting. Such things are not easily renounced. It is unrealistic, therefore, to expect the success of any movement aiming at the global redistribution of resources by means of pres-sure on consumers to scale back on their desires. Whatever new thoughts MacFarquhar may have about Klein after writing *Strangers Drowning*, a heroic exercise in extending her sympathies to people she describes as "vir-tuous ambulance chaser[s]" (5), her 2008 profile of Klein looks today like a corrective. It's hard to argue that the corrective was not and is not neces-sary. But it leaves various questions unanswered. If Klein is not asking for excessive and unrealistic self-sacrifice, what is she asking for? Her vision of global justice as a goal pursued by an international network of local groups and activists, both environmentalist and anticapitalist, is one of the least depressing accounts on offer of how humankind is presently grappling with the apocalyptic mess it has made of the planet, or could come to grapple with it. How does Klein address her fellow beneficiaries, absorbed as she knows them to be in the pleasures and privileges of their ordinary lives? What alternative to consumer asceticism or moral perfectionism might she be helping us imagine?

Klein's chances of appearing in the *New Yorker* in 2008 no doubt got a boost from her almost uncanny timing. Inspired by parallels between the US makeover of postinvasion Iraq (2003) and the radical free-market measures taken after the tsunami of 2004 and Hurricane Katrina (2005), *The Shock Doctrine: The Rise of Disaster Capitalism* (2007) had been written well before the collapse of the financial sector, but it came out right in the middle of the crisis and bailout. The coincidence didn't hurt its sales. Klein's first book, *No Logo: Taking Aim at the Brand Bullies* (2000), had also been blessed with good publishing luck. It was at the printer's, MacFarquhar notes, when "enormous crowds of protesters suddenly materialized outside a meeting of the World Trade Organization in Seattle." Just as suddenly, there the book was, ready to explain all the commotion. It was as if the antisweatshop and counterglobalization protesters had had access to advance copies.

Like her fashion sense, Klein's timing has the ring of what the antiutilitarian philosopher Bernard Williams has called "moral luck." Gauguin had moral luck when, after abandoning his family and moving to the South Pacific to become a great painter, he really did become a great painter, thereby vindicating a bit of conduct that might at the time he undertook it have looked ethically questionable. Is ethical questioning appropriate to actions that need luck in order to acquire their shape and meaning? As I understand him, Williams is arguing that if you recognize that what you do and even what you are is largely the product of historical accidents, lucky or unlucky, there are limits to what you can legitimately be held responsible for. Thus there are also limits to the relevance of morality itself. In *Moral Luck* Williams writes, "Justice requires not merely that something I am should be beyond luck, but that what I most fundamentally am should be so, and, in the light of that, admiration or liking or even enjoyment of the happy manifestations of luck can seem to be treachery to moral worth" (38). For Williams, the amoral moral seems to be: protect your enjoyment. Enjoy the good luck that made you a beneficiary of the system, or else you risk allowing each and every kind of enjoyment to drain out of your life. It's not quite "What's wrong with having a good time?," but it's a challenge to the logic of the beneficiary. Looked at from the outside, Klein's career through *This Changes Everything* seems at every step to have been inviting a spirited and unpredictable back-and-forth with Williams. She wants global justice without sacrificing more enjoyment than has to be sacrificed.

"This book is hinged on a simple hypothesis," Klein prophesied in *No Logo*: "that as more people discover the brand-name secrets of the global logo web, their outrage will fuel the next big political movement, a vast wave of opposition squarely targeting transnational corporations, particularly those with high brand-name recognition" (xx). Klein based this hypothesis, which turned out to be quite astute, on her perception that something had changed in capitalism, or at least in the face capitalism turned toward the world. Brand names had floated free of the places where the products were manufactured and the people who did the manufacturing. Now image, as the saying goes, was everything. This left the image owners vulnerable to bad publicity about what went on behind the closed doors of the distant factories. As Klein puts it: "A select group of corporations has been attempting to free itself from the corporeal world of commodities, manufacturing and products to exist on another plane. Anyone can manufacture a product, they reason. . . . Such menial tasks, therefore, can and should be farmed out to contractors and subcontractors whose only concern is filling the order on time and under budget (ideally in the Third World, where labor is dirt cheap, laws are lax and tax breaks come by the bushel)" (22).

It was to the Third World, then, that the intrepid activist-investigator would have to travel in order to dig up the "brand-name secrets" on which the system rested. And travel the book does. Long sections are devoted to visiting export-processing zones such as Rosario in the Philippines. The book's geography divides the world, roughly speaking, into an "us" of relatively prosperous consumers in the metropolis and a distant "them" of more or less destitute producers elsewhere, with only Klein and a few fellow activists moving back and forth between them and informing the first group about the second.

There is nothing unfamiliar about the notion that capital has shipped off manufacturing jobs to offshore zones of unregulated cheap labor like Rosario. That's hardly a secret. So what exactly *are* the "secrets" that Klein sets out to expose? As Klein tells the story, the companies she has in her sights are not, as one might have expected, simply pursuing the lowest possible wages and the highest possible profits. They are also acting out a psychodrama of body and soul, materiality and immateriality. "After establishing the 'soul' of their corporations," Klein writes, "the superbrand companies have gone on to rid themselves of their cumbersome bodies, and there is nothing that seems more cumbersome, more loathsomely corporeal, than the factories that produce their products" (196). This may sound plausible. But wait. Who ever said that corporeality was loathsome? Capital's motive in running away from production, "transcending the need to identify with [its] earthbound products" (195), treating its workers "like detritus—the stuff left behind" (197), and "sloughing [off] responsibility" (198) turns out to be something instinctive and unreasoned, like physical disgust. Corporate CEOs "are resolutely intent on evading any and all commitments" (223). It's as if fleeing from commitment were somehow just a thing capitalists inexplicably do, whether it serves their self-interest or not. This sounds less like an analysis of capitalism than an analysis of men.[1]

Is capitalism somehow masculine? Has it somehow *jilted* us? That's the suggestion lurking in the words "evading any and all commitments." The idea of a bunch of masculinized brand-name corporations romancing and then dumping a feminized the-rest-of-us seems a bit far-fetched, implying as it does (among other things) that once upon a time we were in fact seduced by the corporate sector, an assumption that does not fit well among Klein's other assumptions. And yet there is something to say for the hypothesis of a prior seduction. *No Logo* does show signs of emotional affinity with consumer capitalism, if only a reluctant and unconscious affinity. Like MacFarquhar's profile, *No Logo* is not shy about bringing in facts or at least sentiments from Klein's biography. In high school, Klein says, she felt a "globo-claustrophobia" (64), and it has never gone away. Speaking on behalf of her generation, she says she craves "metaphorical space: release, escape, some kind of open-ended freedom" (64). This craving sounds like high school, but it also sounds just like the corporate ethic as she has described it. By her own analysis, what the corporations have sought is also open-ended freedom—freedom conceived as virtuality, as cool images and logos no longer pinned down to "cumbersome bodies," as the successful evasion of binding commitments.

Bhaskar Sunkara has called Klein an "anarcho-liberal," and the "anarcho" half of the term captures an impulse to evade binding commitments that has always in fact been part of Klein's anti-institutional, nonparty politics.[2] Yet she is of course also, as the saying goes, a committed writer. Taking the idea of commitment in the broadest sense, its politico-economic connotations jumbled together with the romantic ones, there seems more to be said about what it might mean to Klein. Klein is bound by commitments as a writer of books, of course—entangled in relationships with her publishers and readers and also with the people she writes about, those whose "secrets" she gets writerly credit for uncovering. Pure disinterestedness is not the name of the game for writers. This is something Klein clearly knows, but like other self-conscious beneficiaries she does not find her knowledge easy to channel, nor does she know what to do with it. Being a writer may not take her out of the ethically intolerable relations that bind beneficiaries to nonbeneficiaries. But it is worth speculating that it perhaps indicates, if not quite models, an alternative that her readers are invited to identify with or strive for.

No Logo begins with a description of the "old industrial" neighborhood in Toronto where Klein lived while writing it, "the ghost of a garment district" (xv). Her landlord, she notes in a subordinate clause, "made his fortune manufacturing and selling London Fog overcoats" (xvi). Within a page the scene has shifted to Jakarta, where she is investigating the conditions of garment workers. Talking to women at a particular factory, she asks what brand of garments they produce. She needs to know, for as she says, "if I was to bring their story home, I would have to have my journalistic hook" (xvii). The brand they are producing turns out to be . . . London Fog. This "global coincidence" provides Klein with her journalistic hook. In discovering where London Fog overcoats come from, she says, she has demonstrated that "the young women in the export processing zone are our roommates of sorts, connected, as is so often the case, by a web of fabrics, shoelaces, franchises, teddy bears and brand names wrapped around the planet" (xviii).

For Klein to confess the need for a "journalistic hook" is to confess that she is working within the domain of self-interest: self-interest for herself as a writer as well as self-interest for her readers, who are consumers when they buy her books as much as when they buy London Fog raincoats. This display of metropolitan self-interest seems an important if neglected aspect of the power of Klein's prose. She is in perpetual danger of self-righteousness—as indeed I am myself when I make myself the vehicle of her arguments.[3] Notice how close to political incorrectness Klein is willing to come—close, critics would say, to an uncritical view of capitalism—in order to avoid the politically debilitating self-righteousness she would risk by more direct indignation at someone else's victimhood. Klein's "roommate" trope—"the young women in the export processing zone are our roommates of sorts"—suggests that consumers and producers are, roughly speaking, equals. Roommates *lend* clothes to each other. To call consumers and producers roommates is to obliterate, at least provisionally, the immense, guilt-producing disparity between what "we" pay for the garment and what "they" are paid to make it—precisely the disparity on which the antisweatshop campaign was founded. As rhetoric, this is noteworthy. To repeat: self-righteousness is an occupational hazard if you are addressing the beneficiaries of a system concerning the victims of the system, even if you make it clear that you too are one of those beneficiaries. What Klein is doing is very nearly the opposite of self-righteousness. For better or worse, it sounds more like the disregard for inequality one associates with cheery, we're-all-connected globalists like Thomas Friedman.

The profile of Thomas "the world is flat" Friedman in the *New Yorker* tells us, as if we needed to be told, that he is a genius at "branding." Branding is of course Klein's target of choice. But Klein is a brilliant brander as well. Consider "no logo," "the shock doctrine," and "disaster capitalism." If Klein is not exactly praising the system, as Friedman is, she is certainly wandering around a good deal in it, as Friedman does, and appropriating as a writer its distinctive and profitable forms of excitement, to which she herself has drawn attention. One of the first things you notice about *No Logo* is the rhetoric of the consumer guide. Speaking in the voice of the tastemaker, full of fashion-conscious winks and nods, she reports on the latest thing in activism. (She is describing the period before September 11, 2001, but perhaps, what goes around having come back around, not solely that period.) The older generation of student activists, Klein says, were concerned with "identity." The identity-politics craze is so *over*. What the young people are into now, she says, is brands and sweatshops. And that is really very cool.[4] "Anticorporate activism," Klein writes, "enjoys the priceless benefits of borrowed hipness and celebrity—borrowed, ironically enough, from the brands themselves" (349). Borrowed hipness is not a bad phrase for one of Klein's own favorite tones.

To be into brands and sweatshops entails tracking down and exposing the secrets of capital's flight. If capital is nomadic, you too have to be nomadic. Otherwise you can't stay on its trail. The implication of this politicized nomadism is that the word "tourist" can no longer be reserved for the bad guys. This makes sense of a certain tonality that Klein shares with Jamaica Kincaid, another notable practitioner of the discourse of the beneficiary. Kincaid's prose in *A Small Place* is both so turbulent and so charismatic in part because, try as she might, she cannot push the tourist "you" far enough away, cannot keep the tourist separate from Kincaid's own status as one who has left Antigua and now belongs to the privileged world of the beneficiaries. However self-ironizing they may be, Klein's reports on sweatshops, like Kincaid's on Antigua, are drawn to the voice of the travel writer. Her tourists are not ugly, like Kincaid's, but they do want to be informed about ugliness. The sights to be visited will include scenes of past unpleasantness and continuing calamity, such as shantytowns, as well as the more traditional ruins. Klein assumes that her tourist-readers will be concerned citizens of the world, people of good conscience who will not be above looking down at other, less conscientious tourists. Irony at the expense of tourism is included in the price of the package.

Speaking in this tone means being willing to sound like the "brand bullies." Since the brand bullies are the book's villains, this is a courageous or perhaps a foolhardy move. Klein comes back again and again to the idea that these corporations, freely moving their plants around in search of ever-lower wages, are behaving like "economic tourists" (208). When she talks about journalists like herself on the well-traveled trail of export processing zones, she cannot avoid the phrase "human-rights tourism." The new-style activism wants to force on the brand-name companies the material realities from which they have tried to escape. But in order to do so, it must disobey the parental injunction to stay at home and do the usual chores. At home, the material realities are assumed to be known and the injustices are assumed to be drab and boring. Enterprising activists must go farther afield in search of injustices that are more sordid and dramatic, more exciting and more profitable to expose. It's the game plan of the brand-name corporations.

Like any corporate advertiser, Klein exaggerates the unique value of her product and how much difference its purchase will make to the purchaser. "The only catch," she says, "is that for the system to function smoothly, workers must know little of the marketed lives of the products they produce and consumers must remain sheltered from the production lives of the brands they buy" (347). The *only* catch? To say so is to suggest that because the system generates secrets, bringing secrets to light will be sufficient to bring the system down. This is both self-aggrandizing and dangerously optimistic.[5] If the system cannot function except by keeping producers and consumers ignorant of each others' lives, then the system's archnemesis is none other than the whistle-blowing go-between who tells each about the other: someone like Klein herself. But as Klein knows, consumers and producers do not share in any obvious way the same self-interest. One group wants decent wages and working conditions, the other wants a bargain on an overcoat. How will mere awareness of each other's common relation to London Fog suddenly become a transcendence of their conflicting desires? As the story gets complicated late in the book, Klein has to retract the idea of a simple unity of interest and effort between supposed roommates. She quotes Filipino union organizers who "don't much like the idea of Westerners swooping into the [export processing] zone brandishing codes of conduct" and who say that the solution "lies with the workers themselves, inside the factory" (440). To her credit, Klein is equally willing to spread this message, even though it doesn't dangle the same hook for the well-meaning Western consumer.

The points I've raised may seem dismissive of Klein's argument. That is not at all how they are meant. They are meant to illustrate Klein's way of raising the question of global economic justice while also asking "What's wrong with having a good time?"—a double-action politics that, however hard to pull off, I see as indispensable. In other words, this is an example of global justice for selfish people. From this point of view, Klein's soft spot for corporate hype would count as a virtue. Addressing those of us who are not virtuous ambulance chasers, she needs to display and elicit desire, not just chasten it. Once our desire has been elicited, we may demand to know more. What does Klein really want? Even if Klein herself enjoys, and puts into her characteristic rhetoric, a version of the corporate wanderlust she complains of, her critique of corporate irresponsibility must also presuppose some alternative vision of commitment or relationship, whether achieved or not, that would perhaps be longer-term and certainly would be emotionally more fulfilling. Erotic inclinations and the possibility of their satisfaction are politically relevant, even politically indispensable. Perhaps what we are dealing with is, after all, a kind of love story.

Infrastructuralism

The prime object of Klein's affections in *The Shock Doctrine* is infrastructure.[6] Klein's "commitment," MacFarquhar says, is "to public institutions." The commitment is loudly affirmed. Disaster capitalism, which Klein defines as "orchestrated raids on the public sphere in the wake of catastrophic events" (*Shock Doctrine*, 6), aims at the institutions associated with the New Deal: "rent control, public housing, and the creation of Fannie Mae." But the targets about which Klein is most protective, the ones that for her are bathed in the warmest emotional glow, are infrastructures like water and electricity. Infrastructures have a special status. Like brand-name commodities, they too help corporations turn a profit. Unlike brand-name commodities, however, they are not associated with privileged consumption, or indeed with privilege at all. They are not matters of taste or fashion. There is no special bond between them and consumers. In this sense, infrastructure allows us to be selfish, or more selfish than we would ordinarily be when thinking of the common good. Infrastructure is not a luxury that has to be renounced or indeed a whim of consumer behavior that *can* be renounced. It is not emotionally demanding. It does not ask to be loved 24/7, and this despite the fact that it is there for you 24/7. Perhaps you don't have to love it at all. Most of the time, indifference to it is not unnatural or reprehensible. When infrastructure breaks down, which is famously the only time it gets noticed, it needs to be repaired, not clasped in a warm and tender embrace.

Like the coal mines that Orwell reported on in the north of England, infrastructure is something on which everyone depends. The fact that *everyone* depends on infrastructure is crucial; so is the fact that everyone *depends* on infrastructure. The phrase "off the grid" is a backhanded affirmation that in the modern world, even electricity must be thought of as more a necessity than a luxury. Those who don't have access to it are not having a good time or, like the tourists on the beach in Antigua, not as a good a time as they imagined they would. On this subject, fashion becomes irrelevant. Klein is obliged to speak instead in the name of survival. And the survival that free-market privatization, deregulation, and cuts in social spending throw into question is not just that of Third World producers onto whom the system has shunted its dirt and pain. In *The Shock Doctrine*, it applies to the beneficiaries as well. Even as Klein notes that the Volcker shock, say, exported the extremes of economic pain to zones where the people don't vote in US elections (159), she sees the shock doctrine as a universal policy, not really discriminating victims abroad from victims at home. The beneficiaries are suddenly much fewer. Suffering is much more evenly distributed. When Klein turns away from brand names, the division of the world between beneficiary and nonbeneficiary tends to fade from view.

Emotionally speaking, infrastructure is perhaps most stirring when it is absent, like the sewage treatment plant in Antigua. But the absence of infrastructure restores the sense of a definitive gap between home and abroad. The missing sewage treatment plant is not the result of local oversight or neglect; it is a symptom of systemic inequality, hence also a reason why the tourist, as a beneficiary of the system, might be induced to feel causal responsibility. Thus it sends us back to the discourse of the beneficiary. More on this below.

The fact that Klein's heart goes out to infrastructure has to do with its vulnerability. But it also has to do with the good-time atmosphere that surrounds those who are trying to stop infrastructural projects of the wrong kind, like the Keystone XL pipeline. She refers to these movements collectively as "Blockadia." The politico-theatrical confrontations they arrange make them sound, in her telling, a bit like block parties, effectual but somehow also festive. Naturally enough, she also displays a fondness for those who join in the fight to protect or reconstruct infrastructure. On the last page of the book these allies are identified as "communities" (466), and more specifically "local people's renewal movements" (466). As Klein climbs the ladder from local community to the state, however, her feelings cool off a bit. The institutions of the New Deal were of course state interventions in the economy, but they can also be seen equally well as victories of the left, the results of "pressure from below" (62–63), and in *The Shock Doctrine* that is how Klein prefers to see them. When rescue is called for, her impulse is not to call on the state—perhaps because she thinks it won't answer, and perhaps for other reasons.[7] But neglecting the state sends her straight back to the problems that infrastructure seemed to be helping her avoid. Like the locavore phenomenon, Klein's preference for local activism leaves localities and their citizens shouldering too heavy a moral burden. It is their individual moral choices that determine whether global justice will sink or swim. And if so, Klein will have trouble fending off the objections she gets from Kolbert and Phillips, among others. The project of consumer renunciation or mass asceticism, they say, asks for too much; it is not going to happen. If it did happen, it would entail an unfair personal sacrifice. I don't know whose responsibility all this is, I announce quietly to myself, but I know it's too big to be mine.

In *No Logo* Klein takes some distance from the consumer-is-responsible position, but at various points she also slips back into it. Whether it is a position that can be definitively escaped is arguably the question that pushes her toward the subject of climate change in *This Changes Everything*. In any event, the only possible escape route would clearly involve shifting much of the responsibility to larger, collective agents, as we saw her shift it in her *New York Review of Books* reply to Kolbert. It would be convenient, therefore, if she could feel more turned on by the state. *This Changes Everything* makes explicit the need for such feeling, if not quite the feeling itself. There the option of "shopping our way out of it" (211) is openly mocked, and we are told why: "If these demand-side emission reductions are to take place on anything like the scale required, they cannot be left to the lifestyle decisions of earnest urbanites who like going to farmers' markets on Saturday afternoons" (90). Klein recognizes that the moral weight must be lifted off consumers, whether alone or in small groups, and placed instead on public policies, including the policies of the state. Only the proven power of state intervention allows us to believe the market can in fact be tamed, as it was by rationing, however briefly, during World War II. No smaller agent can even approach the scale of collective action that the linked subjects of global justice and climate change presuppose—without which, to put this more strongly, the issue of global justice cannot even begin to be conceived or formulated.

It's not easy to imagine Klein submitting to a reeducation of desire. But perhaps her desire doesn't need so much reeducating after all. For her, the state is something of a Gothic villain—possibly sexy, if seen in a certain light, even if definitely and deeply unreliable in its motives and behavior. Governing is itself authoritarian, and as MacFarquhar says, Klein does not like authority. "In principle, she is a Keynesian, but she distrusts institutions, platforms, theories—anything except extremely small, local, ad hoc, spontaneous initiatives. Basically, she really, really doesn't like being told what to do. It is clear, in *The Shock Doctrine*, just how deeply she disdains the political" ("Outside Agitator," 68). MacFarquhar, it's interesting to note, is even more disdainful of politics than she judges Klein to be. When Klein speaks of "violent autocrats of the free-market persuasion" such as Pinochet, Yeltsin, and Suharto, MacFarquhar says, she "holds capitalism guilty of all their sins" (71). MacFarquhar herself would be more comfortable, she seems to hint, pointing the finger at guilty individuals rather than at abstractions. For her, individuals are real, whereas the reality of abstractions such as capitalism and the state seems open to question. The contrast favors Klein, who seems to have a partial but perceptible receptivity to government. You can see at least a glimmer of attraction for the wielding of political authority as it should be wielded: "A government shouldn't play the market," Klein tells MacFarquhar, "it should govern" ("Outside Agitator," 62). Asserting itself, Klein now assumes, is the government's proper business. Taking on climate change "requires heavy-duty interventions, seeping bans on polluting activities, deep subsidies for green alternatives, pricey penalties for violations, new taxes, new public works programs, reversals of privatization" (39)—all of them vigorous state interventions.

Klein's feelings for the state's traditional masculinity seem most positive when, looking for evidence that humans will be able to do something about climate change, she finds it in the memory of popular support for the military. The amount of money that would be needed to transition to a non-fossil-fuel-based economy seems staggering, she admits. As does the popular will that would be needed to cut back consumption, especially in rich countries like the United States and Canada. But both have a precedent: World War II rationing. "In Britain and North America during World War II," she writes "every strata of society was required to make do with less, even the very rich. And in fact, although overall consumption in the UK dropped by

16 percent, caloric intake for the poor increased during the war, because the rations provided low income people with more than they could otherwise afford" (*This Changes Everything*, 115). She quotes a government pamphlet titled "What Is Rationing?," and she cites US government crackdowns on the wealthy who broke the rules. What the movement for climate change needs now, she concludes, is both "war-time levels of spending" and the wartime "perception of fairness—that one set of rules applied to players big and small" (116). In an epigraph she also quotes Orwell: "The lady in the Rolls-Royce car is more damaging to morale than a fleet of Goering's bombing planes" (96).

With a quotation from Christopher Lasch (about his White House speech-writing stint during the Carter administration), Klein bolsters her claim that the lessons of World War II can be applied in peacetime: "What was needed was a program that called for sacrifices all right, but made it clear that the sacrifices would be distributed in an equitable fashion" (116). In the conclusion to *Strangers Drowning*, MacFarquhar shows an interest in the same line of thinking. In wartime, she says, the self-sacrificing impulses of the do-gooder appear less eccentric, more sympathetic. For better or worse, commitment to the good of others normally seems praiseworthy in times of national danger. Why then should the same not hold now, surrounded as we and others are by dangers of all sorts? "For do-gooders," MacFarquhar concludes, "it is always war-time" (296).

It is always wartime: this is a hard pill to swallow. Who wants to contemplate a life of perpetual wartime, with no peacetime to look forward to and no leave in the meantime? One might imagine that the sacrifices of wartime seem bearable only because they are assumed to be temporary as well as evenly distributed. It's a bit of a surprise, then, to find that there has been something of a retro fashion for the moment of wartime rationing. You see it for example in the republication of instructional leaflets circulated during the war such as *Make Do and Mend: Keeping Family and Home Afloat on War Rations*. "Recycling, more popular in today's 'green' society than at any time since the years of wartime austerity," Jill Norman writes in the foreword, "was the order of the day in the forties, with paper, old pots and pans and all manner of scrap salvaged to help the war effort" (5).[8]

It's an ironic nostalgia, of course, in an era when austerity is still being imposed with some frequency as an official political-economic program, if only as a temporary measure imagined to enable further growth. That is the problem when Klein tries to attack austerity as economics while at the same time proposing a version of austerity as environmental necessity and (in the metropolis) as a step toward global economic justice. There is the very real possibility that these projects will simply peel away from each other. Can austerity be both punishment and virtue, depending on the lens through which it's viewed? Normally you would say yes. Leigh Phillips, in his critique of what he calls "eco-austerity" (*Austerity Ecology*, 33), notes that from the viewpoint of curbing emissions, the best moment in recent history was the Great Depression—not a period anticapitalists will want to send their constituents back to.

Nevertheless, there is encouragement to be taken, as I have suggested, from the fact that collective asceticism was once state policy. Sacrifice no longer looks so utopian when it has been successfully decided upon by a government, and in an at least minimally democratic way, and then (so Orwell attests) ratified by public opinion. If it succeeded once, why would the experiment not be repeatable? The question seems pertinent even if few if any of those consulted at the time were thinking, as George Orwell was, that wartime rationing might one day show itself to have been a move in the long game of equalizing global resources.

Sacrifice Zones

In a critique of *The Shock Doctrine*, Doug Henwood suggests that there is a problem with "the central role that 'shock' and 'disaster' play in the narrative. By so emphasizing 'shock'—and so much of that shock being extreme repression and torture—Klein skirts the difficult question of how the right developed enough popular consent and legitimation to win election after election, sometimes in landslides."[9] According to Henwood, Klein makes it seem as if the ideologues of the free market hoodwinked the population into accepting their solutions only by taking advantage of disasters. They hit us when our guard was down. But free-market ideology did not *need* disaster, Henwood replies, in order to make itself loved. Society did not hook up with free-market capitalism on the rebound, as it were. What Klein leaves out is the fact that it had already won widespread consent. To return to the vocabulary of high school, it was already popular. Capitalism was one of the cool kids.

Why doesn't Klein see that capitalism, with a tidy budget to lay out on lavish dates and trendy self-adornment, was already scoring big in the political popularity contest? The answer seems to be that she prefers not to consider her metropolitan addressees as *bought off*, won over by goodies they will enjoy too much ever to want to give up. She does not want to see them as selfish. Which implies she has mixed feelings about seeing them, after all, as beneficiaries. Having worked within the discourse of the beneficiary for some time, perhaps she is looking for the exit. As we saw above, Klein's focus on infrastructure in *The Shock Doctrine* tends to erase the geopolitical line separating image-hungry First World consumers from food-deprived, materially dirtied Third World producers, the line around which *No Logo* was organized. It's as if she had become impatient with the morally lopsided and (to some) simplistic division of the world on which the logic of the beneficiary is premised.

If so, how should we feel about it? Giving up on the beneficiary/nonbeneficiary divide may seem like a move in the right direction. Orthodox Marxism would certainly think so, as would the antidialectical but orthodoxly universalistic Marxism of a journal like *Jacobin*. For each, capitalism is the one common enemy that must define the common struggles of everyone, wherever we happen to be situated. No, our motto cannot be location, location, location. In their view, that is the big mistake that the discourse of the beneficiary makes. Getting out of that discourse would also have added virtues that are visible beyond the orthodox left. It would take more weight off the ethical consumer. If you are not the cause of distant suffering, then your self-divestment choices are no longer so politically consequential. Denying that you are in any important sense a beneficiary would also allow you to give your full attention to the variety of urgent issues that face you at home, undistracted by how fuzzy those issues may start to appear if you step back and look at them in more global perspective.

On the first page of *This Changes Everything*, Klein tells the story of a small commuter plane in Washington, DC, that sank into the melted tarmac on a very, very hot day, then was pulled out and continued on its way. Airline travel is of course a major factor in global warming. But Klein does not set herself up to pass judgment. "I am in no position to judge these passengers," Klein concludes. "All of us who live high consumer lifestyles, wherever we happen to reside, are metaphorically, passengers on Flight

3935" (1–2). If those "who live high consumer life styles" belong to an "us," as Klein's "all of us" suggests, then Klein appears to be still speaking from within the discourse of the beneficiary. But the climate change argument pushes her away from it. For the discourse of the beneficiary, those who are excluded from this "us"—the people elsewhere in the world who don't live such "high" lifestyles—are a scandal. Whether or not they live in absolute deprivation, they certainly suffer from intolerable inequality. From the point of view of climate change, however, the "low" lifestyle people are not scandalous at all. On the contrary, they are a model of lower, sustainable consumption that, for the good of the planet, should be followed by everyone. To put this very crudely: they are not having a good time now, and they should not expect to have a good time in the future. A good time is not what anyone has in store.

In what is perhaps a gesture toward equality, Klein suggests, at some risk of self-contradiction, that even her fellow beneficiaries have not actually been having a good time. Perhaps they were never even beneficiaries at all. Speaking of the sacrifices made in the name of austerity over the past thirty years, Klein writes, "It seems to me that if humans are capable of sacrificing this much collective benefit in the name of stabilizing an economic system that makes daily life so much more expensive and precarious, then surely humans should be capable of making some important lifestyle changes in the interest of stabilizing the physical systems upon which all of life depends" (*This Changes Everything*, 17). It's a good debater's point. But if we have been sacrificing, then we can't also have been benefitting, can we? Isn't it one or the other? Perhaps not, but there is still a conundrum here. It's the same conundrum Klein enters into when critics of environmentalism object that no one will choose to sacrifice their present for their future. Klein answers that it's less their future they are trying to change than their present. This answer is politically pious, but it isn't satisfactory. If their present is in such dire need of change, then under capitalism they are already sacrificing. Klein seems to have forgotten here that she has been presenting them as beneficiaries. The premise that the sum total of austerity's effects in the metropolis has been sacrifice collides head-on with the idea that metropolitan consumers have been bought off with creature comforts and that these comforts explain their allegiance to the system, hence also the difficulty of addressing both climate change and global justice. From the standpoint of the beneficiary, the idea that we are all suffering is a way of evading structural inequality. To think we are all equally austerity's victims is to tilt the balance of "What is to be done?" away from global justice and back toward local politics, or toward politics as such. It thereby calms the free-floating anxiety that any mention of global justice is sure to arouse: the anxiety that one is about to take one's leave from politics altogether and float off into the airy domain of ethics.

Instead of calming that anxiety, we should cherish it.

Is the metropolitan reader a beneficiary or not? You can't resolve this question by doing what you probably most want to do. What you most want to do (allow me to inform you) is to separate off, within the metropolis, those who are benefitting from those who are sacrificing. But the majority of them are the same people, viewed at different scales. You can't let go of the local scale, but neither can you let go of the global scale. The World Bank numbers are unambiguous and insistent: most of those who have sacrificed, in the metropolis, have also benefitted. Economic Orientalism is a reality. Structural inequality has not been disappearing. You can't expect the discourse of the beneficiary to disappear either.

As an example of what she calls "sacrifice zones," Klein describes the Pacific island of Nauru. "Sacrifice zones" are "places that don't count and therefore can be poisoned, drained, or otherwise destroyed, for the supposed greater good of the economic process" (*This Changes Everything*, 169–70). Once pillaged for its phosphates and now an ecological disaster as the water levels rise around it, Nauru has been taken over as an offshore refugee center where Australia dumps many boatloads of mostly South Asian migrants and leaves them in limbo for up to five years. Klein describes it as a trash bin for the rest of the world. It's a pungent metaphor, but it also suggests something that Klein may not have intended to say: that the rest of the world, though of course it is also subject to global warming, is *not* a trash bin, not yet, or at any rate is to some appreciable degree better off than the island of Nauru. It may seem like a quibble, but sacrifice zones can be pointed out only because the whole world is not (yet) a sacrifice zone. Nauru can serve as a warning and a reproach to the world only if the world does not already resemble Nauru. It's a still stronger reproach if—and this is clearly what Klein assumes—the "supposed greater good of the economic process" is not just "supposed" but a very *real* greater good, at least for some people: for example, those who live in places that do not resemble Nauru, people who do not live in the midst of garbage because Nauru does, people whose cheap food was grown with the help of Nauru's phosphates. However reluctant Klein may be to commit herself to the discourse of the beneficiary, her "sacrifice zones" pull her back into it.

And this is a good thing. It is easy to ridicule the assumption, in Leigh Phillips's words, "that all Westerners are equally, lavishly affluent these days and so the most harrowing experience we can undergo is having too much goat cheese in our salad, and that we have nothing in common with people in the developing world" (*Austerity Ecology*, 25). But Klein says none of this. She does not say that all Westerners are *equally* affluent. She does not say all Westerners are *lavishly* affluent. She does not say that all Westerners are utterly and absolutely different from all non-Westerners. You can be clear about all this, as Klein is, and still affirm that on the whole, at the largest scale, there is a large difference between people living in the West and people not living in the West. That difference is that people living in the West have much greater access to the world's goods and services. That's what the figures tell us. Being poor outside the affluent West is a different experience from being poor within it. Phillips says it's grotesque to lump the rich and poor together in the West so as to arrive at the notion of an "average" Westerner (54) or calculate "the greenhouse gas emissions of the average American" (55). As we have seen, Klein herself is eloquently critical of the notion that greenhouse gas emissions can be reduced at the scale that's necessary by demanding changes only or primarily from individual consumers. But that is not an argument against national averages, or against averages as such. What about, say, a comparison between the average *poor person* in the United States and the average *poor person* in Sierra Leone? That's exactly the kind of comparison George Orwell was making. What's the problem with it? If Orwell is roughly right in his calculations, which are roughly Branko Milanović's calculations, then it makes no sense to pretend we are not beneficiaries.

Other Business

As a hypothetical agent of global economic justice, the state is of course too small. At its theoretical best, it looks out for its own citizens and only for its own citizens. Beyond its borders, most of what it is in the habit of doing would be hard to describe as public-spirited, let alone altruistic. There is a well-known paradox whereby the state demands and gets self-sacrifice from its citizens, most visibly in time of war, and then in its dealings with other states takes advantage of all that altruism in order to assert its own self-interest in a thuggish and bullying manner. Individual altruism translates into collective self-interest. (History has shown that this dynamic cannot be reversed: the idea that numberless acts of individual self-interest will miraculously result in the disinterested good of the whole, a good that no individual was seeking, has proven itself to be a globalizer's fantasy: *everyone* having a good time.) Why then even raise the subject of the state's possible role in global justice? Why not pin all our hopes on the nongovernmental organizations that make global justice their explicit and exclusive business? The answer is that though of course the increasing clout of the NGO sector is hugely important and a reason for cautious optimism, although it was miraculous that the great powers ever ceded any of their sovereignty at all to the United Nations, flawed as the United Nations is, the question of global economic redistribution most often presents itself, or rather hides itself, in political issues that seem to be about something else, like military budgets or jobs or refugees or, as in Klein's *This Changes Everything*, climate change.[10] It is rarely an agenda item in its own right. If it is mentioned at all, the topic of global justice will come up under "other business."[11]

In a book called *Climate of Corruption*, to which Klein alludes, Larry Bell writes that climate change "has little to do with the state of the environment and much to do with shackling capitalism and transforming the American way of life in the interests of global wealth distribution" (xi). Like abandoning the American way of life, global wealth redistribution is not something Bell favors. He is wrong, of course, about climate change: people talk about it because it is scary and very real. But he's right that attention to climate change necessarily encourages big government intervention. And he's right again that the issue overlaps with the issue of "global wealth redistribution." Here the political right is willing to say something that, however true it may be, the political left finds it more awkward to talk about.

Consider the phenomenon of remittances. According to Ester Hernandez and Susan Bibler Coutin, quoted above, the World Bank describes remittances sent home by foreign workers as "unrequited transfers." By this unintentionally emotive phrase the World Bank apparently means that nothing of monetary value, such as sugar or coffee, is thought to leave El Salvador, say—nothing for which these payments could be seen as an exchange. Thus remittances are a sort of gift. This description seems contestable. What El Salvador has given the United States in exchange for the dollars that travel back to El Salvador is its people, people whom El Salvador has paid a great deal to raise and educate. I do not know how to measure the cost of raising and educating the migrant workers against the value of the remittances they send back. Still, it is true that raising and educating those Salvadorans who did *not* go to work in the United States presumably cost just as much. That cost was not offset by remittances. That's why the remittances make the difference they make in El Salvador. If so, then the unrequited transfer is not the piece of grotesque, out-of-control bureaucratese that it sounds like. It marks a small but real redistribution of resources across the border between rich and poor areas of the world.

This is a graceless thing to acknowledge. Most of the migrant workers in question lead very hard lives, some of them unimaginably so. Their personal sacrifices have often been described. They are not merely mistreated in the faraway places where they work but exploited in the technical sense: they are a source of surplus value for their employers. At the same time, however, they are also agents of redistribution, globally considered. Through them, money flows from the world's richer regions to its poorer regions. From a global perspective, then, they too have to count as beneficiaries, though they are hardly the sort of more prosperous beneficiaries one imagines Klein is addressing. The designation will seem callous and, for orthodox Marxists, revisionist. I make the case for it above in discussing world-systems theory, which has also been castigated as a form of Adam-Smithian revisionism. One cannot hold this position without stretching the traditional Marxist concept of exploitation; Étienne Balibar has declared it in need of stretching, if not more radical reinterpretation.[12] To call them beneficiaries is not to justify in any way their ill treatment. The suspicion that it might seem to do so—might make the global capitalist system seem acceptable—is probably a major motive why people shy away from the subject of remittances altogether. Yet it's mainly under such oblique and embarrassing rubrics that global economic redistribution comes up, when and if it does.

The subject implicates the state. One could imagine currency controls that would keep foreign workers from expatriating the meager savings that they send home to their families. The fact that the state allows this money to leave no doubt has to do with its higher commitment to a set of rules that permits corporations and especially financial institutions to send incomparably larger sums of money across national borders, and with incomparably greater frequency and consequences. Still, the fact that this flow of remittances exists—that even very low-wage workers in the metropolis earn enough to save and pass on a portion of it—and the fact that though it could be cut off, it is not: these facts count as evidence that the systemic inequality between beneficiaries and nonbeneficiaries is not eternally fixed in place, like the solar system. This is why facing the awkwardness is mandatory. There are things that can be done to quicken the flow of remittances. The most obvious would be improving wages and working conditions so that sending the money would be less of a sacrifice. But there are others. In this sense domestic politics makes room for issues of global economic equality even if it is extremely awkward for anyone to say so.

The awkwardness extends to Klein herself. She raises the question of remittances with regard to Filipino workers in export processing zones who left their villages but not their country. "When the recruiters came to their villages," workers in Rosario told Klein, "they promised that workers would earn enough in the factories to send money home to their impoverished families. . . . The problem, they said, is that no matter how long they work in the zone, there is never more than a few pesos left over to send home" (*No Logo*, 220–21). There is no reason to doubt that here, as so often, entrepreneurs broke their promises. But this anecdote cannot stand for everyone everywhere, as if being only a few pesos removed from absolute immiseration were the general case. Filipino workers who leave their country now account for more than 10 percent of its gross domestic product. One result is the government's unhealthy dependence on the personal sacrifices of citizens who cannot see their families for years on end and its failure to live up to its own responsibilities. But other results have to be calculated as well. "Despite their absence," Norimitsu Onishi writes of Overseas Filipino Workers, or OFWs, "the workers have contributed money to help build roads, schools, water grids and other infrastructure usually handled by local governments. They pay for annual fiestas that were traditionally financed by municipalities, churches and local businesses. Thanks to their help, Mabini became a 'first class' municipality last year in a government ranking of towns nationwide, leaping from 'third class.'"[13] Whatever else you want to say about them, remittances sent home from the United States, among other places, to the Philippines and Haiti and El Salvador, among other places, amount to more than a few pesos. Given Klein's special concern for infrastructure, it must be noted that remittances contribute to it. As everyone can see, the sacrifices that make remittances possible are enormous, but the sums involved are not insignificant, especially for those at home receiving them. This fact tells us something about transnational subjectivity, but also about the perhaps unexpected possibility of taking future steps toward the global redistribution of resources.

These unrequited transfers are inspired by love and by a sense of family and community obligation. The love and the sense of obligation may not have any clear equivalent in other, more prosperous beneficiaries and their own relations with distant places. But like wartime rationing, the channels through which remittances currently flow prove a point about what is possible in general. Possible between Klein's global "roommates," who, she seems to be suggesting, in one way or another might yet become roommates, as the saying goes, with benefits.[14]

Chapter 6

LIFE WILL WIN

At the end of *Strangers Drowning*, Larissa MacFarquhar looks back on the gallery of characters she has profiled and concludes that, crazy and unappetizing as many of them seem in their obsession with the welfare of strangers, the world would be a worse place without them. If you are not as obsessed as they are, she says, you will probably leave the world as it is. Why the option of leaving the world as it is seems ineligible to her, why choosing that option would require an undesirable insensitivity or moral obtuseness—these are questions that MacFarquhar doesn't push hard on, perhaps because their inescapable earnestness would endanger her lightness of tone, which is to say her critical distance from her subjects.

Instead, as if to justify the critical distance, she spends time discussing the genre of the novel. Novelists, she says, have been very hard on do-gooders. "The embracing of messiness and imperfection, the dislike of preaching, the prizing of the complex and particular and distrust of the abstract, the injunction to love real people close to you rather than an ideal of people in general"—what this novelistic vision amounts to is "an implicit exhortation to accept the human condition. You should love humans as they are, not as they should or could be. You should embrace human nature, with all its suffering and sin, and accept that it will always be thus. You should accept the role of fate and luck in human life, and the limits of man's ability to alter his lot" (273–74). In other words, the novel is committed to life, and life does not encourage the reckless doing of good. "If there is a struggle between morality and life," the book concludes, "life will win" (295).

If you care about global economic justice, this is not an encouraging axiom. Life has a lot going for it. Justice doesn't have enough. The perception that one is a beneficiary is not rich in practical suggestions about how one might live differently. If it's a bad thing that there *are* beneficiaries, how can there be any good way of *being* a beneficiary? I will have more to say about this below. In the meantime, I will speculate that perhaps, as MacFarquhar's "if" hints, the struggle for global economic justice does not need to be framed as an opposition between morality and life. Perhaps we can keep both terms but reconceive them so they no longer seem so absolutely opposed to each other. In a sense that was the suggestion Bonnie Klein made when she imagined her daughter Naomi asking, "What's wrong with having a good time?"

Life is short. As a word, however, "life" is notoriously open-ended. Some of the word's meanings would obviously blunt the force of morality, as Mac-Farquhar suggests. "Life" might mean, for example, the *best things* in life, as in the philosopher Derek Parfit's argument against both egalitarianism and utilitarianism in "Overpopulation and the Quality of Life": "Even if some change brings a great net benefit to those who are affected, it is a change for the worse if it involves the loss of one of the best things in life" (quoted in Bull, "Levelling Out," 18). The best things in life, for Parfit, seem to be high aesthetic pleasures. He therefore imagines (here I quote a paraphrase by Malcolm Bull) that, as egalitarian redistribution proceeds, first "Mozart's music is lost, then Haydn's; then Venice is destroyed, then Verona, until eventually all that is left is a life of muzak and potatoes" (18).

Either Parfit or Bull seems to be remembering Orwell's herring and potatoes. For Orwell in 1937, as for Parfit, leveling down to a life of herring and potatoes was "a repugnant conclusion"—the title of the book in which

Parfit's essay was published. Having announced that "in order that England may live in comparative comfort, a hundred million Indians must live on the verge of starvation," Orwell used the repugnance of a herring-and-potato diet to back off, explaining why the global leveling and international solidarity he seemed in quest of were probably not in the cards. Then, as we have seen, rationing during World War II made him reconsider. The English were suddenly living on herring and potatoes, more or less, but knowing the reasons why, and knowing that this was more or less true for all of us without exception, they were not complaining. Knowing the reasons made it all right, and even more than all right. It made everyday life more meaningful. One meaning of the word life comes from thinking, despite much evidence to the contrary, that in some sense life might *have* a meaning.

In that sense, what Orwell called "abolishing a part of yourself," which rationing transformed into a collective, impersonal project, would not after all mean giving up on your life or, more precisely, on what made your life meaningful. Caring about life and caring about global justice would not be mutually exclusive. This is the argument that Malcolm Bull makes in his commentary on Parfit. What anti-utilitarians like Parfit actually mean by "leveling down," Bull suggests, is often something closer to "leveling out," that is, adding extra people from outside the given political community and treating them as if their standard of living mattered as much as that of those inside. Leveling out was exactly Orwell's issue. Bull describes this project as accommodating an "additional population of non-beneficiaries" ("Levelling Out," 15). The pressure to accommodate seemingly limitless and therefore impossible numbers of nonbeneficiaries is not a problem of democracy as such but specifically a problem of *planetary* democracy. The fact that leveling out is not much discussed doesn't mean its planetary scale is not recognized or not feared. If it were not, one would surely hear more argument against national borders—the argument that capital has benefitted from the privilege of being freer to move than labor is, and that global justice demands there should be no more restriction of the movement of labor than there is restriction of the movement of capital. Which of course might imply only that the movements of capital should be more regulated.

The threat, which emanates from the foreigner's more radical nonbelonging, involves nonrecognition of the value of the objects that would now have to be shared. What is feared (Parfit is one of many who fear it) is that planetary egalitarianism will breed nihilism: a denial of the value of the good life, of good things, of good times. Bull accepts the term "nihilism," citing Nietzsche, but turns nihilism into an argument in *favor* of leveling out. Sharing your goods with outsiders helps you to see that after all you were not as attached as you thought you were to certain things you used to value very highly.[1] Some goods, including objects that were once cherished or are still cherished, can be tossed or given away. The process can be exhilarating. It's a sort of spring-cleaning of the soul. Like shopping, which it does not inherently contradict, it is one of life's proven pleasures. Perhaps it is even one of life's definitions.

Ways in which the program of global economic justice might be pursued at home, which is to say integrated into everyday life and the pursuit of everyday happiness, might lead us to the subject of refugees. Refugees are already right here, on everyone's minds, on everyone's agenda, even if the United States has thus far been extremely ungenerous in opening its borders to them and even if the issue is rarely if ever seen as an engaging with the prospects for global economic redistribution. The mention of Nauru above suggests the bigger picture, but consider for the moment only a smaller one: the hundreds of thousands of people who have streamed into Europe in 2015 and 2016, many and perhaps most of them fleeing the violence in Syria and environs. Borders have tightened; the Schengen agreement, which allows freedom of movement within much of Europe, is no longer functioning. The impulse of the European policy makers has been to push the blockage back toward the source. In terms of getting at the underlying causes of the mass migration, that's insufficient but not stupid. There is much to say for example on behalf of David Graeber's proposal that Turkey's president, Recep Tayyip Erdoğan, be induced to stop bombarding and blockading the Kurds, the most effective opponents of Isis on the ground. What we don't want is any more closing off of borders, whether in Turkey or in Greece. The island of Lesbos, where the inhabitants have struggled nobly in the midst of their own crisis of diminished resources to help the crowds coming up the beaches, has been in chaos. The refugees wouldn't be arriving in Europe if Syria weren't a more violent chaos.

But of course, not all the refugees are fleeing the violence in Syria. Many are fleeing the only slightly-less-out-of-control violence in Iraq, Afghanistan, and numerous other less newsworthy places. And violence is not what all are fleeing. Many refugees have been quoted as saying that they left home because there is no life where they live or no chance to make a life. In other words, they are in danger of being labeled migrants rather than refugees. But is there really a defensible line between refugees, who are victims of violence, and migrants, who are merely victims of impoverishment? Wars destroy economies; economics causes wars. Where do we see violence without also seeing, not far in the background, scarcity and inequality? Does anyone believe that the bleeding and leading news on the front page can be explained by a conflict of civilizations? In private, at least, this may be the moment to dust off the unfashionable materialist doctrine that most conflicts in fact have material roots.

No, one does not want to say so publicly. Refugees have a claim to entry. Migrants do not. The European Union has no immigration policy. No European nation except Albania has ratified the International Convention on the Protection of the Rights of Migrant Workers, which came into force in March 2003, just as the United States was invading Iraq. As of late November 2015, Macedonia was barring entry to people carrying Pakistani, Bangladeshi, and Moroccan passports on the grounds that they are not fleeing military conflict. Anyone moving for economic reasons already has to lie. Those perceived to be lying are more likely to be perceived as criminals. To be perceived as a criminal is one step from being perceived as a terrorist even if one is not, like the Syrians, already presumptively associated with the terror one is running away from. In practice, domestic law and the manner of its enforcement have a direct impact on global access to resources. But the state of the conversation about global justice being what it is, it would be bold and perhaps irresponsible to allow the issue to be framed as such.

On Thursday, November 12, 2015, the day before the Paris terror attacks, European leaders were meeting in Malta with their African counterparts to discuss measures to reduce the flow of migrants—that is, economic migrants. In the 735 words of his opening address, European Council president Donald Tusk used the word "responsibility" five times. His message was clear. Responsibility for dealing with the migrants does not rest on Europe alone. The so-called sending countries must share that responsibility. The premise seems to be that African leaders are responsible not merely for corruption and human rights violations but also for poverty. The responsibility for poverty is local? That premise would be worth discussing at length. Alas, anyone who might have wanted to query it and push the linked questions of poverty and responsibility forward would have had her attention distracted by the events of the following day. And indeed, why tarnish the sacredness of the word "refugee," which for the moment at least seems capable of holding off some of the anti-immigrant backlash?

The only excuse for doing so, even very hesitantly, is to try to focus on the global situation. After all, the Malta conference was not just about Syria. The recent state of emergency, with its corpses in parked trucks and its photo of the drowned four-year-old, Aylan Kurdi, is part of a longer-term emergency in which thousands of others, mostly unphotographed, have drowned elsewhere in the Mediterranean. A responsible policy is needed. But perhaps we also need some irresponsible speculation.

What if all these movements of people could be imagined as a movement? A movement for global economic justice. In that case, well-intentioned beneficiaries would have something to work on, here and now.

No single image of what a movement for global economic justice would look like has managed to stick in the public imagination. If we were to see one, would we even recognize it? There is nothing we currently think of as politics that would register as such a movement. As Nancy Fraser puts it in *Scales of Justice: Reimagining Political Space in a Globalizing World*, the present system channels the claims of the global poor "into the domestic arenas of relatively powerless, if not wholly failed states." Thus "the system denies them the means to confront the offshore architects of their dispossession" (146). The meeting in Malta, organized by the offshore architects, was the poorest of substitutes for such a confrontation.

Images are there to be watched of the have-nots of the global South, forever on the move. Few of these images posit any causal linkage with the places we are watching them from. But some do. Science fiction writers at least since Doris Lessing have fantasized that one day there would be literal battles on the borders of Europe as the hungry barbarians climb over the walls. The fashion for zombie stories holds this idea at a relatively safe distance while sneaking the occasional peek at it. Of course, the actual violence that has struck the heartland of Europe does not on the whole come from the actual refugees. They are not violent or aggressive. On the contrary, they are risking everything merely to get their loved ones a piece of Europe's prosperity and security. And that is what we as their defenders will want to emphasize. Humanitarian solidarity demands that we see ourselves as generous, not as forced by the weight of ominous numbers to share the possessions we have worked so hard to gather around us. Apocalyptic scenarios are not helpful.

Strain as we might, perhaps we just can't see the mobility as a political movement, even an embryonic one. Still, it's good for the mind to switch occasionally from policy to politics in a larger and looser sense and from politics to what now lies beyond politics, if only as an exercise of the appropriate muscles. Thinking responsibly, we have reason to expect the worst. Youth unemployment in Greece and elsewhere in the south of Europe, on the front lines of migration, is over 50 percent. In France, which in the winter of 2016 was still bleeding internally from the shock of Le Bataclan, unemployment hits hardest among the children of immigrants. All over Europe, it is the most vulnerable, those with the least education and the fewest marketable skills, who will be most tempted to fear for their jobs and culture and to react accordingly. For many Europeans, chronically high unemployment is a sign that the elites are not listening to them. That's why no merely technocratic solution to the refugee crisis, carried out behind the backs of the general population, is going to fly.

Technocratic solutions certainly won't fly, of course, if they seem to come only from German industrialists eager to pay Syrian labor less than the minimum wage or from bleeding-heart liberals who will pay nothing at all. But it is at least possible to imagine, in the longer term, something less technocratic, something with more input from below. The sense of generalized disempowerment could result in something other than an anti-immigrant backlash. Why not, say, an anti-austerity program shared between migrants and nonmigrants? In Greece, and not just on Lesbos, that does not seem at all inconceivable. Maybe this is a chance for the already unemployed and underemployed to say to the offshore architects of dispossession, "Help them by all means, but raise the level for everyone."

It is a bad time, a very bad time, to ask people to make extra room in their homes and neighborhoods, to help others make a life or have a life, which is what a more equitable distribution of the world's resources comes down to. It's always a bad time. It's always been like this. And it's never been like this.

Getting On with Your Life

Life figures again in Thomas Haskell's contribution to the shallow pond debate. Flying off to Mexico City to help rescue the victims of an earthquake cannot be a true moral obligation for him, Haskell says, because it would disrupt his life, or disrupt his life "too much" ("Capitalism," 299). Here life is the target not of devaluation but of disruption; it seems to signify not the *best* things in life but rather *customary* life, my right to continue on with a majority of the habits, possessions, and comforts to which I have become accustomed. But how much disruption of life *is* too much disruption? If quantity is ruled out entirely, the refusal to be disrupted or disturbed would begin looking like what I once described (with reference to Richard Rorty's case for American patriotism) as the identity politics of the rich.[2] As with any identity politics, this position takes as sacred the identity I now assert and the props that help me assert it, laying down in advance a prohibition on making any part of that identity an agenda item in future negotiations about justice within some larger social whole. The premise is that anyone else's proposal to change my identity, however slightly and for whatever reason, would constitute a violation of that identity. As with any identity politics, the identity politics of the rich has on its side the considerable power of inertia. And it too could be described as Nietzschean. A defining example of slave morality in *The Genealogy of Morals* was the demand that birds of prey start behaving like lambs, a demand that made a lot of sense to lambs, Nietzsche suggested, but from the perspective of birds of prey would violate their carnivorous nature. Unsurprisingly, it was also an engagement with Nietzsche that helped Bernard Williams to formulate his suspicions of Kantian and utilitarian ethics, including arguments for economic redistribution such as Peter Singer's. For Williams, "what gives life its meaning" is "selfish partiality": "To grant morality the power to adjudicate impartially in situations like this [you must choose between saving your wife or two drowning strangers] would be to abandon what gives human life its meaning. Without selfish partiality—to people you are deeply attached to, your family and friends, to place—we are nothing. We are creatures of kinship and loyalty, not blind servants of the world."[3] If life itself is selfish partiality, then the imperative to achieve global economic justice would count as another expression of slave morality.

Nietzsche himself often argued in the name of life. But nothing could be further from Haskell's sense of life as custom or Williams's sense of life as family commitments than what Nietzsche meant by "life." What Nietzsche had in mind was, roughly speaking, a Dionysian energy, rowdy and revolutionary, that had been repressed by the degenerate, enfeebled, nihilistic customs of his time. In Nietzsche's opinion, his era's everyday life was life-denying. He might well say the same about the comfortable habits that Haskell does not want to disturb too much by an expedition to Mexico City. Nietzsche's vitalism can also be understood in terms of what he came to call the will to power. Life as will to power cannot be safely opposed to the radical transvaluation of values that would be entailed by a program of global economic equality.

Power, both as will and as accomplished fact, is essential to the peculiar and uncomfortable form of radicalism that this book has tried to espouse. Sliding as it does toward humanitarianism, the discourse of the beneficiary risks being a good deal less radical than ordinary left-wing politics. But in a sense it also tends to be *more* radical. Whether because it is not organic to a national movement with a multivoiced constituency to answer to and with local achievements to protect, or for some other reason, it tends to declare the present state of things absolutely intolerable. The English novelist and art critic John Berger, about whom much more might be said under this heading, uses the word "intolerable" often and in a distinctive sense. In "Image of Imperialism," his meditation on the famous photograph of the dead Che Guevara, Berger writes, "Guevara found the condition of the world as it is intolerable." But what follows is a strange twist: "It had only recently become so. Previously, the conditions under which two thirds of the people of the world lived were approximately the same as now. The degree of exploitation and enslavement was as great. The suffering involved was as intense and widespread. The waste was as colossal. But it was not intolerable because the full measure of the truth about these conditions was unknown—even by those who suffered it" (*Selected Essays*, 110). Berger suggests that this truth about the world's intolerability has become known thanks to movements of national liberation. But he also seems to be saying something more general: that in order to find the world intolerable, you must have the power to change it, to have sensed or tasted or anticipated that power, or at least to have understood that such power exists. His next sentence could have been an epigraph for this book: "The world is not intolerable until the possibility of transforming it exists but is denied" (116). Here Berger refuses the liberal orthodoxy that would make extreme suffering into a moral absolute. In a historical, one might say Hegelian, mode, he makes suffering historically relative—relative to power and knowledge. This bestows a certain significance on purveyors of power and knowledge, wherever they might be located. Often, like him, they are located in a privileged metropolitan space. One might say that Berger's underlying subject is the beneficiary.

To occupy a metropolitan location means, as we frequently insinuate, to enjoy proximity to power. To some, any proximity to power will disqualify the speaker's opinions. To many speakers, proximity to power will be undesired, unarticulated, and embarrassing. But it is also, I am suggesting, politically and even epistemologically useful. Useful because (following Berger's insight about Guevara, whose own political career could be usefully understood within the discourse of the beneficiary) it makes available the metropolitan's confidence that the world can indeed be transformed, that the capacity to transform it exists. And without this capacity, I repeat, the world would not rise to the standard of absolute intolerability.

Thus power becomes part of Berger's fraught sense of structural inequality between himself and his subjects. The phrase from John 4:38 that Berger chose for his peasant trilogy, "Others have labored and ye have entered into their labors," is a succinct restatement of the discourse of the beneficiary. Indeed, the new international translation of "entered into" is "reaped the benefits of." An old peasant woman who remains behind in the village when the others have left divides the world into two kinds of people, peasants and those who feed off peasants. Berger gives no evidence of disagreeing. If he doesn't, then his peasants are not just an expression of what he and many others have called his romanticism. They are also a way of sustaining the discourse of the beneficiary.

I will come back to the association of life with power. But first I want to touch on another sense of life that, like custom and high aesthetic pleasure, seems to work against attributing moral responsibility for global economic inequality to anyone in particular. Life is also *complex*. Complexity matters in the sense that it confuses lines of responsibility that morality, looking at things more abstractly, might prefer to see as simple.[4] In *Reason in a Dark Time: Why the Struggle Against Climate Change Has Failed*, Dale Jamieson takes the everyday example of Jack stealing Jill's bicycle and proposes that, as the paradigm adapts to the more complex givens of an issue like climate change, its simple attribution of responsibility very quickly disappears. In a case like climate change, he says, the causality linking Jack and Jill looks more like this: "Acting independently, Jack and a large number of unacquainted people set in motion a chain of events that causes a large number of future people who live in another part of the world from ever having bicycles" (149–50). Here the agency is shared but not conspiratorial. The victims are plural, geographically distant, and in the future. Above all, there is no intention to do harm. As a result, Jamieson comments, for many people this will be "just an abstract description of normal, everyday behavior. There is nothing suspect about it at all" (150). For others, he concedes, there will still be "something morally questionable about it" because the moral center of the Jack-and-Jill theft is still there: "Some people have acted in a way that harms other people" (150). Even for them, however, "the wrongness of the acts and the culpability of the agents is greatly diminished" (*Reason*, 150) by comparison with the theft of a bicycle.

Here life enters again. "The fact that they will not have bicycles is just a consequence of Jack and others getting on with their lives" (150). Life is something you get on with, in fact what you *have* to get on with. In a system of great social complexity, not getting on with your life will also cause harm, harm to others (who will have to take care of you if you don't get on with your life) as well as to oneself. Thus life as complexity turns into life as its own kind of moral or perhaps amoral imperative: to get on with living. This sense of complex-but-imperative life explains why in a case like climate change (and, I add, global economic justice) "it is difficult for the network of moral concepts that involve responsibility and harm to gain traction" (150).[5]

Jamieson is clearly touching on something real. His subject is what Orwell called "the system," and he is trying to account for why, despite the damage the system causes, the moral weight of belonging to it does not translate into the sense of quasicriminal liability Orwell wants, or sounds like he wants. In a system, Jamieson suggests, you do not cause something, you merely contribute to it.[6] The remarkable thing here is the key causal element that Jamieson inexplicably forgets. When Jack steals Jill's bicycle, he gets to ride the bicycle that Jill can no longer ride. He benefits from the theft. In the scenario that Jamieson substitutes for it, which supposedly corresponds better to climate change because the responsibility is now shared and the harm is no longer intentional, the benefit goes unmentioned. It has simply disappeared. Yet in fact benefit remains no less pertinent than it was. In the climate change case, as in the case of bicycle theft, I get to have the benefits of air conditioning and air travel and all the other environmentally expensive amenities that the prime victims of climate change will not have. And the same holds for the overlapping case of global economic justice.

The point here is not Jamieson's blindness to his own quite enlightening illustrations, interesting as that is, but rather how putting back what he has omitted changes his conclusion. The absence of any intention to cause damage is of course morally significant, as is the sharing of responsibility for that damage with others. But if you add to the damage caused, which Jamieson does not doubt, *the benefits enjoyed as a result of causing it*, as in the case of the stolen bicycle, then the prospects that moral responsibility will seem relevant again are a good deal brighter.

Life as something you are supposed to get on with remains, of course, a factor that can never be discounted. Transposed onto the international stage—and there can be no doubt that personal morals are always informing what happens or doesn't happen on bigger and deadlier stages—getting on with your life will also mean, for example, that the United States too should get on with its life, which is to say get on with the business of asserting its interests by whatever means necessary. It should not be held back, for example, by a nagging sense that in so doing it is losing its hold on higher ideals. In the aftermath of the revelations about what went on in the Abu Ghraib shower room when American interrogators acted out various fantasies upon the bodies of Iraqi prisoners, many of whom turned out (as if this mattered) not even to have been combatants, Joseph Lelyveld observed that despite all the "genuine outrage in predictable places about what was soon being called a 'torture scandal,' . . . the usual democratic cleansing cycle never really got going. However strong, the outcry wasn't enough to yield political results in the form of a determined Congressional investigation, let alone an independent commission of inquiry; the Pentagon's own inquiries, which exonerated its civilian and political leadership, told us a great deal more than most Americans, so it would appear, felt they needed to know."[7] Americans did not want the truth, at least not where the ill treatment of foreigners was concerned, at least not in wartime. Lelyveld concludes:

An implicit understanding has been reached . . . between the governed and those who govern: that the prime task is the prevention of future attacks on our own soil as opposed to the punishment of past attacks; that extralegal excesses, not excluding kidnappings and physical abuse, may be necessary in the effort to suppress terrorists seeking to implant sleeper cells in our midst and equip them with deathly substances and bombs; that in pursuit of this goal, much can be forgiven, including big mistakes (the abuse and infinite detention of innocent people, the tacit annulment—for foreigners, anyway—of legal guarantees, not to mention a costly war of dubious relation to the larger struggle); and the less we know as a people about our secret counterterrorism struggles and strategies, the less we contemplate the possibly ugly consequences, the easier it will be for those in authority to get on with the job of protecting us. (39)

There are many reasons for curbing one's enthusiasm about American cosmopolitan common sense, and in particular about its moral prospects. The recent trend has been toward a hard-bitten, disillusioned realism. Realism assumes that outside our borders, it's a state of nature. Thus the rules are off. George Packer, reviewing John Sifton's recent book on human rights, *Violence All Around*, makes a belated but inevitable defense of Iraq War hawks like himself by suggesting that America is not exceptional but just like other nations, a member in good standing of an international club where brutality is the unquestioned norm.[8] It's an imperfect world. What's a little invasion here or there? Don't be too hard on yourself. I have not heard questions raised in the mainstream media about the double standard that is applied on issues like the proliferation of nuclear weapons (it's okay for us to have them, but not for any country that doesn't have them yet) or military bases (it's okay for us to have them, and we don't complain that others don't). No one asks how we would feel about might makes right if, the veil of ignorance being lifted, we were suddenly to find ourselves the weak rather than the mighty. The sense that we must take our own side, right or wrong, helps explain the recent fad for adding zombies to whatever the subject under discussion happens to be, whether Jane Austen or Abraham Lincoln. Suddenly no subject feels complete unless we have added to it the idea of an unthinkable but violent and decisive outside. In *Theories of International Relations and Zombies*, Daniel W. Drezner notes that "well over one-third of all zombie films have been released since the September 11, 2001 terrorist attacks" (2).

The philosophy of life as something to get on with could be also detected during and after the financial disaster of 2008. Why was more not made of the personal and institutional responsibilities involved? Of course, the banks and other financial institutions saw to it that their lobbyists applied cash in all the right places. But other logics were also at work. As Julia Ott shows in *When Wall Street Met Main Street: The Quest for an Investors' Democracy*, the mentality of Wall Street had made inroads into moral common sense via investment in retirement funds. Before 2008, a sizeable slice of the population could already be described in effect as beneficiaries of the financial sector. But now our pensions and retirement savings are more directly hooked into finance. (To be fair, it was also her retirement that George Eliot was trying to protect with the guaranteed 5 percent return on her Indian railway stock.) With end-of-life scenarios at stake, which is to say life itself, people will *feel* the status of beneficiary in a way that makes them more hesitant to point the finger, or to keep it pointed.

What You Live Off, or On

Here life becomes what you live off or live on. We have already encountered the beneficiary in the guise of the rentier.[9] The rentier can be loosely defined as someone who "has" a fixed income from property or investments. A more restricted definition makes the return on accumulated wealth, perhaps accumulated by someone else and then inherited, into a larger proportion of the rentier's total income and thus also a crucial fact about his selfhood or life: the rentier is someone who "lives off" income from property or investments. She or he is someone who does not depend on income from work that she or he actually performs. "Live off" sounds like the parasitism Orwell was hinting at when he spoke of the system as what we live "on" rather than merely in.

The word *rentier* (in italics, to indicate it has not yet split off from French) has a featured place in Orwell's much-admired essay on Dickens. Yoking Dickens's disinclination to represent work in his fiction with his penchant for characters who don't have to work—those who enjoy what was then called "an independence"—Orwell expresses his disappointment that, with the possible exception of David Copperfield, "one cannot point to a single one of his central characters who is primarily interested in his job. . . . The feeling, 'This is what I came into the world to do. Everything else is uninteresting. I will do this even if it means starvation,' which turns men of differing temperaments into scientists, inventors, artists, priests, explorers and revolutionaries—this motif is almost entirely absent from Dickens's books" (Dickens, 87). When Orwell speaks in *The Road to Wigan Pier* of "worthless idlers," worthy or meaningful work is the standard by which he is judging them. When he evokes the rentier, however, it is not as a mere antithesis of virtuous industry, hence a cheap target of ridicule. Rather, he associates the figure with a certain confusion about power and its uses. The rentier emerges in Dickens, he says, as a replacement for "the Good Rich Man," a figure who "is usually a 'merchant'" (we are not necessarily told what merchandise he deals in), and is always a superhumanly kind-hearted old gentleman who 'trots' to and fro, raising his employees' wages, patting children on the head, getting debtors out of jail and, in general, acting the fairy godmother. Of course he is a pure dream figure. . . . Even Dickens must have reflected occasionally that anyone who was so anxious to give his money away would never have acquired it in the first place (52). In the later, darker novels, Orwell then notes, "the good rich man has dwindled from a 'merchant' to a rentier. This is significant. A rentier is part of the possessing class, he can and, almost without knowing it, does make other people work for him, but he has very little direct power. Unlike Scrooge or the Cheerybles, he cannot put everything right by raising everybody's wages" (53). Someone who cannot put everything right, though it is hinted that he might want to; someone who makes other people work for him, but not directly or consciously; someone who has power, but "very little direct" power: these characteristics do not preclude satire of love-me-I'm-a-liberal complacency, but they also suggest a more widespread and interesting predicament, one with which Orwell himself seems to feel an uneasy intimacy. The passage from Good Rich Man to rentier offers another perspective on the history of the beneficiary.

As we have seen, being a rentier seems to Orwell inexplicably unobjectionable: "We tamely admit to being robbed in order to keep half a million worthless idlers in luxury."[10] Orwell seems sure that imperialism is much more objectionable, from the viewpoint of common or uneducated decency, and this although imperialism is usually understood to have been quite popular among the populations that practiced and benefitted from it. The surprise is not that the rentiers themselves have no qualms of conscience about their source of income, but that society at large finds little or nothing wrong in it either—at any rate, not enough to act on. Why not?

There is a kind of paradoxical logic, I think, behind the popular reluctance to blame those who live off unearned income, and it has to do with the "get on with it" sense of life. A zone of special tolerance surrounds the issue of how people make a living—where their money comes from. Life in this sense has its own ethical microclimate. It means live and let live, mind your own business—and don't mind the ultimate, distant consequences of your own or anyone else's business. The imperative not to intrude is akin to the tacit assumptions about the proper space between bodies or the proper loudness of speech that underlie the rules of ordinary sociability.

A long literary and theatrical tradition exposed characters such as peasants and preachers, merchants and lawyers, to being gently or not so gently mocked for sounding like their occupations, thereby revealing that their natures are subdued to what they work in, or on. Occupational satire arguably has its social basis, like so much of the canon, in a society that was culturally dominated by an aristocracy, which is to say a rentier society. What I am talking about is the inverse of this sensibility. Little by little, the rentier has faded away as a cultural touchstone, vanquished by the increasingly cross-gendered assumption that most people most of the time will work for a living wage, or will try to. One result of this cultural democratization is that it is no longer quite so embarrassing to expose your nine-to-five activities involuntarily by your habits of after-hours conversation and favored choices of metaphor. Another, trickier effect is a version of the work ethic that, if not immune to raillery, resists any more serious critique of what people do to earn a living. For most people most of the time, it has been and is still assumed that we have a strong obligation to take care of ourselves and those closest to us. Our obligation is to do so by any means necessary.

This unarticulated common sense could be described as amoral, like life as MacFarquhar sees it. It is what her do-gooders are up against, and it is a formidable adversary. When the issue is survival—life-or-death, as we say—we don't have to be told that the moral rules are suspended. Necessity makes its own rules, which are beyond good and evil. Haskell, in his commentary on Bernard Williams, sums up this logic as "evil necessity."

Hence there are unspoken limits to the questions we permit ourselves to ask about the source of someone else's income, and this is so even when that income is inherited or otherwise unearned. Rentiers benefit from a general dispensation that is not especially meant for them—from the fact that we working people give everyone around us a pass because it is assumed that where work is concerned most of us don't really have much choice. Beggars can't be choosers.

For those of us who would like to see the rentiers held to moral account and, more generally, to see the rewards of work and the resources of the world distributed more equally, the conclusion would seem to be that we must do whatever we can to ensure that survival is no longer an active anxiety. The best name for this project has been and still is socialism. But for the moment at least, steps in this direction can only be undertaken by the state we have. It is ironic in the extreme, therefore, that another misguided political effect of the work ethic is antistatism. Misguided because, as I suggested above, it's the state that has provided the best demonstration that as yet exists that the link between paid work and moral worth can be broken. Breaking this link was the work of the welfare state, which has taken for its premise that no one should have to fear for their survival, whether because of the vagaries of the job market or for any other reason. There should be no beggars. Then everyone can be more of a chooser.

We need more of this project, not less. We need the state to use its powers of regulation against the financial industry, to render financial instruments transparent, to tax financial transactions—and perhaps also to introduce a serious inheritance tax, thereby leveling the playing field of work, so to speak, and thereby reinvesting work with meaning. And we need the state to diminish as far as possible that amoral sense of ultimate responsibility for our own survival that protects from the scorn they deserve even the creative inventors of intentionally toxic derivatives. But in order to draw this conclusion, we also need to realize that we are beneficiaries. The most tempting way to scorn the rentiers is of course by accusing them of being parasites and contrasting them with those who work hard to maintain themselves. That's the comparison Orwell clearly has in mind when he calls them worthless idlers. But many and perhaps most of those who live in or off the financial sector do work hard. And in any case, hard work is the wrong criterion. Those of us outside the world of finance who live and work at the metropolitan core do not escape from structural parasitism by virtue of our personal industriousness. No matter how hard we work, we still benefit from the international system that skims off the surplus from the countries of the periphery and silently distributes so much of it (by no means all of it via return on investments) into our bank accounts. Faith in hard work is another part of decency, and of himself as a representative of it, that Orwell was logically proposing we try to abolish. Globally speaking, it is a pillar of an unjust system. The problem with finance is not laziness; the problem with it is that it is injurious to the common good. It must be answered, therefore, in the name of the common good and by institutions that stand up for the common good.

That said, it may not be such a bad thing that the beneficiary's power—very little direct power, as Orwell says, but indirect power, which is to say *some* power—is associated with life or even that it benefits from an undeserved moral toleration.

Linking the saintliness of Mohandas K. Gandhi to that of the aged Tolstoy, Orwell suggested that Tolstoy, despite his commitment to nonviolence, had not renounced "the principle of coercion, or at least the desire to coerce others. . . . The distinction that really matters," he goes on, "is not between violence and non-violence, but between having and not having the appetite for power."[11] Orwell may not have wanted say that power was also an appetite for Gandhi, but he nevertheless praised Gandhi for making good if unofficial use of it, and his praise of Gandhi's effectiveness offsets at least in part his critique of Gandhi's otherworldliness, which MacFarquhar cites: "The essence of being human is that one does not seek perfection, that one *is* sometimes willing to commit sins for the sake of loyalty, that one does not push asceticism to the point where it makes friendly intercourse impossible" (*Strangers*, 8–9). Gandhi's life "was not a failure," Orwell concluded. "His main political objective, the peaceful ending of British rule, had been attained" ("Reflections on Gandhi," 469–70).[12] This was not seeking "perfection" but acting—we would now say, thinking of the horrors of Partition, acting very messily and imperfectly—in a messy and imperfect world.

Currently Dominant, Conventional, Normative, or Institutional

The critic Leela Gandhi, who locates herself in the line of thinking laid out by her more famous namesake, proposes "an inclusive and transnational quotidian ethics of the victim or underdog." Such an ethics, she says, would be against "whatever is currently dominant, conventional, normative, or institutional" ("Utonal," 83). This description does not quite fit Mohandas K. Gandhi, at least as Orwell sees him, but it does underline with precision what the discourse of the beneficiary is not. The discourse of the beneficiary also defines itself in relation to the victims, globally considered. But by holding on to what might be seen as a transcendental sense of victimage—the economic deprivation of the global South—it relativizes all other forms of victimage. It thereby suggests that, globally speaking, many of those who are in the habit of thinking of themselves as victims or underdogs, including many of Leela Gandhi's favorite characters, would be better described as beneficiaries. More important still, it assumes that the one speaking is not such a victim. The speaker is part of the "currently dominant, conventional, normative, or institutional." She or he shares in its power. The political risks involved in making such an assertion have already been discussed—notably, the risk of inhibiting the righteous and effective indignation of the locally aggrieved. The advantage, on the other hand, is to encourage the use of power by those who, because they are beneficiaries of the system, have some power. This may sound outlandish, but it is actually nothing more than what is already assumed by most of what is said and done in the name of politics or change by people like ourselves, people who have the relative leisure to read and write about such matters. When we speak, we assume that unequal power can be used to diminish inequalities of power. We even assume that their diminishment will give us pleasure. I think we're right. Life is power: Nietzsche's polemical redefinition lays out the common ground between Naomi Klein and Bernard Williams, between justice and having a good time.

"Workers of the world, unite!" remains an indispensable slogan, whatever the riders and amendments, friendly and not so friendly, that it has accumulated. I am not making the ludicrous proposal that "workers" here be replaced by "beneficiaries." But I am not the first to suggest that the workers of the world will have a much easier time of it if a slice of the stratum above them, those who are simultaneously (but unequally) victims and beneficiaries of the system, come to see what the two groups share, in terms of values and even of self-interest. The case for shared self-interest has come to be associated with arguments like Naomi Klein's that arresting climate change requires regulating global capitalism. (That is one reason why I have spent so much time on her work.) George Orwell became this book's central figure both because of an itch to take him away from his Cold War admirers, who don't deserve him, and because, from this perspective, he suddenly came to look like one of Klein's missing ancestors. My Orwell is the heroic figure that recognized that the inequality between rich and poor at the global scale was a massive hindrance to political progress anywhere. That recognition threatened him again and again with political paralysis. Yet he kept groping for evidence that it was not as immovable as it seemed, and he found some.

Luckily, Klein is by no means alone in linking the idea of decreased consumption in the West with the idea of greater economic equality between the West and the rest. "Just as it is certain," Jared Diamond writes, "that within most of our lifetimes we'll be consuming less than we do now, it is also certain that per capita consumption in many developing countries will one day be more nearly equal to ours. These are desirable trends, not horrible prospects."[13] Klein is less confident than Diamond about the trends of long-term capitalist development. For her, climate change is another disaster, bringing the possibility of radical change for the worse (as in *The Shock Doctrine*) as well as an opportunity to achieve change for the better. No trends are guaranteed. But since people are going to be shaken loose from habits that had seemed unshakable parts of themselves, the inequalities that were wrapped up in those habits are now fair game, open for revision as well, or more open for revision than they had ever seemed to be.

Despite their differences, however, both Klein and Diamond are now voices of common sense, a common sense that has come a long way, even if it also still has a long way to go. My subject here has been the making of this rough version of common sense, the emergence and increasing coherence of marginal, dissonant elements of moral vision connecting people in the prosperous West with faraway others. As a cultural historian, my impulse in writing this book has been to treat with more respect than they seem to merit images of symbolic or pseudologic such as the starving child next to the vending machine that are not ready to be translated into policy proposals but convey a rich discomfort out of which future policy proposals can perhaps be expected. I have tried to string these scraps of discourse together so as to sketch out a history of moral sense making in situations in which people in relatively prosperous countries choose to see themselves against a backdrop of people in less prosperous countries who don't have as much to eat. I have tried to suggest that, taken together, they help explain the real if partial common sense that today makes George F. Kennan's proposal that America do everything to sustain its economic advantage sound scandalous, a common sense that is certainly not majoritarian but that does make the unmaking of economic Orientalism possible to conceive and desire.

This common sense is of course insufficient. "The corpus of our moral judgments is incomplete, indeterminate, inconsistent, and incoherent," Dale Jamieson very properly notes (*Reason in a Dark Time*, ix–x). And he concludes, "The challenges that climate change presents go beyond the resources of commonsense morality" (5–6). The same is true for global justice. Much of life continues to stand against it, telling us every morning to get on with our business whatever that business may be, whatever distant consequences our quotidian activities may obscurely produce. But it helps to know that some transformation in commonsense morality has already happened and that the project of further transforming the moral concepts linking us to the rest of the world is therefore not merely quixotic, utopian, and silly—that it has something substantial and persistent to build on. If our ordinary moral conceptions are not adequate to the system, it remains an accomplishment to have changed them as far as we have. Even guilt, impractical as it may appear, should be understood as a historical accomplishment. New and more adequate moral conceptions will perhaps have the luxury of leaning on it less.

It may be that a leveling in the world's resources will happen by means of violence. That is arguably the most likely scenario. It may be that it will result from market forces, though neither the United States nor the Chinese government has ever allowed market forces to work unhindered. It may be, of course, that this leveling will not happen at all. None of these possible outcomes seems to me as desirable as a leveling that would happen by means of democratic decision making at a planetary scale—by a planetary equivalent to the once-equally-unimaginable process by which the United States decided democratically, against strong opposition, that it would have a graduated income tax. If we would like to equalize at least somewhat the life chances of the residents of Planet Earth, and if we would prefer to see that happen in a peaceful and democratic way, then we should surely value whatever evidence we can find, however skimpy and unsatisfying, that people who have more than their fair share are willing to imagine living on less, just as we should value all evidence that people are capable of seeing their lives as causally related to the suffering of others. In any event, these questions about how we live can no longer be separated off from what we mean by life.

For many, they are now part of everyday life. Thanks to the Internet and to administrative changes, Hua Hsu wrote on New Year's Eve of 2015, student protests today are actually better connected to the wider world than those of the 1960s. Today "you might actually walk across campus, knock on a door, and meet a representative of the power structure."[14] Campus activists have "the means to escalate their grievances with relative ease" ("The Year of the Imaginary College Student"). Black Lives Matter may or may not lead to hesitant, overcautious police forces, but the movement has certainly intensified "the desire to see injustices in one's immediate surroundings as part of larger struggles that once might have seemed distant and abstract, to draw connections and recognize broader patterns linking everyday indignities with systemic problems." It is among the ambiguous privileges of the youngest generation of beneficiaries to be more and more capable of seeing and knowing the system they live on and explaining the discomfort that goes with that. Perhaps something will come of it.

YOU CAN'T HANDLE THE TRUTH

"You can't handle the truth!" So begins one of the most quoted passages in Hollywood history, the speech delivered by Jack Nicholson at the climax of the movie *A Few Good Men* (1992). Even if you haven't seen the movie, you will probably remember the passage, and not just because it was a chance to watch a very charismatic actor do a slow time release of his inner wild man. The Nicholson character, a colonel in the marines, is on the witness stand, testifying in the court-martial of two enlisted men accused of causing the beating death of another, Santiago. Their attorney, played by Tom Cruise, says he wants the truth—that Nicholson ordered the beating. Nicholson, goaded into a rage, responds,

> You can't handle the truth! Son, we live in a world that has walls, and those walls have to be guarded by men with guns. Who's gonna do it? You? You, Lieutenant Weinberg? I have a greater responsibility than you

can possibly fathom. You weep for Santiago and you curse the marines. You have that luxury. You have the luxury of not knowing what I know, that Santiago's death, while tragic, probably saved lives. And my existence, while grotesque and incomprehensible to you, saves lives! You don't want the truth, because deep down in places you don't talk about at parties, you want me on that wall. You need me on that wall. We use words like "honor," "code," "loyalty." We use these words as the backbone of a life spent defending something. You use them as a punch line. I have neither the time nor the inclination to explain myself to a man who rises and sleeps under the blanket of the very freedom that I provide, and then questions the manner in which I provide it! I would rather you just said "thank you," and went on your way.[1]

These words are a confession; they mark Cruise's victory, Nicholson's defeat, and the acquittal of the men who followed Nicholson's orders. But if this speech is remembered so widely and so gleefully, it's not just because of its place in the plot. It has a vision, a vision in excess of its standard-issue militarism, a vision that is mysteriously hard for liberals such as Aaron Sorkin, the film's talented screenwriter, to refuse, or to refuse without some admixture of ambivalence. Sorkin, who went on to create the TV shows *The West Wing* and *The Newsroom*, came to be known for snappy, ratings-grabbing repartee. The most plausible target of his line about using words like "honor," "code," and "loyalty" as a punch line is himself. Whatever else that line is, in other words, it is also a flash of self-consciousness on Sorkin's part, a moment in which he authorizes his character to present him with a truth that he himself suspects to be indigestible, something he might hesitate to talk about at parties.

At this advanced stage in the argument, this truth should have a familiar ring. If some part of Sorkin does feel he needs men like Nicholson on that wall (while reserving the right to imprison them when necessary), if he does think that he rises and sleeps under the blanket of protection that violent, lawless people like Nicholson provide, if he agrees that whatever else Nicholson deserves, he also deserves a thank you, then what Sorkin has arranged to be told is, in effect, that he is a beneficiary. Your life, Nicholson is telling him, depends on mine. You depend on me. The reason why you and your witty, urbane friends owe me thanks is because all of you are my beneficiaries.

Nicholson is of course not an assembly-line silicon chip maker in a Fox-conn plant or a picker of coffee beans in an intemperate zone. As things are presently ordered, Third World manual workers are not in a position to de-mand thanks, as the marine colonel does, from those who benefit from their labors. When the day comes for them to make demands, whether for grati-tude or for something more than gratitude, much else will have changed and will go on changing. In the meantime, Nicholson's famous words slip loose from their military context. They insinuate that whatever our political principles, we are all in fact beneficiaries.

Since Nicholson's arrest ends the film, and on an upbeat note, Sorkin does not leave himself time to answer the questions Nicholson's speech poses. For example: Is it possible to withhold one's gratitude from the Nicholsons of the world without also cutting the chain of dependence and obligation to the coffee pickers and chip makers? Is the discourse of the beneficiary inev-itably aimed at global justice? If it isn't, how can we distinguish more and less desirable forms of beneficiary thinking? And more generally, questions that have haunted this book since the first chapter: What would it take to stop being a beneficiary? If being a beneficiary is intolerable to you, what are your options?

Logically speaking, options obviously exist. One is to renounce the bene-fits. And if the benefits cannot be renounced, another option is to see that the benefits (and risks) are shared equally.

Nicholson does not seem eager to see either of these things happen, per-haps because they would entail forfeiting the moral advantage he clearly thinks he enjoys. But both are at least theoretically possible, if not histori-cally likely. In the specific context of national defense, sharing the risks might entail, say, reinstituting universal conscription, as recommended in Fredric Jameson's *An American Utopia: Dual Power and the Universal Army*.[2] Re-nouncing the benefits would entail America's giving up on its self-assigned role of world policeman or at least scaling back its recent understanding of its national interest, which has been expansive, protective of the free flow of money and goods, hence hawkish. It would mean renouncing militarism.[3]

But Nicholson's speech would not be so powerful if it did not also touch on realities other than national defense. So the question has to be rephrased in more abstract terms. Why is it so tempting to assume that there is no way out of dependence, however unendurable it may seem? Why does escape from the status of beneficiary seem so implausible? Why are we so willing to grant that being a beneficiary may be a truth we can't handle?

The reason, I think, takes us away from Nicholson's speech and from the specifics of militarism. It takes us into the dimension of time. Advantages accruing to us in the present can be dealt with, at least theoretically and partially. The same does not hold, or hold with equal clarity and ethical force, for advantages that have accrued to us because of actions that were performed by others (perhaps our venerated ancestors) in some more or less distant past and that have made their way down to us, without our conscious consent, simply because of who we are and where we live. History is not what Nicholson is speaking about, but it is what many of his listeners will think of. It is as a fact about the past—rather than, say, as a fact about the economic system of the present—that the logic of the beneficiary is most readily recognized and, I have to say, respected. And this temporal dimension turns the logic of the beneficiary into something very different.

Consider Ari Shavit's much-acclaimed book *My Promised Land: The Triumph and Tragedy of Israel* (2013). In a long section of the book, Shavit, an Israeli journalist for *Haaretz*, goes in search of the story behind one of the most harrowing episodes of the military conquest of Palestine: the Israeli army's massacre of Palestinians at Lydda, a once-thriving city between Tel Aviv and Jerusalem. As he recounts it, in July 1948 the army moved through the streets, tossing grenades into houses and firing on Palestinian civilians. They came upon Palestinians taking sanctuary in a mosque and gunned them down. Others, many of them women and children, died on a forced march to Jordan after being "permitted" to leave with the possessions they could carry. Shavit speaks with the brigade commander and other now elderly soldiers in an attempt to reconstruct the story. He tries manfully to explain the atrocity on its own terms: there were misunderstandings, provocations, unfortunate improvisations by soldiers on the ground. But ultimately, he concludes, there was a deliberate strategy of expulsion. Thus he comes face to face with Israel's founding idea and what it means for him. He concludes:

> Do I wash my hands of Zionism? Do I turn my back on the Jewish national movement that carried out the deed of Lydda? Like the brigade commander, I am faced with something too immense to deal with. Like the military commander, Gutman, I see a reality I cannot contain. Like

the training group leader, I am not only sad, I am horrified. For when one opens the black box, one understands that whereas the small mosque massacre could have been a misunderstanding brought about by a tragic chain of accidental events, the conquest of Lydda and the expulsion of Lydda were no accident. They were an inevitable phase of the Zionist revolution that laid the foundation for the Zionist state. Lydda is an integral and essential part of our story. And when I try to be honest about it, I see that the choice is stark: either reject Zionism because of Lydda, or accept Zionism along with Lydda.

One thing is clear to me: the brigade commander and the military governor were right to get angry at the bleeding heart Israeli liberals of later years who condemn what they did in Lydda but enjoy the fruits of their deed. . . . If need be, I'll stand by the damned. Because I know that if it wasn't for them, the State of Israel would not have been born. If it wasn't for them, I would not have been born. They did the dirty, filthy work that enables my people, myself, my daughter, and my sons to live. (131)

This is Shavit's version of the Nicholson speech. It too is a bit of a rant, though it does not demand gratitude so much as thank Israel's Nicholsons, and there are many. It is spoken in a voice that is both tormented by an unwanted and uncomfortable debt and, finally, grateful. This is one of the voices of the beneficiary. The speech is Shavit's way of handling a truth that, like Nicholson, he doubts most of his readers will be able to handle. He presents the truth as sublime, "too much to contain," "too immense to deal with." Deep down, he suggests, in places he doesn't talk about at parties, he is honest enough to admit that he wants people like the brigade commander and the military governor on that wall. (At Lydda, the participants in the slaughter included such national heroes-to-be as Moshe Dayan and Yitzhak Rabin.) He can't say no to what they did for him because to do so, he says, would be to will his own undoing. Having admitted that the massacre and expulsion were policy, not accident, he goes on to say that this truth is "essential"—essential in the sense that it has to be confessed, but also essential in that it had to happen if there was going to be a state of Israel. And because it's essential, it can't be condemned. He is the beneficiary of that "dirty, filthy" violence, enjoying "the fruits of their deed." As a beneficiary he would be a hypocrite if he did not stand with the damned souls on whose violence his very existence depends. He makes it sound as if that is the only choice.

As far as I can see, Shavit's account of Lydda in July 1948 is not grossly inaccurate. If you compare it with that of, say, the more critical Israeli historian Ilan Pappé, you will note that it does not give the total number of the Palestinian dead, even as an estimate. It does not mention the fact that Dr. George Habash, who went on to found and lead the Popular Front for the Liberation of Palestine, was working that day as a physician in the local hospital. Habash was on duty when survivors of the massacre began to ferry in the dead and wounded. To mention what Habash saw during those hours would have suggested good reasons for the kind of Palestinian violence that Shavit, like most non-Palestinian Israelis, wants to present as unreasoned and unreasonable. Shavit mentions but doesn't dwell on how Israeli soldiers systematically looted jewelry and other valuables from the refugees, as testified to by all observers, Israelis included. Images of uniformed thugs robbing and ridiculing a column of helpless civilians come too close for comfort to iconic scenes of Jewish deportees under the Nazis. However, his account is more vivid and, where individual acts of violence are concerned, even more accusatory than, say, the firsthand account of Palestinian volunteer and paramedic Spiro Munayyer, who emphasized the heroism of the city's vastly outnumbered Palestinian defenders.

If you are ready to be called a bleeding-heart liberal, you may respond to this by dusting off some old-fashioned moral principles, as Cruise does when he stands up in court for truth and law. For example, the Golden Rule. Shavit refuses to condemn an atrocity. By the same standard, any Palestinian could refuse to condemn suicide bombers, and would arguably have at least as good a case. How would Shavit like *that*? If you adopt his version of the beneficiary's gratitude, there's no way out of the conflict; you choose the certainty of unending vendetta over the still not entirely hopeless project of peace-with-justice. An equally immediate response would be that past atrocities are not the point. We can assume that there were atrocities on both sides, in fact (even if the atrocities are not evenly matched) that one atrocity story can always be paired with another from the opposite side. Soon everyone's patience will have worn thin, and the time allotted for the discussion will have run out. No one will be occupying the moral high ground. The Occupation will continue.

The only way to decide the issue is with reference to the present. The ethnic cleansing of Palestine did not stop at Lydda; it is still happening. A few rockets that cause some eagerly documented Israeli anxiety but don't hit anything can't really be compared to the deliberate massacre of two thousand people, most of them civilians, in Israel's latest (2014) foray into Gaza, not to speak of other forays or the consequences of the blockade. What Shavit's repugnant gratitude is really defending, without saying so, is a procession of self-propagating and apparently limitless atrocities. Not just amorality in the past, but amorality that is ongoing. I will come back to the word "ongoing."

When Americans think of themselves as beneficiaries, the context in which the idea is likely to make the most intuitive sense is probably as a version of white privilege. The benefits that come to mind first are those that have accrued to members of America's white majority as a result of slavery, the massacres that accompanied the removal of Indians from their lands, the theft of so much of what was once Mexico, and the ongoing consequences of these extended acts of founding violence. In conversations about official apologies and reparations, the concept of white privilege has enjoyed a real if limited success. Thus far I have more or less ignored its inroads into mainstream common sense, which are limited but not inconsequential.

One reason why African Americans, Native Americans, and Latino Americans have played so negligible a role in my argument has already been mentioned: an argument that takes its rationale from injustice at the global scale is at perpetual risk of derailment each time it dwells on the domestically disadvantaged. It's not true, of course, that "all of us without exception" are beneficiaries vis-à-vis the nonmetropolitans on the other side of the international division of labor. Extreme poverty in the metropolis is an exception. But how extreme must the poverty or powerlessness be in order for its victims to be struck from the list of global beneficiaries? It's the kind of question that is never asked. We are much more comfortable adding items to the inventory of the injured and aggrieved, usually with no vetting of the candidates or any sense that the group as a whole might be devalued if it came to have too many members. Perhaps some vetting is called for. Otherwise, "all of us without exception" are in danger of counting among the injured—a sick parody of how the concept of the beneficiary ought to operate. That concept would be better understood as an invitation to get real about the most actionable locations of injustice.

That said, I for one will not be whittling the list down. Having claimed that the category of beneficiary includes even migrant workers living hand to mouth in the United States who nevertheless manage to send home meager remittances to the Philippines and El Salvador, I am not well placed to welcome arguments that Group X or Group Y ought (or ought not) to be allowed an exemption. I merely concede again, as I did above, that the concept of the beneficiary is often accompanied by a certain exaggeration and even a willful blindness. Orwell presents the English in general as hailers of taxis and nibblers at strawberries and cream even though his account of Midland mining communities included no evidence of such luxurious habits. In the context of contemporary America, it is more than a bit grotesque to imagine that the class of those who habitually enjoy these or other minor luxuries include large proportions of, say, African American victims of drug violence in Chicago and elsewhere who have also paid lifetime taxes for being black or Native Americans suffering almost genocidal rates of unemployment, alcoholism, and suicide. Whatever the picture of injustice at the scale of the planet, it seems perverse to look away from them.

If this is culpable negligence, there is at least one extenuating circumstance. Like Shavit's confession about Lydda, consideration of the atrocities of slavery and Native American genocide encourages us to think that the beneficiary is first and foremost benefitting from actions performed *in the past*. And the turn to the past threatens to sidetrack the whole enterprise— as indeed it does in Shavit.

It is easy enough to run together the logic of the beneficiary as it applies to the present and the logic of the beneficiary as it applies to the past. I do so myself above when I fail to stress the difference between Orwell, who talks exclusively about the present, and Sartre, who talks about the past—about how Europe has constituted itself by means of the plunder and exploitation of its colonies. Orwell was of course writing before anticolonialism had scored any victories, before it was even in sight of the finish line. Sartre, writing later, in the heyday of the anticolonial movements, did not pretend the plunder and exploitation were finished, but he was closer to the postindependence era. He could therefore begin to imagine the very specific moral dilemma of a future Europe that, having surrendered its colonies, might nonetheless see itself as guilty in a permanent and irrevocable sense, indeed *should* see itself as guilty *in its very being*.

Guilty in its very being: it is a perversely attractive and, of late, a widespread thought. After all, Europe invented the modern nation-state. And that is why there are so many walls and men with guns on them. "All Nation-States are born and found themselves in violence," as Jacques Derrida writes in his essay "Forgiveness": "The moment of foundation, the instituting moment, is anterior to the law or legitimacy which it founds. It is thus outside the law, and violent by that very fact" (57). This is a philosophical translation of Nicholson's speech. By now its truth has entered into educated common sense. Who has not nodded sagely at the idea that the state of exception reveals the secret truth of the norm and that every liberal democracy has its origins in bloody atrocities that it then has to cover up? But this is one way in which, as it does enter common sense, the logic of the beneficiary can go awry. Though it remains alien to uninhibited racists such as Benjamin Netanyahu, it is increasingly what we hear from the more sophisticated apologists for Israel, the ones like Shavit who are willing to name the Nakba and to admit Israel's crimes against the Palestinians in 1948. After all, they will say, don't expect nation formation to resemble high tea. It cannot be decorous. Its aim is not universal justice. Look at what the United States did in its process of self-formation and more or less got away with. To paraphrase certain critics of Boycott, Divestment, and Sanctions against Israel (BDS): people in glass houses shouldn't throw stones. If your country has behaved no better than mine, what right do you have to single mine out? If your land was stolen from the Native Americans, what right do you have to point the finger at me for my treatment of the Palestinians? Who the hell are we Americans to boycott anyone? Look at our blood-soaked history! Shouldn't we just boycott ourselves?

Such inward-turning paralysis is what can follow all too naturally from seeing oneself as the beneficiary of atrocities in the past, atrocities that can never be erased. You begin in distressed self-accusation, but with nowhere else to go (after all, the clock can't be turned back), you shift from self-accusation to a tough-minded lockdown on political initiatives of any sort, a steely eyed embrace of the status quo. This too is the logic of "all of us without exception."

The concept of the beneficiary would not be worth expending so much energy on if it did not give us somewhere to go. That premise will perhaps help explain my restriction of the concept as far as possible to the present and thus my saying so little about the cases of gross historical injustice in America that will spring most readily to mind. I hope it is clear that I am not thereby embracing the radical presentism of cosmopolitans like Walter Benn Michaels. Michaels (no bleeding-heart liberal he) suggests that for Americans today to apologize to the Native American victims of genocide or the African American victims of slavery would mean "apologizing for something you didn't do to people to whom you didn't do it (in fact, to people to whom it wasn't done)" (*Trouble with Diversity*, 122). In other words, it's fine for me to live on stolen land as long as I myself did not commit the theft and those whose land was stolen are safely dead, and this is so even if that theft has reduced generations of them to poverty.[4] Here I return to the word "ongoing." The most eloquent champions of reparations to African Americans, such as Ta-Nehisi Coates, insist on how a racism that is now illegal nonetheless continues to push its dirty fingers into the present, choking off black lives by such palpable, measurable means as redlining. By the criterion of continuity between past injustice and present suffering, the same is easy enough to show for the Palestinians and the Native Americans (in early December 2016, as I prepare to send this manuscript in, everyone's eyes have been riveted by the confrontation at Standing Rock and the extraordinary apology to the Sioux issued there by Wes Clark). Those who are still on the fence about BDS may be encouraged by the thought that it is not first and foremost about true and full redemption for past wrongs—that is beyond the power of any program or policy, however ambitious. It is a response to an active call for solidarity from Palestinians today whose rights are, to say the least, not respected. Yes, any debt to the living takes precedence over any debt to the dead. But some debts to the dead really *are* debts to the living. The recognition that we inhabit the site of violent injustices committed long ago matters now if (1) we can see that we still benefit from those injustices, and (2) there is something to be done by or for those now alive whose lives have been visibly shaped by those injustices.

It is this position—call it a moderate presentism—that has informed this book, which has maintained a relatively single-minded focus on the beneficiary as a present-tense relation to present economic realities. For some, this choice will still sound too presentist. So be it. I will stand by the proposition that arguments in favor of reparations are not equally valid in every case. It can't be taken for granted that effects always do persist into the present in a meaningful way and to a meaningful degree. The presentness of the past should not be treated as if it were a moral postulate and thus did not need the verification that Coates's research so amply offers. It is tempting to assume that in terms of consequences, all past injustice is ongoing. But before you assume it, it would be wise to reflect on what it would mean to take seriously the idea that each action lives forever; that nothing is ever over; that the passage of time is morally meaningless; that time has no power to heal or obscure or heal by obscuring. Faced with blatant injustice, it is disorienting and frankly upsetting to think that the mere passing of years should make any ethical difference at all. And yet there is no denying that to some degree it does, and it must. It seems necessary to work on the opposite premise that, like the conquests of Genghis Khan or Alexander the Great (though all examples will get you in trouble somewhere), some past atrocities should be treated as pedagogical opportunities but otherwise left substantively unwept and uncommemorated. Close off the possibility of letting the past go, and you risk an inflation of moral responsibility that will make all debts seem unpayable, hence will make them easier to ignore.

It is ongoing debts, debts in and to the present, debts that are most often ignored, that I have tried to highlight in this book. Of course even debts to the present can be inflated and made to seem unpayable. In their eagerness to get off the grid or out from under the burden of being a beneficiary, some would hold that global economic interconnectedness is itself a moral scandal, whether or not too much fossil fuel is involved in getting commodities to distant markets. This is a misleading simplification. The problem is not the division of labor but the inequality that the division of labor coincides with and disguises. Yet that inequality is not as easy to deny as the champions of globalization make it seem.

To underline this point, I will enlist in the ranks of beneficiary talkers another extremely unlikely writer. Thomas Friedman, in *The Lexus and the Olive Tree*, before making the discovery that the world is flat, had described the United States as "the country that benefits most from today's global integration" (437) and again as global capitalism's "biggest beneficiary" (463). He admits to no qualms about the country's beneficiary status. The assumption seems to be that we have earned our benefits by outcompeting our rivals or at least by doing more than our fair share of the work of sustaining the system. Friedman writes, "My message to [my daughters] is very simple. Girls, when I was growing up my parents used to say to me, 'Tom, finish your dinner. People in China and India are starving.' I say to my girls, 'Girls, finish your homework. People in China and India are starving for your jobs'" (Ross, *Fast Boat to China*, 6).

This is capitalism's official line: globalization has eliminated actual starvation. MacFarquhar's Aaron should not be worrying about the starving child next to the vending machine. Starvation is now merely a metaphor. There are no real victims, only competitors. The only imperative Aaron should worry about is the imperative to compete. For Friedman, who fancies himself a humorist but would not I think claim to be a moralist, morality is therefore not involved. His daughters are not invited to reach across the geographical distance in order to help anyone. It is the people starving for his daughters' jobs who are already reaching across it, and they are doing so in order to threaten his daughters' future livelihood. This threat does not quite rise to the level of a moral scandal, though given the apparent newness and menace of this global reach, the elements of potential economic nationalism are in place. Friedman does not see that before anyone felt any hunger for American jobs, his daughters' livelihood was *already* causally connected, and perhaps harmfully so, to the past, present, and future livelihoods of the Indians and the Chinese. His daughters may be in danger of having their (future) jobs stolen by foreigners, but no attention is paid to the question of how Americans first obtained those jobs and who, perhaps, might have complained at the time that *their* jobs were being relocated to America. No harm, no foul.

And yet even Friedman seems unable to keep the harm of inequality entirely out of sight. He tells his daughters that they lose if people in India and China win. But in his own much-publicized view, there is something they have already lost. One extraordinary aspect of Friedman's best-selling *The World Is Flat* is that the book recognizes American loss as an accomplished fact. One might even suggest that, in a somewhat oblique way, it recognizes the loss as a taste of future justice. The metaphor of the flat world, a world in which as Friedman says the playing field has been leveled, has somehow not been widely interpreted as saying one thing it clearly does say: if the world *is* flat, if the playing field *has* been leveled, then the world we lived in *before* the leveling of the playing field was an uneven, unequal one. The world in which America was the system's "biggest beneficiary" was a world in which Americans enjoyed unfair advantages. How can the "world-is-flat" metaphor be read without drawing this conclusion? We know Friedman is a champion of free trade and is optimistic, perhaps to the point of criminal negligence, about free trade's social consequences. But in his title, staring us in the face, is a recognition not only of the jobs that may be lost at some time in the future but also of advantages America has already lost—and, by implication, rightly so. Friedman comes to praise the system, not to bury it. But both the metaphor and the cheeriness suggest some acknowledgment that, from a planetary perspective, up to now the system has been extremely unfair, and the current loss of national privilege is a step in the direction of greater fairness.[5]

To illustrate one more time how far variants of the discourse of the beneficiary extend beyond the obvious sites and suspects, from Orwell and Sartre to Klein, Kincaid, and Berger, let me recall the bright but annoying teenager in Don DeLillo's novel *White Noise* who mocks his father's ignorance of how everyday gadgets and technologies work, his inability to understand or remake the objects on which he has allowed his life to depend:

> "It's like we've been flung back in time," he said. "Here we are in the Stone Age, knowing all these great things after centuries of progress but what can we do to make life easier for the Stone Agers? Can we make a refrigerator? Can we even explain how it works? What is electricity? What is light? We experience these things every day of our lives but what good does it do if we find ourselves hurled back in time and we can't even tell people the basic principles much less actually make something that would improve conditions. Name one thing you could make. Could you make a simple wooden match that you could strike on a rock to make a flame? . . . Could you rub flints together? Would you know a flint if you saw one? . . . Explain a radio." (147–48)[6]

At first, this monologue is about what "we" don't know, such as how to make a refrigerator. By the end, the "we" has become an aggressive "you," a you who wouldn't know a flint if you saw one and can be issued the abrupt command to name something you could make, to explain radio. Like Orwell and Kincaid, the teenager both does and does not include himself. This characteristic of the discourse of the beneficiary, structured as it is by an appetite for a universalistic speech that it angrily knows itself unable to satisfy, is the rhetorical analogue of the desire that sits right out on the surface of the passage: a desire to get off the grid, to get out from under the weight of dependence on the labor of others. To be materially independent would mean not to be a beneficiary. That's what the boy wants. But what we see is his knowledge that he can't have it. The annoying teenager plays out the humanitarian fantasy of rescue, represented here as what "our" technical expertise would have to offer the inhabitants of the Stone Age, whether in the past or (assuming an apocalyptic "airborne toxic event" like the one the novel conjures up) in the near future. But his point of course is that neither he nor his father would be capable of playing Twain's Connecticut Yankee. The scandal is that no one possesses adequate knowledge—especially not his father. A whole civilization would be needed. Seeing beyond the beneficiary does not encourage or require anything so drastic as the sacrifice of that civilization. What it requires is erasing the structural inequality by which the beneficiary is defined. Postapocalyptic narratives are all around us, but partial self-abolition is a smaller and more accessible goal than apocalypse.

As I have been suggesting, debts to distant others whose labor and undercompensation make possible the relative abundance of life in the metropolis shed a different light on humanitarianism. Humanitarianism insists on what we owe to all fellow members of the species. If you add the fact that our prosperity is causally linked to the sufferings that humanitarians such as Peter Singer ask us to be charitable about, as I have proposed, we would seem to owe a good deal more, or owe in a different way. Think of the discourse of the beneficiary as what is added to Singer by Jack Nicholson. Singer speaks in the name of the traditional cosmopolitan premise that all lives everywhere should matter to you as much as the lives of those around you. Nicholson speaks in the name of particular loyalty to those around you. (The "truth" he comes bearing is also the now archaic "troth," or pledged loyalty.) One reason why I am willing to claim Nicholson's character for the discourse of the beneficiary, holding my nose at his odious politics, is that concern for global justice needs loyalty. As his critics have observed, Singer constantly flirts with nihilism: compared to the rescue of the starving, everything else seems insignificant and even valueless. If you feel impelled to sacrifice everything you have, if sacrifice becomes so central to your life that (to cite again Naomi Klein's mother) you can never permit yourself to have a good time, and once rescued others will not be able to have a good time either, then what is it you are rescuing people *for*? Why is it even worth being rescued? Loyalty, dangerous as the virtue has always been to cosmopolitanism, is a component of good times; as Bernard Williams would say, it makes life worth living. And loyalty should not be considered merely local or essentially anticosmopolitan. This has been key to my argument throughout: loyalty is also a way of describing the extra intensity of attachment and responsibility one can feel for those who make one's life possible, wherever they happen to reside. It's thus another way of describing the synthesis of cosmopolitanism with belonging. The as yet unnamed amalgam of humanitarianism and politics that will be necessary in order to move toward global economic redistribution cannot ground itself either in do-gooders or in planetary demographics. It will require forms of North/South loyalty that remain inchoate (that is no doubt one reason why they were not on Bernard Williams's radar) but for which, as I have tried to show, some foundations have been laid.

When I began writing about cosmopolitanism in the early 1990s, I was impatient both with the old culture-blind universalism and with recent celebrations of the local and the situated that seemed just as blind to the larger situatedness of all localities in planetary context, economic and political. The formula I adopted for what would come to be called "new" cosmopolitanism was "multiple and overlapping loyalties." That formula has never seemed entirely satisfactory; in *Perpetual War: Cosmopolitanism from the Viewpoint of Violence* (2012), the volume to which this is a sequel, I asked whether the diasporic groups to which it most obviously applies were in fact demonstrating the kind of resistance to, say, patriotic militarism without which the term cosmopolitan would seem a grave misnomer. In the context of global economic inequality, however, the phrase "multiple and overlapping loyalties" seems newly pertinent. How else can one describe the simultaneous obligation to the poor at home and to the even poorer abroad? How else to account for the need both to say, and not to say, that we are the 99 percent? And how else can you make the point that in both cases, and not just the one, what you are talking about is indeed a feeling of loyalty?

The fact that beneficiaries exist is evidence that the world is out of joint. There should be no such thing as a beneficiary. There can be no good way to be a beneficiary, therefore, except by trying not to be one—trying to do away with the divide between beneficiaries and nonbeneficiaries, the stark geometry of global injustice by which beneficiaries are defined. The point of the category is not to persist in its being but to abolish itself. But this is the stuff of paradox: one becomes conscious of oneself as a beneficiary only by trying to be morally consistent—that is, recognizing what one's existence depends on. And yet the project of self-abolition necessarily involves acknowledging and accepting a large quotient of seemingly irreducible inconsistency. Inconsistency (most saliently, between global and domestic commitments) will be irreparable as long as there are beneficiaries. This is a truth that will not be easy to handle. Even harder to handle, perhaps, is the related fact that there is no list of satisfying and immediately accessible things to do about global economic inequality. My hope is that, without encouraging Singer-like self-sacrifice, this book will nevertheless leave its readers grasping for a less perfect to-do list made up of items that are less accessible and less satisfying. Perhaps we can all find some satisfaction in the (to me, still surprising) knowledge that our awkward ambitions do not come from nowhere and that they are widely if still insufficiently shared.

NOTES

INTRODUCTION

1 On the origin and history of the Kennan line, see d'Aymery, "Context and Accuracy."
2 Diamond, "What's Your Consumption Factor?"
3 See Caparrós, "Counting the Hungry."
4 For an example of an appeal to pride, consider a passage found early in Adam Smith's *The Wealth of Nations*: "If we examine, I say, all these things, and consider what a variety of labour is employed about each of them, we shall be sensible that without the assistance and cooperation of many thousands, the very meanest person in a civilized country could not be provided, even according to, what we very falsely imagine, the easy and simple manner in which he is commonly accommodated. Compared, indeed, with the more extravagant luxury of the great, his accommodation [Smith means "level of comfort"] must no doubt appear extremely simple and easy; and yet it may be true, perhaps, that the accommodation of an European prince does not always so much exceed that of an industrious and

frugal peasant, as the accommodation of the latter exceeds that of many an African king, the absolute master of the lives and liberties of ten thousand naked savages" (13). The explicit meaning of this last sentence is that a European peasant is more prosperous than an African king, and that there is a greater difference between the prosperity of European peasant and African king than between a European prince and a European peasant. Smith's intention seems to be to preempt the grievances of the European poor as they resentfully contemplate "the extravagant luxury of the great" by offering them the flattering picture of their putative economic superiority to African kings. This is a subgenre of what I will be calling the discourse of the beneficiary.

5 Dale Jamieson quotes John Nolt, 6.

6 Valuable commentary on the eighteenth century's new awareness of causal chains extending across vast distances comes from Laqueur, "Bodies, Details."

7 See, for example, Charles Isherwood, "Moral Issues behind iPhone and Its Makers," *New York Times*, October 17, 2011.

8 Žižek and Horvat, *What Does Europe Want?*, 170.

9 "From the standpoint of creating an *effective* transitional regime, bystanders are beneficiaries who are yet to be blamed and beneficiaries are bystanders who are yet to be absolved" (Meister, *After Evil*, 28).

10 I like to imagine a discussion of the loss of American jobs that have been shipped overseas in which someone asked how Americans got those jobs in the first place and in particular whether someone else possessed them at the time, someone (for example, steelworkers somewhere in Europe) who might have complained with equal justice that their jobs had been "stolen."

11 I have written elsewhere about the larger issue that Meister raises under the heading of "reparations": namely, how feeling oneself a beneficiary of past violence can lead one's judgments of the present astray. The book I am currently writing, on the literary history of atrocity, addresses questions of ethics and temporality that are raised below, especially in the conclusion, but that I leave undeveloped.

12 Orwell, *Road to Wigan Pier*, 140.

13 Samuel Fleischacker, in his *A Short History of Distributive Justice*, notes how slow the world was to arrive at the moral conviction that poverty is harmful and "that people do not deserve their socioeconomic place" (116) and how many presuppositions had to change in order for this to happen even on the domestic scale.

CHAPTER 1. THE STARVING CHILD

1 Vernon, *Hunger*, 275.

2 It would be useless for me to deny that this project is motivated by the same kinds of concerns as Singer's. I am grateful to Singer and his philosophical companions even if I try to dispute the ethical bases of effective altruism. My double premise here is (1) that it's not good for the cause of global economic justice for utilitarians to have a monopoly on it, and (2) that Singer needs to be argued with by people,

unlike his usual array of critics, who are less complacent about economic inequalities and/or about global capital.

3 The Samaritan, it turns out, may not have been as disinterested as he seemed. Guidebooks locate the biblical scene on the road between Jerusalem and Jericho, on what is now the West Bank, in fact near one of the larger fortified settlements. And they make the Good Samaritan out to be, like me, a sort of Jew. The story is that when most of the Jews were sent into exile after the Assyrian conquest around 720 BC, some were left behind. Returning from exile a couple of centuries later, the Jews shunned the Samaritans for their intermarriage with the conquerors, although (or perhaps because) the Samaritans claimed a stricter adherence to the Mosaic Law than the exiles. There is thus some question as to whether the Samaritans were simply enemies of the Jews or something more intimate and more confused, and thus whether the Good Samaritan can stand for something as simple as a disinterested spectator. Perhaps this charitable action was closer to solidarity, or to the specific overcoming of a specific hostility.

4 On "we," consider Peter A. French. In "Morally Blaming Whole Populations," French makes a distinction between two senses of blame: "the determination of causes or faults" (267), on the one hand, and "to hold responsible" (267), on the other. The determination of cause or fault and the "expression of displeasure" that accompanies it can of course aim at small children or at inanimate objects such as the weather that cannot or should not be held responsible. French calls this "non-moral blame." The more relevant sense comes from the following example. "Anyone sincerely saying [that the American people are to blame for Vietnam atrocities] must be able to show that (1) there exists a recognizable or referable collectivity designated by the term 'the American people'; (2) that events describable as 'atrocities' took place in Vietnam; (3) that a causal relationship can be drawn from acts of the collectivity to the 'atrocities' in question; (4) that the American people should have acted (collectively) in a manner different from the manner in which they did act; (5) that the American people were not completely unaware of the nature of their behavior (that is, the American people did not believe they were authorizing a cultural exchange of ballet troupes with the Vietnamese; and (6) that the collectivity could have acted (had the ability and opportunity of acting) in those alternative ways cited in (4), that is, there were conceivable alternative courses of collective action which had they been tried would have made less likely the perpetration of atrocities in Vietnam" (282). Fulfilling criteria like these is by no means guaranteed, but it seems to be within the zone of possibility.

5 Psychologically speaking, MacFarquhar also notes, the fantasy of rescue includes a component of aggression: the one who fantasizes being a rescuer takes a perverse pleasure in imagining someone else in the state of extreme suffering from which rescue would be necessary (*Strangers Drowning*, 109).

6 Hitchens, *Trial of Henry Kissinger*, 44.

7 A detailed history of the episode is available in Gary J. Bass's *The Blood Telegram: Nixon, Kissinger, and a Forgotten Genocide*. A broader but pertinent backstory

comes from Nick Cullather's *The Hungry World: America's Cold War Battle against Poverty in Asia*.

8 Maher, "Food Fights," 37.

9 The section of Rushdie's novel *Midnight's Children* that deals with the events of 1971 makes its protagonist a participant as well as an observer and therefore guilty, even if he suffers from amnesia.

10 Thanks to John McClure for this handy formulation and for much else.

11 Orwell, *Road to Wigan Pier*.

12 Orwell, *Road to Wigan Pier*, 126.

13 Working on an analogy between one moral revolution that has happened, the abolition of slavery, and another that has not, vegetarianism, Haskell asks, "If vegetarianism should someday become the mainstream point of view, how would the historians among our vegetarian descendants view us, their carnivorous ancestors?" ("Capitalism," 250). Would they be correct to assume "that because some twentieth-century people are ethically opposed to eating meat, others must know in their hearts that it is wrong and can only maintain a clear conscience by deceiving themselves"? (251). Should they decide, for example, that "exaggeration of the harsh consequences of poverty, the pain of discrimination, the penalties of class, and the horrors of human warfare" were all means of self-deception allowing the carnivorous to "give tacit sanction" to what they knew in their hearts was wrong, "the systematic slaughter of non-humans"? (251). Haskell's answer is, obviously, no. The view that the slaughter of nonhumans is morally wrong, however obvious it may now seem to some, had not become a foundational one, any more than the view that wage labor is as exploitative as slavery. The sense of moral responsibility to end slavery, like the sense of moral responsibility to end the eating of animals, is, as we have come to say, a historical construct.

14 Moyn, "Spectacular Wrongs."

15 Fassin, "Inequality of Lives," 239.

16 On fracking leading to earthquakes in Ohio, see Klein, *This Changes Everything*, 329.

17 See my "All of Us without Exception: Sartre, Rancière, and the Cause of the Other."

CHAPTER 2. YOU ACQUIESCE IN IT

1 Orwell, *Road to Wigan Pier*, 140.

2 George Orwell, *Review of Letters on India*.

3 "If it's appropriate for you to have the share of things which in fact you have, and it's appropriate for all the people who are like you all over the world to have the share that they have, that means that it's not inappropriate for all of the others to have the share that remains. You know that what you have is what you deserve, and that means that what they have is what they deserve" (Shawn, *The Fever*, 59–60).

4 I treat Wallerstein at length in "Blaming the System." Fredric Jameson's use

of "world-system" in *The Geopolitical Aesthetic* seems to include political actors while it also, characteristically for Jameson but of course not for Wallerstein, sees the totality as an "absent, unrepresentable totality" (10). For Orwell, as for Wallerstein, "An economic system on the scale of the globe itself" (Jameson, 9) will not necessarily be beyond the capacities of the human perceptual apparatus.

5 World-systems theory has had many critics over the years, and its status in the scholarly community is anything but assured. See, however, the measured support from outside it receives in Sebastian Conrad's judicious *What Is Global History?* (2016).

6 Anthony DePalma, "15 Years on the Bottom Rung."

7 See, for example, Hernandez and Coutin, "Remitting Subjects."

8 See Basch, Glick-Schiller, and Blanc, *Nations Unbound.*

9 DeParle, "Good Provider," 57.

10 Sartre, Daniel Just notes, "considered guilt to be a vital political force . . . guilt must be cultivated because it stimulates action" (*Literature, Ethics, and Decolonization*, 113). Sartre insisted on this point with special force during the Algerian war.

11 See Branko Milanović, *Worlds Apart: Measuring International and Global Inequality* and *The Haves and Have-Nots: A Brief and Idiosyncratic History of Global Inequality.* It is worth noting that Wallerstein would disagree about the timing here. For him, inequality between countries has been more significant than inequality within countries since the beginning of the world capitalist system in the 1500s. For a judicious overview of Milanović's views of global inequality, see Therborn (2017). For recent corroboration, see Hickel (2017).

12 The substance of this position is given by the economist Yanis Varoufakis. Well before his brief but memorable stint as Greece's finance minister during the negotiations over the Greek sovereign debt, Varoufakis had argued "that the defining characteristic of the global political economy was the reversal of the flow of trade and capital surpluses between the United States and the rest of the world. The hegemon, for the first time in world history, strengthened its hegemony by willfully enlarging its deficits, once it had lost its surplus global position" (*Global Minotaur*, x). That was in 2003. After the financial collapse of 2008, Varoufakis reiterated his position: the United States is "a giant vacuum cleaner, absorbing people's surplus goods and capital" (22).

13 For an eloquent and informative restatement of this position, see Beckert, *Empire of Cotton.*

14 Ahmad, *In Theory*, 182; emphasis his.

15 Lloyd, *Man of Reason*, 96.

16 If you do an Internet search for "zero-sum economics," most of what you get is apologists for capitalism seizing upon the zero-sum, my-gain-is-your-loss logic in order to explain triumphantly that though capitalism's moralistic enemies are forever trying to oversimplify things, this is not how capitalism actually works. However, googling "zero sum" also gets you some critics of capitalism, such as a Salon piece from 2013 by Robert Reich called "Economic Prosperity Is Not a Zero-Sum

Game." Reich makes the basic Keynesian point that "even the very wealthy" should realize that their success depends on "a broader-based prosperity. That's because 70 percent of economic activity in America is consumer spending. If the bottom 90 percent of Americans are becoming poorer, they're less able to spend. Without their spending, the economy can't get out of first gear." It's the point that European leftists and social democrats have made about Germany's relation to its neighbors to the south: we northern Europeans won't stay prosperous if we impose austerity on our Mediterranean neighbors. It's the difference between family budgets and national budgets: the family budget really is zero-sum in the sense that if you spend more than you take in, you lose, whereas for a nation in a world of other nations, what you spend comes back to you as what they are able to buy of your products. On problems with the concept of exploitation, see Balibar, "Exploitation."

CHAPTER 3. A SHORT HISTORY OF COMMODITY RECOGNITION

1 George Orwell, "Not Counting Niggers," in *The Collected Essays: Journalism and Letters*, Vol. 1, ed. Sonia Orwell and Ian Angus (Harmondsworth: Penguin, 1970), 434–438. George Orwell, "Review of Letters on India by Mulk Raj Anand," *Tribune*, 19 March 1943, in Peter Davison (ed.), *The Complete Works of George Orwell*, Vol. 15, "Two Wasted Years" (London: Secker & Warburg, 1998), 33.

2 It seems likely that Orwell is channeling the perspective of Indians he knows personally, such as Mulk Raj Anand, with whom he had shared the antifascist struggle in Spain and whom he invited to participate in the BBC broadcasts.

3 During Orwell's childhood, as Hitchens recalls, the "family's meal ticket" was the employment of Orwell's father in "the degrading opium trade between British India and China" (*Why Orwell Matters*, 6).

4 Louis Menand, "Honest, Decent, Wrong."

5 For further nuance on Smith and poverty, see Istvan Hont, *Jealousy of Trade: International Competition and the Nation-State in Historical Perspective*; Istvan Hont and Michael Ignatieff, eds., *Wealth and Virtue: The Shaping of Political Economy in the Scottish Enlightenment* (1986); and Gareth Stedman Jones, *An End to Poverty? A Historical Debate*.

6 In *The Lexus and the Olive Tree* (1999), Friedman offers a putatively amusing "five gas stations theory of the world" that has its own backhanded recognition of poverty: "First there is the Japanese gas station. Gas is $5 a gallon. Four men in uniforms and white gloves, with lifetime employment contracts, wait on you. . . . Second is the American gas station. Gas costs only $1 a gallon, but you pump it yourself. You wash your own windows. . . . And when you drive around the corner four homeless people try to steal your hubcaps. Third is the Western European gas station. Gas there also costs $5 a gallon. There is only one man on duty. He grudgingly pumps your gas and unsmilingly changes your oil, reminding you all the time that his union contract says he only has to pump gas and change oil. . . . Fourth is the developing country gas station. Fifteen people work there and they are all cousins. . . . Gas is only 35 cents a gallon because it is subsidized by the

government, but only one of the six gas pumps actually works. . . . The gas station is rather run-down because the absentee owner lives in Zurich and takes all the profits out of the country. . . . Lastly there is the communist gas station. Gas there is only 50 cents a gallon—but there is none, because the four guys working there have sold it all on the black market for $5 a gallon" (379–81). Friedman's ostensible point is that "through the process of globalization everyone is being forced toward America's gas station" (380). But notice how (as so often) Friedman says more than he wants to say. The real cost of Americanization here isn't having to pump your own gas: it's being one of the homeless, unemployed men who are reduced to trying to steal hubcaps. (Trying, and not even succeeding—what losers!) The image of the four hubcap stealers is a confession that Friedman would otherwise never make: American-style globalization demands a well-populated class of have-nots.

7 Thucydides, *History of the Peloponnesian War*, Book 2, xxxv–xlvi.

8 Swift, *Gulliver's Travels*, part 4, chapter 6, 229–30. See the commentary in Sussman, *Consuming Anxieties*, 9. Another locus classicus for commodity recognition in the period is Alexander Pope's *The Rape of the Lock*. See, for example, Kroll, "Pope and Drugs."

9 Emeralds were largely mined in Colombia and Africa, though some came (perhaps through the Baltic, in which Eliot's Mr. Brooke fails to interest voters in his speech) from Russia and Austria. The largest source of diamonds had been India, but in the nineteenth century excited attention had turned to Brazil. And then in 1866 the discovery of diamonds in South Africa led to a diamond rush. Amethysts, which Dorothea does not choose, could also be found in Russia and Austria, though Brazil and Uruguay and Mexico were more prominent sources. The exhaustion of the German deposits of agate in the nineteenth century had led to mining in Brazil, hence to the discovery of amethyst deposits there.

10 On this point Sebastian Conrad agrees.

11 Among the commentaries on this famous passage that stress the growing sense of global system, see in particular "Killing a Chinese Mandarin: The Moral Implications of Distance" by the Italian historian Carlo Ginzburg. Ginzburg comments on the passage in Balzac's *Père Goriot* where the hero, Rastignac, agonizes over the "pact with the devil" he's just been offered by the diabolical but charismatic Vautrin. All he has to do to make a rich marriage and ensure his fortune is acquiesce in a murder of someone he will never see. He reformulates this offer, in a conversation with his friend, as the question of "what he would do if he could become wealthy by killing an old Chinese mandarin, without leaving Paris, just by an act of will . . . all you'd need to do would be nod your head" (54–55). The friend says no, but the point about Rastignac's eventual upward mobility is made anyway. As Ginzburg writes, the passage gestures toward "the emergence of a worldwide economic system" that has built its rewards on "distance" and on the indifference to suffering that distance makes possible: "Somebody's financial gains can be related, more or less directly, to the distress of distant human beings, thrown into poverty, starvation, and even death" (56).

12 For a glimpse of actual Chinese subjectivity on earthquakes, see Solnit, *Paradise Built in Hell*. "Since the Chou dynasty," Solnit writes, "earthquakes in China have often been seen as signs that the rulers had lost the mandate of heaven. Even in modern times, many interpreted in this light the death of Chairman Mao two months after the colossal 1976 Tang Shan earthquake killed hundreds of thousands" (151). Solnit sees revolutionary potential in this logic but makes no mention of the stronger conclusion that one might prefer to see drawn: that there is something wrong with the very notion of heavenly mandate for human government. It's perhaps worth adding that Solnit's emphasis on spontaneous, face-to-face community making in moments of disaster such as earthquakes overrides the problematic of the overcoming of distance and gives no special role to literature.

13 On Smith and religion, see Fitzgibbons, *Adam Smith's System*.

CHAPTER 4. NATION-STATE AS AGENT OF COSMOPOLITANISM

1 I discuss the connection between "It's not your fault" and the welfare state in *Upward Mobility and the Common Good: Toward a Literary History of the Welfare State*.

2 In a sense, then, self-blame (as an effect of mercantile misogyny) leads to the realization (under the welfare state) that self-blame is a mistake.

3 I take the idea of self-flagellation from Lamouchi's Jean-Paul Sartre et le tiers monde: Rhétorique d'un discours anticolonialiste: "Certes, il y a un peu d'auto-flagellation dans cette violence verbale de l'intellectuel, obligé d'être contre son propre pays" (176). See also Arthur, *Unfinished Projects: Decolonization and the Philosophy of Jean-Paul Sartre*.

4 Hence Orwell's intense interest in Sir Stafford Cripps and Cripps's 1942 mission to India. (For what it's worth, Cripps was Anthony Appiah's maternal grandfather.) The failure of that mission, which the British blamed on the intransigence of the Congress Party, is sometimes given as a reason for Orwell's decision to quit the BBC. He declared in his letter of resignation that his efforts were useless. Cripps was also associated with the ascetic, anticonsumer tendency that I will be discussing below. On February 28, 1942, Orwell writes, "The chief event has been the entry into the Government of Sir Stafford Cripps, late Ambassador to Moscow. It can be taken for granted that Sir Stafford would not have accepted office without being certain that large political changes were contemplated, both in Britain's home and foreign policy." About the foreign policy, the referent here is obvious: antiimperialism. But what about domestic policy? "In his first speech in his new post," Orwell continued, "he has already forecast a tightening up of social legislation, which will have the effect of suppressing many useless luxuries, and in general making the way of life of all classes more equal. It is also known that the relationship between Great Britain and India is to be debated in Parliament next week, and it can be taken for granted that the relationship is the subject of most earnest discussion and is about to undergo a great change. Public opinion in this

country is very anxious for a solution of the Indian political deadlock, and equally anxious to see India a willing and active ally of Britain against the Fascist powers. This popular feeling has crystallized around Sir Stafford Cripps" (*War Broadcasts*, 59). It is also worth noting that Cripps put up the money for *Tribune*, the journal at which Orwell began working after he quit the BBC. Orwell listened to Cripps's speech from Delhi to get a clue of how he himself sounded from India.

5 Orwell, *Orwell: The War Broadcasts*. W. J. West's theory is that his time as talks producer in the Indian section of the BBC's Eastern service was "the key to Orwell's evolution from the slightly pedantic and unpolished author of pre-war days" (13). West opposes "the received view . . . that these were lost years for Orwell" (13). "There were constraints and frustrations certainly," but he didn't stop writing, he wrote some of the talks himself, and saw what he said as "essentially truthful" (13).

6 West comments in another footnote, "The welcoming of austerity and the rationalising of the necessity for it were always, from the first outline of the book, part of the background of *Nineteen Eighty-Four* and Orwell was at first not averse to those sentiments. Later, with the experience of post-war austerity, the bitterness of the parody in *Nineteen Eighty-Four* took over" (59).

7 Also censored was Orwell's reporting of new taxes on tobacco and alcohol and the political spin he puts on those taxes: "The wiping out of class distinctions which is happening in Britain as a result of the war" (*War Broadcasts*, 79).

8 For other and more detailed readings of wartime rationing, see Collingham, *The Taste of War*, and Carruth, "War Rations and the Food Politics of Late Modernism."

9 Sacrifice in the defense of a nation at war could plausibly be described as self-interested. My argument requires a motive other than war, and perhaps one that would also exceed or at least trouble the bounds of self-interest. Is it possible to imagine a moral equivalent of war that could generate as much will to collective self-fashioning as the Nazi threat did while also extending its solidarity beyond the collectivity of wartime allies? I can't pretend to know. But the most obvious answer to the "moral equivalent of war" question is of course the threat of ecological catastrophe. That threat is the major nonracist impulse that the locavores and other new ascetics are responding to. Whether you consider this self-interested or altruistic will depend on how far into the future you consider that your self extends. I would not like to think that it's only those of us with offspring who recognize ourselves in future collectivities, even if we can't know them, as well as in our present, delimited selves—which we don't know all that well either. Do I see striking evidence of people stretching themselves in time to anticipate severe ecological harm the way they anticipate coming to belong to the top 1 percent? Not for the moment. But I don't think the case is closed.

10 Klein and MacFarquhar both have Orwell in mind. MacFarquhar quotes him on Gandhi: "The essence of being human is that one does not seek perfection, that one is sometimes willing to commit sins for the sake of loyalty, that one does not push asceticism to the point where it makes friendly intercourse impossible"

(*Strangers Drowning*, 8–9). This is why people don't want to be saints. Yet as Mac-Farquhar observes, Orwell genuinely admired Gandhi.

11 To this Kolbert's response is unconvincing—that Klein is erring "on the side of optimism" by suggesting that "dealing with climate change is something that can be done with minimal disruption to ordinary people's (i.e. voters') lives" ("Can Climate Change Cure Capitalism?," 16). The issue might be better framed as a choice between telling people to deal with obesity by dieting and addressing the infrastructure of industrial food production and marketing. Thanks to Bonnie Honig for the suggestion.

CHAPTER 5. NAOMI KLEIN'S LOVE STORY

1 For what it's worth, the historian Thomas Haskell draws exactly the opposite conclusion about capitalism and commitment in his analysis of abolitionism: for Haskell, as noted above, capitalism encourages a *tighter* sense of commitment.

2 In *This Changes Everything*, Klein is critical of the "fetish for structurelessness, the rebellion against any kind of institutionalization" that she and the movement have shared (157). According to MacFarquhar, Klein was at first taken with the "anarchic formlessness" of the antisweatshop movement, then changed her mind. "Seeing how easy it was for everything to evaporate, without institutions taking that energy and nailing it down—we were too ephemeral" (MacFarquhar, "Outside Agitator," 67–68).

3 Let's say I, the speaker, see someone suffering somewhere and talk about it to you. Before you have a chance to say or do anything, I am claiming a moral advantage. For in the very instant of conversation, we both know about the suffering, but by the very act of telling you, I seem to be doing something about it. Not much, but something. Whereas you (by the very act of listening passively) are just sitting there, *not* doing anything about it. Which you may reasonably enough resent. Having found myself in the passive, morally disadvantaged position more often than I would like, I don't mind saying that I find this analysis quite liberating. It liberates me from the resentment I tend to feel, the tendency to want to criticize the messenger bringing me the bad news, and to use my ill will toward the messenger as an excuse for forgetting about the message.

4 Of course, much of the capitalist economy doesn't depend on brand names. Hence the danger that anticorporate campaigns will miss the point and "degenerate into glorified ethical shopping guides: how-to's on saving the world through boycotts and personal lifestyle choices" (Klein, *No Logo*, 428).

5 Doug Henwood's critique of *The Shock Doctrine*, "Awe, Shocks," accuses Klein of pretending things are secret so as to be able to uncover them.

6 For more on the term "infrastructuralism," see the special issue of *Modern Fiction Studies* edited by Michael Rubenstein et al.

7 One of the smartest discussions of Klein focuses on her reluctance to call on the state or to consider a politics that involves capturing the state's power for progressive purposes. See Battistoni, "How to Change Everything."

8 *Make Do and Mend: Keeping Family and Home Afloat on War Rations*, a collection of reproductions of official instructional leaflets circulated during the war. One commentary on the nostalgic fashion for wartime deprivation is Silcoff, "Pig Swill and Bones," 51.

9 Henwood, "Awe, Shocks." http://www.leftbusinessobserver.com/Shock.html.

10 Jeremy Corbyn's "criticism of the absurdly high level of military expenditure," Tariq Ali writes, "is echoed by some prominent US economists in relation to their own country. Joseph Stiglitz (a Corbyn adviser on the economy) and Linda Bilmes have argued that America's spending on wars since 2003, estimated now at nearly $8 trillion, is crippling the country. 'A trillion dollars,' they note, 'could have built eight million additional housing units, could have hired some 15 million additional public school teachers for one year; could have paid for 120 million children to attend a year of Head Start; or insured 530 million children for healthcare for one year; or provided 43 million students with four-year scholarships at public universities. Now multiply those numbers by three.'" They do not add the more complex but perhaps even more dramatic effects that such a shift in funds might have on global economic inequality. Ali, "Corbyn's Progress." http://tariqali.org /archives/3098.

11 To these issues must be added the issue of immigration. The ease or difficulty of transnational labor migration of course makes a huge difference to the intensity of global exploitation. If capital is free while labor is stopped at the border, capital wins and labor loses. But both sides run away from any argument over immigration that would wield a vocabulary of global economic justice. This systematic shunning suggests a certain consciousness of the unsayable.

12 Balibar, "Exploitation."

13 Onishi, "Toiling Far from Home."

14 Benefits have to be recognized. "Rosario has all the problems of industrialization— pollution, an exploding population of migrant workers, increased crime, rivers of sewage—without any of the benefits" (*No Logo*, 209). Here, if only in passing and out of the corner of her eye, Klein recognizes that industrialization *does* have benefits.

CHAPTER 6. LIFE WILL WIN

1 Bull argues that nihilism undercuts existing judgments of "value," such as the superiority of Mozart to potatoes, by imagining "the potential disappearance of what at the start of the process is the good being distributed ... the revolutionary tradition has actually been inspired by the idea of advancing to that point where the absence of limits negates the existence of those things the limit seeks to preserve and distribute—property, class, law, or the state—and which equality serves to maintain precisely because it presupposes them. There is indeed a sense in which, as Nietzsche said, this is 'the secret path to nothingness'" ("Levelling Out," 24). Bull redefines equality, accordingly, as "a form of socially realized skepticism about

value. Equality already functions like this in the case of positional goods, where sharing in, and diminishing the value of, are effected simultaneously" (24).

2 On the identity politics of the rich, see my "Sad Stories in the International Public Sphere: Richard Rorty on Culture and Human Rights."

3 Quoted in MacFarquhar, *Strangers*, 67.

4 On what might be called the "innocent beneficiary" and what can be done where straightforward restitution for wrongs done is impossible, see Goodin and Barry, "Benefiting."

5 In the chapter of *Distant Suffering* devoted to the rhetoric of denunciation, the act by which the spectator of suffering accuses those responsible, Luc Boltanski follows out a similar argument. He writes, "The greater the distance between the persecutor and his victim," the longer the "causal chain between the unfortunate and the agent who causes his suffering," and the more rhetorical work has to be done to establish a connection (62). Consider "an unfortunate who dies of hunger in a shanty-town. His persecutor, who has never seen him, occupies an office in Paris or New York at the head office of a holding company from which he works on the financial markets. How can the connection between unfortunate and persecutor be made to stick?" (62). The ability to denounce successfully under these conditions, Boltanski says, requires the mediation of a "theory of power" (62). For only a theory of power will be able to distinguish such cases from cases of "suffering which, however distressing it may be, is inherent in the human condition" (62)—that is, from suffering that cannot properly be described as political. The chapter ends by facing an even more sobering difficulty: the denunciation of "system," a theory of power that demands that accusation be "shifted from *persons* on to larger deindividualized entities such as *systems* or *structures*" (73). Where denunciation is concerned, every baby step away from pity for a particular individual and indignation at a particular perpetrator is presented as fraught with extreme danger. Whether an individual sufferer is made representative of some larger collectivity, or a system rather than an individual is held responsible for the suffering, the emotional intensity of the listener would also seem to suffer. The same theory of power that is needed to enforce the link between sufferer and accused would also seem to threaten the latter's freedom to act otherwise, hence his or her accountability: "Accusation cannot abandon all orientation towards responsibility without falling into self-contradiction. It is the very possibility of things happening otherwise and, consequently, the existence of responsibility, which distinguishes the denunciation of suffering about which it seems reasonable to be *indignant* from the attitude of *resignation* which prevails in the case of sufferings about which nothing can be done" (75).

6 Meister, *After Evil*, chapter 8, offers a useful commentary on the complexity problem with regard to the case for reparations.

7 Joseph Lelyveld, "Interrogating Ourselves," *New York Times Magazine*, June 12, 2005, 38.

8 Packer, "Dark Hours."

9 See my "On the Rentier."

10 Today's more substantive match for the rentier would be, alas, "the shareholders," that shadowy group in whose name so much corporate mayhem is committed. But "the shareholders" are a sublimely unknowable collectivity, anonymous because infinitely dispersed. They can't even be personified, let alone told to go get a real job.

11 Orwell, *Collected Essays*, 4:301.

12 Orwell's Gandhi is not a humanist; he did not assume "our job is to make life worth living on this earth"; *Collected Essays*, 4:468). The attraction of saintly non-attachment for him was "a desire to escape from the pain of living" (467), which is partly the pain of "loving some people more than others" (466). Still, he was also someone "who enriched the world simply by being alive" (465).

13 Jared Diamond, "What's Your Consumption Factor?"

14 Hsu, "Year of the Imaginary College Student."

CONCLUSION

1 *A Few Good Men*, directed by Rob Reiner, Castle Rock Entertainment, 1992.

2 Note that Nicholson's "You? You, Lieutenant Weinberg?" is a reminder that, whoever dials it up, the discourse of the beneficiary is likely to result in a hyperaggressive amplification of the second person. "You" are told that you took a deferment or found some other way of not serving in Vietnam. You were not on that wall then and will not be getting up on it anytime soon.

3 Both Sorkin's attraction to this solution and his inability to embrace it fully are woven into the seven highly successful seasons of *The West Wing*, in which an ideal president who is not looking for trouble is nonetheless forced to agonize heroically over whether to send the military into one trouble spot after another and to express again and again his sense of debt to the servicemen he puts in harm's way. Yet the series' next president comes into office committed to a less combative foreign policy. Opinions will of course differ as to whether, as the global system is presently constituted, an American government would be capable of renouncing militarism. The coffee pickers Wallace Shawn suddenly sees below the horizon have been beaten and kicked. Can refugees be set apart from economic migrants? Coercion may be inseparable from labor itself, and inseparable from the system that organizes that labor and ships off its rewards to beneficiaries far away. In that case, it would not be only the do-gooder or the nomad activist who can divulge the horrible and secret truth on which the system is based. In *A Few Good Men*, it's the one who applies the coercion, the uniformed overseer with the whip, who speaks the unspeakable.

4 I comment on this position in a review of *The Trouble with Diversity* in *n+1*: "Notice that you exist, for Michaels, entirely in the present tense; no part of you extends into the past or future. That's why he can speak of the disappearance of languages as a 'victimless crime.' There cannot be a victim, for no one is actually injured by anything that merely affects the memory of her ancestors or the future

of his children and grandchildren. Granted, much dangerous drivel is said in the name of ancestors and unborn grandchildren. Granted, remembering isn't always a solution or a satisfaction, even in the case of the Holocaust and the Middle Passage. There have to be protocols (difficult and complicated ones) regulating what and when and how much to remember, what and when and how much to forget. Otherwise you get Serbs butchering Albanians in the 1990s in the name of the betrayal at the Battle of Kosovo in 1389. But this doesn't mean ruling out transgenerational identification as if it were a bizarre pathology or a feudal survival. To ask one obvious question among many: what would become of the environmental movement if we agreed in advance not to recognize ourselves and our interests as exceeding the present moment?"

5 All appearances to the contrary, the rhetorical setup in Friedman (who includes no item for "sweatshop" in the index of *The World Is Flat*) has something in common with the stance of an antisweatshop writer such as Naomi Klein. Klein is telling her readers in effect that their economic self-interest—getting a really good deal on a cheap raincoat—works against the interest of the producers of their apparel, and shames them into surrendering something of that self-interest, or at worst reformulating it.

6 A relevant ancestor for the DeLillo passage and for much postapocalyptic discourse generally is Max Weber. Talking about scientific progress in "Science as a Vocation," Weber asks whether it means "that we, today, for instance, everyone sitting in this hall, have a greater knowledge of the conditions of life under which we exist than has an American Indian or a Hottentot? Hardly. Unless he is a physicist, one who rides on a streetcar has no idea how the car happened to get into motion. And he does not need to know. He is satisfied that he may 'count' on the behavior of the streetcar, and he orients his conduct according to this expectation; but he knows nothing about what it takes to produce such a car so that it can move. The savage knows incomparably more about his tools. . . . The savage knows what he does in order to get his daily food and which institutions serve him in this pursuit. The increasing intellectualization and rationalization do not, therefore, indicate an increased and general knowledge of the conditions under which one lives" (139). In this respect, envy of the so-called savage remains alive and well. I'm grateful to John Guillory, in a discussion years ago at the University of Washington, for pointing out to me that, if he shared some of Weber's nostalgia for romantic prespecialization, I was perhaps too uncritical of Durkheim's more positive take on the division of labor.

BIBLIOGRAPHY

Ahmad, Aijaz. *In Theory: Classes, Nations, Literatures.* London: Verso, 1992.

Ali, Tariq. "Corbyn's Progress." *London Review of Books,* March 3, 2016. http://tariqali.org/archives/3098.

Anderson, Amanda. "The Temptations of Aggrandized Agency: Feminist Histories and the Horizon of Modernity." *Victorian Studies* 43:1 (2000), 43–65.

Appadurai, Arjun. *Modernity at Large: Cultural Dimensions of Globalization.* Minneapolis, MN: University of Minnesota Press, 1996.

———, ed., *The Social Life of Things: Commodities in Cultural Perspective.* Cambridge: Cambridge University Press, 1986.

Appiah, Anthony. *Cosmopolitanism: Ethics in a World of Strangers.* New York: Norton, 2006.

Arthur, Paige. *Unfinished Projects: Decolonization and the Philosophy of Jean-Paul Sartre.* London: Verso, 2010.

Balibar, Étienne. "Exploitation." *Political Concepts: A Critical Lexicon.* 2016 (online). https://www.politicalconcepts.org/balibar-exploitation/.

Barry, Norman. *Welfare.* Milton Keynes, UK: Open University Press, 1990.

Basch, Linda, Nina Glick-Schiller, and Cristina Szanton Blanc. *Nations Unbound: Transnational Projects, Postcolonial Predicaments, and Deterritorialized Nation-States*. Amsterdam: Gordon and Breach, 1994.

Bass, Gary J. *The Blood Telegram: Nixon, Kissinger, and a Forgotten Genocide*. New York: Vintage, 2013.

———. *Freedom's Battle: The Origins of Humanitarian Intervention*. New York: Knopf, 2008.

Battistoni, Alyssa. "How to Change Everything." *Jacobin*, December 11, 2015 (online). https://www.jacobinmag.com/2015/12/naomi-klein-climate-change-this-changes -everything-cop21/.

Beckert, Sven. *Empire of Cotton: A Global History*. New York: Random House, 2014.

Bell, Larry. *Climate of Corruption*. Austin, TX: Greenleaf, 2011.

Berger, John. *Selected Essays*. Edited by Geoff Dyer. New York: Vintage, 2001.

Boltanski, Luc. *Distant Suffering: Morality, Media and Politics*. Translated by Graham Burchell. Cambridge: Cambridge University Press, 1999.

Börner, Stefanie. *Belonging, Solidarity, and Expansion in Social Policy*. Basingstoke, UK: Palgrave Macmillan 2013.

Bull, Malcolm. "Levelling Out." *New Left Review* (NEW SERIES) 70 (July/August 2011), 5–24.

Caparrós, Martín. "Counting the Hungry." *New York Times*, September 28, 2014, 4.

Carruth, Allison. "War Rations and the Food Politics of Late Modernism." *Modernism/Modernity* 16:4 (November 2009), 767–95.

Coe, Sophie D., and Michael D. Coe. *The True History of Chocolate*. London: Thames and Hudson, 1996.

Collingham, Lizzie. *The Taste of War: World War II and the Battle for Food*. New York: Penguin Books, 2013.

Conrad, Sebastian. *What Is Global History?* Princeton, NJ: Princeton University Press, 2016.

Cullather, Nick. *The Hungry World: America's Cold War Battle against Poverty in Asia*. Cambridge, MA: Harvard University Press, 2011.

d'Aymery, Gilles. "Context and Accuracy: George F. Kennan's Famous 'Quotation.'" *Swan's*, March 28, 2005 (online). http://www.swans.com/library/art11/ga192.html.

DeLillo, Don. *White Noise*. New York: Viking Penguin, 1986.

DePalma, Anthony. "15 Years on the Bottom Rung: Mexican Immigrants and the Specter of an Enduring Underclass." *New York Times*, Ma6 256, 2005, A1, A20, A21.

DeParle, Jason. "A Good Provider Is One Who Leaves." *New York Times Magazine*, April 22, 2007, 51–123.

Derrida, Jacques. *On Cosmopolitanism and Forgiveness*. Trans. Mark Dooley and Michael Hughes, with a preface by Simon Critchley and Richard Kearney. London: Routledge, 2001.

de Waal, Alex. *Famine Crimes: Politics and the Disaster Relief Industry in Africa*. Bloomington: Indiana University Press, 1997.

Diamond, Jared. "What's Your Consumption Factor?" *New York Times*, January 2, 2008, Op-Ed page.

Drezner, Daniel W. *Theories of International Relations and Zombies*. Rev. ed. Princeton, NJ: Princeton University Press, 2015.

Eliot, George. *Middlemarch: An Authoritative Text, Backgrounds, Reviews, and Criticism*. Edited by Bert G. Hornback. New York: Norton, 1977.

———. *Miscellaneous Essays*. Edited by Esther Wood. New York: Doubleday, 1901.

Fassin, Didier. "Inequality of Lives, Hierarchies of Humanity: Moral Commitments and Ethical Dilemmas of Humanitarianism." In *In the Name of Humanity: The Government of Threat and Care*, edited by Ilana Feldman and Miriam Ticktin, 238–55. Durham, NC: Duke University Press, 2010.

Fitzgerald, F. Scott. *Tender Is the Night*. New York: Scribner, 1933.

Fitzgibbons, Athol. *Adam Smith's System of Liberty, Wealth, and Virtue: The Moral and Political Foundations of The Wealth of Nations*. Oxford: Clarendon, 1995.

Fleischacker, Samuel. *A Short History of Distributive Justice*. Cambridge, MA: Harvard University Press, 2004.

———. *On Adam Smith's "Wealth of Nations": A Philosophical Companion*. Princeton, NJ: Princeton University Press, 2004.

Frank, Dana. *Buy American: The Untold Story of Economic Nationalism*. Boston: Beacon, 1999.

Fraser, Nancy. *Scales of Justice: Reimagining Political Space in a Globalizing World*. New York: Columbia University Press, 2009.

French, Peter A. "Morally Blaming Whole Populations." In *Philosophy, Morality, and International Affairs*, edited by Virginia Held, Sidney Morgenbesser, and Thomas Nagel, 266–85. New York: Oxford University Press, 1974.

Friedman, Thomas L. *The Lexus and the Olive Tree: Understanding Globalization*. New York: Anchor, 2000.

———. *The World Is Flat*. New York: Farrar Straus, 2005.

Gandhi, Leela. "Utonal Life: A Genealogy for Global Ethics," in Bruce Robbins and Paulo Lemos Horta, eds., *Cosmopolitanisms*. New York: New York University Press, 2017, 82–113.

Garfield, Simon, *Mauve: How One Man Invented a Color that Changed the World*. New York: Norton, 2001.

Gately, Iain. *Tobacco: A Cultural History of How an Exotic Plant Seduced Civilization*. New York: Grove Press, 2001.

Ginzburg, Carlo. "Killing a Chinese Mandarin: The Moral Implications of Distance, *Critical Inquiry* 21:1 (autumn 1994), 46–60.

Giraud, Pierre-Noël. *L'inégalité du monde: Economie du monde contemporain*. Paris: Gallimard, 1996.

Goodin, Robert E., and Christian Barry. "Benefiting from the Wrongdoing of Others." *Journal of Applied Philosophy* 31:4 (November 2014), 363–76.

Grandin, Greg. *Kissinger's Shadow: The Long Reach of America's Most Controversial Statesman*. New York: Metropolitan Books, 2015.

Haskell, Thomas. "Capitalism and the Origins of the Humanitarian Sensibility, Parts One and Two." *American Historical Review*, 90:2 (April 1985), 339–61, and 90:3 (June 1985), 547–66. Reprinted in Thomas Haskell, *Objectivity Is Not Neutrality: Explanatory Schemes in History*. Baltimore, MD: Johns Hopkins University Press, 1998.

Hayot, Eric. *The Hypothetical Mandarin: Sympathy, Modernity, and Chinese Pain*. Oxford: Oxford University Press, 2009.

Henry, Nancy. *George Eliot and the British Empire*. Cambridge: Cambridge University Press, 2002.

Henwood, Doug. "Awe, Shocks." *Left Business Observer* 117 (March 2008) (online), http://www.leftbusinessobserver.com/Shock.html.

Hernandez, Ester, and Susan Bibler Coutin. "Remitting Subjects: Migrants, Money and States." *Economy and Society* 35:2 (May 2006), 185–208.

Hickel, Jason. "Aid in Reverse: How Poor Countries Develop Rich Countries," *The Guardian*, 14 January 2017

Hitchens, Christopher. *The Trial of Henry Kissinger*. London: Verso, 2001.

———. *Why Orwell Matters*. New York: Basic Books, 2002.

Hochschild, Adam. *Bury the Chains: Prophets and Rebels in the Fight to Free an Empire's Slaves*. Boston: Houghton Mifflin, 2005.

Hont, Istvan. *Jealousy of Trade: International Competition and the Nation-State in Historical Perspective*. Cambridge, MA: Harvard University Press, 2005.

Hont, Istvan, and Michael Ignatieff, eds. *Wealth and Virtue: The Shaping of Political Economy in the Scottish Enlightenment*. Cambridge: Cambridge University Press, 1986.

Hsu, Hua. "The Year of the Imaginary College Student." *New York Times*, December 31, 2015 (online). http://www.newyorker.com/culture/cultural-comment/the-year-of-the-imaginary-college-student.

Jameson, Fredric. *An American Utopia: Dual Power and the Universal Army*. London: Verso, 2016.

———. *The Geopolitical Aesthetic: Cinema and Space in the World System*. Bloomington: Indiana University Press: BFI Publishing, 1992.

Jamieson, Dale. *Reason in a Dark Time: Why the Struggle against Climate Change Failed—and What It Means for Our Future*. New York: Oxford University Press, 2014.

Just, Daniel. *Literature, Ethics, and Decolonization in Postwar France: The Politics of Disengagement*. Cambridge: Cambridge University Press, 2015.

Kincaid, Jamaica. *Lucy*. New York: Farrar Straus, 2002.

———. *A Small Place*. New York: Farrar Straus, 2000.

Klein, Naomi. *No Logo: Taking Aim at the Brand Bullies*. New York: Picador, 2000.

———. Response to Elizabeth Kolbert. *New York Review of Books*, January 8, 2015, 60.

———. *The Shock Doctrine: The Rise of Disaster Capitalism*. New York: Metropolitan Books, 2007.

———. *This Changes Everything: Capitalism vs the Climate*. New York: Simon and Schuster, 2015.

Kolbert, Elizabeth. "Can Climate Change Cure Capitalism?" *New York Review of Books*, December 4, 2014, 14–16.

Kowaleski-Wallace, Elizabeth. *Consuming Subjects: Women, Shopping, and Business in the Eighteenth Century*. New York: Columbia University Press, 1997.

Kriegel, Lara. *Grand Designs: Labor, Empire, and the Museum in Victorian Culture*. Durham, NC: Duke University Press, 2007.

Kroll, Richard. "Pope and Drugs: The Pharmacology of *The Rape of the Lock*." *English Literary History* 67:1 (2000), 99–141.

Kurlansky, Mark. *Cod: A Biography of the Fish That Changed the World*. New York: Penguin, 1997.

Lamouchi, Noureddine. *Jean-Paul Sartre et le tiers monde: Rhétorique d'un discours anticolonialiste*. Paris: L'Harmattan, 1996.

Laqueur, Thomas. "Bodies, Details, and the Humanitarian Narrative." In *The New Cultural History*, edited by Lynn Hunt, 176–204. Berkeley: University of California Press, 1989.

Lelyveld, Joseph. "Interrogating Ourselves," *New York Times Magazine*, June 12, 2005, 36–69.

Lloyd, Genevieve. *The Man of Reason: "Male" and "Female" in Western Philosophy*. Second Edition. Minneapolis: University of Minnesota Press, 1993.

MacAskill, William. *Doing Good Better: How Effective Altruism Can Help You Make a Difference*. New York: Gotham, 2015.

MacFarquhar, Larissa. *Strangers Drowning: Grappling with Impossible Idealism, Drastic Choices, and the Overpowering Urge to Help*. New York: Penguin, 2015.

———. "Outside Agitator." *New Yorker*, December 8, 2008, 61–71.

Maher, Katherine. "Food Fights." *Bookforum*, December/January 2011, 37.

Make Do and Mend: Keeping Family and Home Afloat on War Rations. No author. With a foreword by Jill Norman. London: O'Mara, 2007.

Maren, Michael. *The Road to Hell: The Ravaging Effects of Foreign Aid and International Charity*. New York: Free Press, 1997.

Massing, Michael. "How to Cover the One Percent." *New York Review of Books*, January 16, 2016.

Meister, Robert. *After Evil: A Politics of Human Rights*. New York: Columbia University Press, 2011.

Menand, Louis. "Honest, Decent, Wrong: The Invention of George Orwell." *New Yorker*, January 27, 2003 (online). http://www.newyorker.com/magazine/2003/01/27/honest-decent-wrong.

Michaels, Walter. *The Trouble with Diversity*. New York: Metropolitan Books, 2007.

Milanović, Branko. *Global Inequality: A New Approach for the Age of Globalization*. Cambridge, MA: Harvard University Press, 2016.

———. *The Haves and Have-Nots: A Brief and Idiosyncratic History of Global Inequality*. New York: Basic, 2010.

———. *Worlds Apart: Measuring International and Global Inequality*. Princeton, NJ: Princeton University Press, 2005.

Moyn, Samuel. "Spectacular Wrongs: Gary Bass's 'Freedom's Battle.'" *Nation*, September 24, 2008.

Nagel, Thomas. "Better Ways to Help." *Times Literary Supplement*, November 18, 2015.

Onishi, Norimitsu. "Toiling Far from Home for Philippine Dreams." *New York Times*, September 18, 2010 (online). http://www.nytimes.com/2010/09/19/world/asia/19phils.html.

Orwell, George. Collected Essays: *Journalism and Letters*, edited by Sonia Orwell and Ian Angus, Harmondsworth, UK: Penguin, 1970.

———. "London Letter." *Partisan Review*, August 29, 1942.

———. *Orwell: The War Broadcasts*. Edited by William John West. London: Duckworth/BBC, 1985.

———. *The Road to Wigan Pier*. Harmondsworth, UK: Penguin, 1962 [1937].

———. "Not Counting Niggers." In *The Collected Essays: Journalism and Letters*, edited by Sonia Orwell and Ian Angus, 434–38. Vol. 1. Harmondsworth, UK: Penguin, 1970.

———. Review of *Letters on India*. by Mulk Raj Anand, *Tribune* 19 March 1943, *The Complete Works of George Orwell*, edited by Peter Davison. Vol. 15, *Two Wasted Years*. London: Secker and Warburg, 1998.

Ott, Julia C. *When Wall Street Met Main Street: The Quest for an Investors' Democracy*. Cambridge, MA: Harvard University Press, 2011.

Packer, George. "Dark Hours: Violence in the Age of the War on Terror." *New Yorker*, July 20, 2015. http://www.newyorker.com/magazine/2015/07/20/dark-hours.

Parfit, Derek. "Overpopulation and the Quality of Life." In *The Repugnant Conclusion*, edited by J. Ryberg and T. Tännsjö, 7–22. Dordrecht, the Netherlands: Kluwer Academic Publishers, 2004.

Phillips, Leigh. *Austerity Ecology and the Collapse-Porn Addicts: A Defence of Growth, Progress, Industry, and Stuff*. N.p.: Zero Books, 2015.

Rancière, Jacques. *Aux bords du politique*. Paris: Gallimard, 1997.

Reich, Robert. "Economic Prosperity Is Not a Zero-Sum Game." *Salon*, January 29, 2013 (online). http://www.salon.com/2013/01/29/economic_prosperity_isnt_a_zero_sum_game_partner/.

Rieff, David. *A Bed for the Night: Humanitarianism in Crisis*. New York: Simon and Schuster, 2002.

———. *The Reproach of Hunger: Food, Justice, and Money in the Twenty-First Century*. New York: Simon and Schuster, 2015.

Robbins, Bruce. "All of Us without Exception: Sartre, Rancière, and the Cause of the Other." In *The Meanings of Rights*, edited by Costas Douzinas and Conor Gearty, 251–71. Cambridge: Cambridge University Press, 2014.

———. "Blaming the System." In *Immanuel Wallerstein and the Problem of the World*, edited by David Palumbo-Liu, Nirvana Tanoukhi, and Bruce Robbins, 41–63. Durham, NC: Duke University Press, 2011.

———. "Do Something, Quick!" *boundary 2* 40:2 (summer 2013), 1–8.

———. "On the Rentier." *PMLA* 127:4 (October 2012), 905–11.

———. *Perpetual War: Cosmopolitanism from the Viewpoint of Violence*. Durham, NC: Duke University Press, 2012.

———. Review of Walter Benn Michaels. *The Trouble with Diversity: How We Learned to Love Identity and Ignore Inequality*. *n+1*, December 2006 (online), https://nplusonemag.com/online-only/online-only/magical-capitalism/.

———. "Sad Stories in the International Public Sphere: Richard Rorty on Culture and Human Rights." *Public Culture* 9:2 (winter 1997), 209–32.

———. *Upward Mobility and the Common Good: Toward a Literary History of the Welfare State*. Princeton, NJ: Princeton University Press, 2007.

Ross, Andrew. *Fast Boat to China: Corporate Flight and the Consequences of Free Trade, Lessons from Shanghai*. New York: Pantheon, 2006.

Rubenstein, Michael, et al., "Infrastructuralism." *Modern Fiction Studies* 61:4 (winter 2015).

Rushdie, Salman. *Midnight's Children*. Harmondsworth, UK: Penguin, 1980.

Sartre, Jean-Paul. Preface to *The Wretched of the Earth*, by Frantz Fanon, 26. Translated by Constance Farrington. New York: Grove Weidenfeld, 1963.

Schivelbusch, Wolfgang. *Tastes of Paradise: A Social History of Spices, Stimulants, and Intoxicants*. New York: Vintage, 1993.

Shavit, Ari. *My Promised Land: The Triumph and Tragedy of Israel*. New York: Spiegel and Grau, 2013.

Shawn, Wallace. *The Fever*. New York: Grove Press, 1991.

Silcoff, Mireille. "Pig Swill and Bones and Bottle Caps and Wire!" *New York Times Magazine*, March 13, 2011, 51.

Singer, Peter. "Famine, Affluence, and Morality" (1972). In *Writings on an Ethical Life*. New York: HarperCollins, 2000.

———. *The Most Good You Can Do: How Effective Altruism Is Changing Ideas about Living Ethically*. New Haven, CT: Yale University Press, 2015.

Smith, Adam. *The Theory of Moral Sentiments*. Edited by D. D. Raphael and A. L. MacFie. Oxford: Oxford University Press, 1976.

———. *The Wealth of Nations*. Edited by Edwin Cannan. Introduction by Robert Reich. New York: Modern Library, 2000.

Solnit, Rebecca. *A Paradise Built in Hell: The Extraordinary Communities that Arise in Disasters*. New York: Viking, 2009.

Stedman Jones, Gareth. *An End to Poverty? A Historical Debate*. London: Profile Books, 2004.

Sunkara, Bhaskar. "The Anarcho-Liberal." *Jacobin*, October 29, 2012. https://www.jacobinmag.com/2012/10/naomi-klein-as-anarcho-liberal/.

Sussman, Charlotte. *Consuming Anxieties: Consumer Protest, Gender, and British Slavery, 1713–1833*. Stanford, CA: Stanford University Press, 2000.

Swift, Jonathan. *Gulliver's Travels*. Edited by Christopher Fox. Boston: Bedford / St. Martin's, 1995.

Terry, Fiona. *Condemned to Repeat? The Paradox of Humanitarian Action*. Ithaca, NY: Cornell University Press, 2002.

Therborn, Göran. "Dynamics of Inequality." *New Left Review* 103 (Jan/Feb 2017), 67–85.

Thucydides, *History of the Peloponnesian War*, trans. Charles Foster Smith. Cambridge: Harvard University Press, 1935.

Varoufakis, Yanis. *The Global Minotaur: America, Europe, and the Future of the Global Economy.* London: Zed Books, 2015.

Vernon, James. *Hunger: A Modern History.* Cambridge, MA: Harvard University Press, 2007.

Warman, Arturo. *Corn and Capitalism: How a Botanical Bastard Grew to Global Dominance.* Translated by Nancy L. Westrate. Chapel Hill: University of North Carolina Press, 2003.

Weber, Max. *From Max Weber: Essays in Sociology.* Translated and edited by H.H. Gerth and C. Wright Mills. New York: Oxford University Press, 1946.

Weinberg, Bennett Alan, and Bonnie K. Bealer. *The World of Caffeine: The Science and Culture of the World's Most Popular Drug.* New York: Routledge, 2001.

Williams, Bernard. *In the Beginning Was the Word: Realism and Moralism in Political Argument.* Edited by Geoffrey Hawthorn. Princeton, NJ: Princeton University Press, 2005.

———. *Moral Luck: Philosophical Papers, 1973–1980.* Cambridge: Cambridge University Press, 1981.

Woolf, Virginia. *The London Scene: Six Essays on London Life.* Introduction by Francine Prose. New York: HarperCollins, 1975.

Žižek, Slavoj, and Srećko Horvat. *What Does Europe Want? The Union and Its Discontents.* New York: Columbia University Press, 2014.

Zuckerman, Larry. *The Potato: How the Humble Spud Rescued the Western World.* New York: North Point Press, 1998.

Antigua, 38, 100, 103
antisweatshop campaign, 9, 20, 59, 82, 99,
    164n2; Klein and, 95–101, 168n5
Appadurai, Arjun, 62–63
Appiah, Anthony, 162n4; *Cosmopolitanism*
    (2006), 17, 21, 27
Apple, 6, 13
asceticism, 20, 95, 162n4, 163n10; collective
    or mass, 90, 104, 107; of Orwell, 83–84
Asia, 4, 43, 52; Four Tigers of, 44–45; as
    home of bulk of British proletariat, 35,
    41; South, 51, 110. *See also specific names
    of Asian countries*
atrocities and massacres, 9, 29, 77, 86,
    156n11; American, 146, 157n4; Israeli,
    142–45; past, 147, 149
austerity, 89, 106, 107, 109, 123, 160n16,
    163n6; in Greece, 7, 11, 45
Australia, 2, 65, 66, 88, 110

Baby Boomers, parents of, 16
Balibar, Étienne, 113
Bangladesh, 10, 13, 91, 121
Barry, Norman, *Welfare* (1990), 80
Bass, Gary J., *Freedom's Battle* (2008),
    29–30
BBC, 43; Orwell and, 43, 85, 86–89, 160n2,
    162n4, 163n4, 163n5, 163n7
Bell, Larry, *Climate of Corruption* (2011),
    112
beneficiary, beneficiaries, 4, 5, 36, 40, 57,
    83, 108, 113, 118, 126, 130, 135, 138, 143,
    145, 152, 156n9, 167n3; Americans as, 13,
    150–51; capitalism and, 29, 53; escape
    from status of, 141–42; in *A Few Good
    Men*, 140–41; globalism and, 43, 48;
    history and, 50, 131; Klein and, 95; logic
    of, 96, 108, 142, 146, 147; Meister on,
    7–9; nonbeneficiaries and, 98, 103, 108,
    114, 154; of Orwell's British imperial
    system, 37, 86–87; of past violence,
    147, 156n11; in present tense, 148; as
    potential rescuers, 31; power of, 134;
    psychology of, 8; sacrifice and, 109,
    110; self-conscious, 98, 133; structural
    inequality and, 7, 152; as term, 5–6;

underdogs as, 135; United States as, 149.
    See also discourse of the beneficiary
Bengal, famine in, 21–23, 44, 73
Berger, John, 9, 126, 151; "Image of Imperi-
    alism" (2001), 125–26
Bhagwati, Jagdish, 70
Bibler Coutin, Susan, 112
Bilmes, Linda, 165n10
binary division of world, 18, 41; economic
    Orientalism and, 19, 31; in Klein, 96–97
Blair, Eric. *See* Orwell, George
blame, 157n4; self-, 52, 84, 162n2
Blockadia, 103
Boltanski, Luc, *Distant Suffering* (1999),
    18, 166n5
Börner, Stefanie, *Belonging, Solidarity, and
    Expansion in Social Policy* (2013), 81, 82
Bosnia, 77
Boston Tea Party, 59, 79
bourgeoisie, 41, 52. *See also* middle class
boycott(s), 59, 79, 147; consumer, 84,
    164n4; sugar, 58–59, 61, 82
Boycott, Divestment, and Sanctions
    against Israel (BDS), 147, 148
brands, 96, 98, 99, 100, 102, 164n4
British East India Company, 73
British Empire, 4, 35, 43, 61, 78, 85; Orwell
    and, 82, 83–84; tea trade and, 72–73
Bull, Malcolm, 118, 119; on nihilism, 120,
    165–66n1
Burma, 51
bystanders, as structural beneficiaries, 7

Canada, 98, 105
capitalism, 24, 69, 100, 105, 107–8, 159n16;
    anti-, 95, 107; arbitrage and, 24, 26;
    Bell on, 112; brands and, 164n4; British
    Empire and, 43; climate change and, 91;
    commitment and, 164n1; commodities
    and, 52–53; consumer, 97; disaster, 102;
    global, 11, 37, 44, 45, 65, 113, 136, 149;
    humanitarianism and, 28, 31; the left
    and, 33, 108; as link, 29; masculinity of,
    97; Orwell on, 9; profits and, 67; prog-
    ress and, 29; sacrifice and, 109; share-
    holders and, 167n10; as system, 49–50;

wage labor and, 48; waste in, 66; Weber on, 20; as world system, 40, 90, 159n11. *See also* corporations; free markets; market, markets

carbon emissions, 91; individuals and, 104, 111; public policy shifts needed to limit, 92

Caribbean, 40, 58

causality, causal linkages, 9, 27, 47, 59, 72, 80; chains of, 38, 72, 141; consciousness of, 26, 138; to distant suffering, 3, 9, 17; humanitarianism and, 23, 25, 28; Orwell and, 34

charity, 3, 17, 24, 29, 157n3. *See also* philanthropy

China, Chinese, 26, 43, 61, 71, 150; chip makers and, 13, 53, 141; earthquake and, 3–4, 11, 68–69; economic rise of, 44–45, 46; hinders market forces, 137; GDP per capita of, 45; opium trade and, 73, 160n3; tea trade and, 72–73

chocolate, 54, 55, 87

Churchill, Winston, 44

Clark, Wes, 148

class and class system, 40, 41, 83, 85; identity of, 40, 163n7; struggle of, 35, 52

climate change, 12, 59, 109, 112; capitalism and, 91; Klein on, 104, 136; morality and, 137; responsibility and, 127, 128; stopping, 92, 136, 164n11

coal mines and miners, 55, 87; Orwell and, 34, 55, 56, 64, 102

Coates, Ta-Nehisi, 148, 149

coercion, 4, 5, 56, 134; labor and, 167n3; world system and, 48

coffee, 90, 112, 141; pickers of, 167n3

Cold War, 8, 9, 35, 82, 86, 90, 136

Collingham, Lizzie, 44

colonialism, 37, 44; anti-, 49, 146; exploitation under, 48, 52, 73, 76; post-, 45

comfort(s), 34, 52, 109, 155n4; of English, 86–87, 88. *See also* luxuries

commitment, 98, 164n1; of Klein, 98, 102

commodities, 5, 24, 58, 63, 64, 73, 74, 79, 149; brand-name, 102; capitalism and, 52–53; consumer and, 12; cultural per-

spective on, 62–63; democratization of, 54–55; fetishism of, 39–40, 60, 90; historians of, 63–64; recognition of, 52–64, 79. *See also names of individual commodities*

common good, 102, 134

common sense, 8–9, 11, 60–61, 79, 129, 132, 136, 147; moral, 130, 137

communism, 33, 34

complicity, 22, 23, 47

consumer(s), 17, 54, 64, 84, 79, 89, 92, 96, 97, 99, 101, 102, 104, 105; consumerism and, 17, 66, 94, 162n4; First World, 10, 108; ethical, 21, 108; power of, 54–55; responsibility of, 64, 92, 104; spending by, 160n16; women as, 56–59, 67. *See also* boycott, boycotts

consumption, 19, 91, 136: ethical, 10; gendered politics of, 58–59; luxurious or affluent, 17, 18–19, 56, 58; restrictions on British wartime, 87–88, 90; work ethic and, 20–21

Corbyn, Jeremy, 165n10

corporations, 26, 114, 167n10; transnational brand-name, 96–101, 102, 164n4

corruption, 27, 40, 61, 69, 73, 121

cosmopolitanism, 2, 11, 13, 61, 79, 80, 91, 129, 153; of Orwell, 9, 82–83

cotton, 61

Cruise, Tom, 139, 140, 144

culpability, 84, 127, 146

cultural economy, global, 62–63

"currently dominant, conventional, normative, or institutional," 135–38

David Copperfield, 130–31

Dayan, Moshe, 143

Deb, Siddhartha, 45–46

debts, 42, 56, 152; civilian, 13, 143, 167n3; to living and dead, 148; past and present, 149

decency, 26, 46, 56, 83, 89, 134

delayed gratification, 20

Deleuze, Gilles, 46, 47

DeLillo, Don, *White Noise* (1986), 151–52, 168n6

fantasy, 70, 71, 157n5

fascism, 51, 86, 163n4; anti-, 51, 52, 89, 160n2. *See also* Nazis

fashion and taste, 64, 87, 95, 99, 102, 103

Fassin, Didier, on humanitarianism, 30, 31

Feeding America (NGO), 15, 16

feeling(s), 2, 3, 6, 13, 39, 55, 104, 131; of Klein, 103–5, 108; of loyalty, 153; organizing, 31; of outrage, 18; of sympathy, 68. *See also* fairness; responsibility

Ferguson, Niall, 43

Few Good Men, A (1992), 139–42, 167n2, 167n3

financial crisis of 2008, 26, 36, 95, 130, 159n12

First World, 2, 41, 42, 46, 51; consumers in, 10, 108. *See also* North, global; West, the

Fitzgerald, F. Scott, *Tender is the Night* (1934), 57–58

food: insecurity of, 16; prices for, 24; rationing of, 12, 43–44, 87–89

foreigners, 79, 128–29, 150; distant, 17, 35, 52

foreign policy, 22, 162n4, 167n3; foreign aid and, 29

fossil fuels, 105–6, 149. *See also* coal mines and miners; oil

Foucault, Michel, 29

Foxconn, 6, 141

fracking, earthquakes and, 30

France, 77, 123, 130, 159n10; Algeria and, 12, 76–78

Frank, Dana, *Buy American!* (1999), 79

Fraser, Nancy, *Scales of Justice* (2009), 122

freedom of transnational corporations, 98, 165n11

free markets, 27–28, 78–79, 95, 103, 105; admirers and champions of, 61, 70, 107, 151; social justice and, 81; welfare state and, 80, 82

Friedman, Thomas, 11, 56, 67, 99, 150; on globalization, 160–61n6; *The Lexus and the Olive Tree* (2000), 149–50; *The World Is Flat* (2005), 53, 150–51, 168n5

Gaza, 145

gaze, the, 49

Gandhi, Leela, 135

Gandhi, Mohandas K., 59, 134, 135, 163–64n10, 167n12

gender: of capitalism, 97; consumption and, 56–57

genocide, 22–23, 146, 148

Genussmittel (articles of pleasure), 64

Germany, 53, 66, 123, 160n16, 161n9. *See also* Nazis

globalization, globalists, 11, 13, 27, 43, 46, 99, 149, 150; anti-, 82, 95

global warming, 108–9, 110. *See also* climate change

God, 42, 70

Golden Rule, 144

Gollancz, Victor, 34

Good Housekeeping, 64

Good Samaritan, 18, 20, 21, 157n3

Gore, Al, 91

government, 17, 40, 76, 105, 114, 160–61n6, 162n12; British, 44, 45, 73, 86–89, 162n4; Chinese, 73, 137, 162n12; climate change and, 112; sacrifice and, 107, 114; U.S., 73, 106, 137, 167n3

Graeber, David, 120

Great Britain, 4, 58; India and, 59, 78, 162–63n4; Ministry of Information, 12, 86, 88; in World War II, 12, 105–6, 163n7. *See also* British Empire; England

Great Depression, 16, 107

Greece, 120, 123, 159n12; ancient, 56; austerity in, 7, 11, 45

Guevara, Che, 125, 126

Guillory, John, 168n6

guilt, 37, 41, 42, 85, 159n10; Orwell and, 52; in Rushdie's *Midnight's Children*, 158n9

Haaretz, 142

Habash, George, 144

habits, 85, 93, 136

Haiti, 115

Haskell, Thomas L., 72, 124, 125; on abolitionism, 28–29, 68; on capitalism, 31, 164n1; on no-fault suffering, 30; progressivism of, 29; on vegetarianism, 158n13; on Williams, 132

Macedonia, 212

MacFarquhar, Larissa, 24, 105, 132, 150, 157n5, 163–64n10; on do-gooders, 91, 92; on Klein, 12, 94, 97–98, 164n2; "Outside Agitator" (*New Yorker*, 2008), 94, 97–98; *Strangers Drowning* (2015), 10, 12, 15–17, 21, 34, 91–94, 117, 134

mainstream media, 129

Malta Conference (2015), 221–22

Maren, Michael, *The Road to Hell* (1997), 29

market(s), 28, 48; demand of, 62, 89; distant, 149; state intervention in, 104, 137

Marx, Karl, 41, 48, 60; *The Communist Manifesto*, 33

Marxism, Marxists, 33–34, 42; orthodox, 48, 108, 113

masculinity: of capitalism, 97; of state, 105

Massing, Michael, "How to Cover the One Percent" (2016), 24–25

Mediterranean, refugees drowned in, 122

Meister, Robert, *After Evil* (2011), 7–9, 156n11

membership, action and, 84

Menand, Louis, 52

mercantilist misogyny, 11

metropolis, metropolitan center or core, 13, 43, 126, 145, 152; austerity in, 107, 109; beneficiaries in, 5, 41, 110; workers in, 114, 134; under world system theory, 40

Mexico, 30, 145, 161n9; illegal immigrants from, 40, 41

Michaels, Walter Benn, *The Trouble with Diversity* (2007), 148, 167–68n4

middle class, 27, 37, 85, 87. *See also* bourgeoisie

migration, migrant workers, 40, 165n11; refugees vs., 121–22, 167n3; remittances and, 112–13, 146

Milanović, Branko, 11, 42, 111; *Global Inequality* (2016), 43; *Worlds Apart* (2005), 47

militarism, 140, 142, 153, 165n10; renouncing, 141, 167n3

military: humanitarianism and, 29, 37, 78; interventions of, 29, 78, 167n3

misogyny, 57, 63, 64; mercantilist, 11, 162n2

mobility, 123

modernity, 29

morality, 3, 29, 47, 61, 67, 70, 71, 72, 95, 118, 124, 134, 137, 144, 164n3; commonsense, 137; critique of, 12, 56; intuitions of, 25, 26, 27, 28; moral improvement and, 29; moralism and, 42, 56; moralizing of commodity and, 58; norms of, 2; Orwell's moral vision and, 46, 47; philosophers of, 17, 25; relevance of, 95; responsibility of, 28, 126–27, 149

moral obligation, 10, 21, 47; local vs. distant, 18, 20, 27

Morocco, 121

Moyn, Samuel, 29–30

Munayyer, Spiro, 144

Nakba, 147

nationalism, 13, 44; commodity recognition and, 79; humanitarianism and, 29–30; Orwell and, 83, 89, 90

nation-states, 12, 42, 78, 80, 90, 91, 122, 147; borders of, 119, 120; climate change and, 92

Native Americans, 145, 146, 147, 148

Nauru island, 110–11

Nazis, 82, 90, 144, 163n9

necessities, 28, 62, 64, 132; infrastructure as, 102–3; luxuries vs., 63, 103

neoliberal hegemony, 8

Netanyahu, Benjamin, 147

New Deal, institutions of, 102, 103–4

Newsroom, The, 140

New Yorker, 12, 94, 95, 99

New York Review of Books, 92, 104

New York Times, 40, 53

NGOs: Feeding America, 15, 16; global justice and, 112

Nicholson, Jack, in *A Few Good Men*, 139–42, 147, 152, 167n2

Nicole, in Fitzgerald's *Tender is the Night*, 57–58

Nietzsche, Friedrich, 12, 120, 125, 135, 165n1; *The Genealogy of Morals*, 124

nihilism, 21, 120, 125, 152, 165–66n1

"99 percent" slogan, 35–36, 85, 153

nonbeneficiaries, 98, 103, 108, 114, 119, 154

Norman, Jill, 106
North, global, 41, 44, 50, 84, 153
novelists, MacFarquhar, 117–18
nuclear weapons, 129

obligation, 47, 115, 153
Occupy Movement, 35–36
oil, 2, 30, 58, 64, 90
ongoingness, 148, 149
Onishi, Norimitsu, 114
opium trade, 4, 61, 64, 72, 73, 84, 160n3;
oppression, foreign vs. domestic, 26
Orientalism, Orientalists; economic, 11, 31,
    48, 50, 110, 137
Orwell, George, 9, 10, 37–38, 41, 47, 64, 72,
    85, 102, 111, 130, 146, 151, 160n2, 162n4;
    admirers of, 136; *Animal Farm*, 35; as-
    ceticism of, 83–84; BBC and, 43, 86–89,
    160n2, 162n4, 163n4, 163n5, 163n7; on
    British imperial system, 26, 34–35, 37,
    51–52, 83, 131–32, 133; British Ministry of
    Information and, 12, 86; career of, 82–83,
    86; colonial wealth of family of, 52, 73,
    84, 160n3; death of, 90; on decency, 26,
    46, 56, 133; on food rationing, 43–44,
    87–89, 107, 119; on Gandhi, 134, 135,
    163–64n10, 167n12; on global injustice,
    84; on India, 10–11, 45, 46, 88; the left
    and, 34; leveling out and, 119; "London
    Letter" (1942), 88; moral vision of, 42,
    118; *1984*, 35, 88, 90, 163n6; present and,
    146; *The Road to Wigan Pier*, 34, 35, 86,
    131; shared structural contradiction and,
    49; state power and, 89–90; use of "you"
    by, 11; on wartime morale, 106; zero-sum
    vision of, 44, 49, 50
Other, 48, 49, 126; cause of, 76, 77, 78;
    faraway, 136, 152
Ott, Julia, *When Wall Street Met Main
    Street* (2011), 130
Overseas Filipino Workers (OFWs), 40, 114

Packer, George, 129
Pakistan, 121
Palestine: ethnic cleansing of, 145; military
    conquest of, 142; Occupation of, 144

Palestinians, 148; crimes against, 147;
    Lydda massacre of, 13, 142–46; under-
    standable violence of, 144
Pappé, Ilan, 144
parasitism, 130, 133, 134
Parfit, Derek, 119–20; "Overpopulation
    and the Quality of Life" (2004), 118
Paris, 76, 77
partiality, selfish, 124
Partisan Review, 88
past, 71, 147, 149; as problematic, 142, 146,
    156n11
peasants, 39, 126, 132, 156n4
Pericles, 56
periphery, 5, 43, 46, 134; core and, 13, 40,
    43
pessimism, 29
philanthropy, philanthropists, 24–25. *See
    also* charity
Philippines, 53, 101, 115; remittances and,
    40, 114, 146; Rosario in, 96, 97, 114,
    165n14
Phillips, Leigh, 94, 104, 107; *Austerity
    Ecology and the Collapse-Porn Addicts*
    (2015), 18–19, 34, 111
politeness, rules of, 6
politics, 5, 9, 62, 76, 83, 85, 92, 103, 105, 114,
    123, 164n7; boycotts and, 58–59; com-
    modity recognition and, 59; double-
    action, 101–2; ethics and, 76, 78; hu-
    manitarianism and, 23, 78, 153; identity,
    49, 100, 124; local, 110; political action
    and, 43; political engagement and, 3, 7;
    political movements and, 43; women
    and, 67–68
pollution, 45, 46, 165n14
Popular Front for the Liberation of Pales-
    tine, 144
postapocalyptic discourse, 168n6
poverty, poor, 111, 156n4, 156n13,
    160–61n6; in Africa, 121–22; in Amer-
    ica, 15, 19, 37; common sense of, 60–61;
    in England, 35, 56, 106; global, 24, 40,
    41, 122; in India, 45–46; in metropolis,
    145; relativity of, 19; responsibility and,
    122; of Third World, 42

power, 68, 70, 90, 166n5; of consumers, 54–55; indirect, 134; of individuals, 70; life and, 126, 135; networks of, 67; proximity to, 126; radicalism and, 125

present, 156n11, 167–68n4; presentism and, 148–49

privatization of infrastructure, 103

privilege, 6, 19, 46–47, 49, 102, 119; of beneficiaries, 138; white, 13, 145

production, 63, 101; distant, 62, 96, 99, 152; invisible, 65–66; Third World, 10, 103, 108

profits, 97, 102

progress, 92, 136, 168n6; humanitarianism and, 29, 30

proletariat, British, 35, 41; Orwell's Proles in *1984* and, 88

propaganda, Orwell and, 86

protests, by students, 138

public opinion, 107

public policy, 107, 136–37; carbon emissions and, 92, 104

psychology, 8, 20

Quakers, 28, 58

quiescence, 25

Rabin, Yitzhak, 143

racism, 30, 76, 147; in United States, 79, 148

Rancière, Jacques, 12, 76; "The Cause of the Other," 75, 77–78

rationing in World War II, 12, 44, 87–89, 91, 104, 107, 119; as precedent, 105–6, 115

realism, 129

recycling in World War II, 106

redistribution of global resources, 7, 8, 12, 27, 92, 153; justice of, 91; movement for, 94; possibility of, 115; remittances as, 113; UN and, 112; violence and, 137–38

redistribution of resources and wealth, 45–46, 79, 82, 90, 112–13. *See also* welfare state

refugees, 12, 110–11, 120–22, 123, 167n3

remittances, 12, 40, 112–13, 146; as sacrifice, 114, 115

rentier, 130, 132–33; Orwell and, 131–32, 133; shareholders and dividends and, 26, 167n10

reparations, 8, 148, 156n11

rescue, fantasy of, 157n5

responsibility, moral, 23, 104, 157n4; attribution of, 127; causal, 3, 23; collective, 23–24; for financial disaster of 2008, 130; guilt and, 37; individual, 11, 27, 64, 80–81, 92; Malta Conference and, 121–22; poverty and, 122; relevance of, 128; vectors of, 41

revisionism, 41, 43, 113

rich, the, 124, 131

Rieff, David: *A Bed for the Night* (2002), 29; *The Reproach of Hunger* (2015), 24, 29

Robbins, Bruce: *Perpetual War* (2012), 10, 153; *Upward Mobility and the Common Good* (2007), 11–12

romanticism, 126

Rorty, Richard, 124

rubber, 65

Rwanda, 77

sacrifice(s), 96, 104, 154; austerity and, 109; beneficiary and, 110; of migrant workers, 113; remittances as, 114, 115; wartime, 106, 112, 163n9; zones of, 110–11

Said, Edward, 49; on Orientalism, 11, 19; *Orientalism*, 48

Sanders, Bernie, 13, 35

Sartre, Jean-Paul, 9, 12, 48, 49, 78, 85, 146, 151, 159n10; Rancière on, 75, 76

Schengen agreement, 120

Schivelbusch, Wolfgang, *Tastes of Paradise* (1993), 64

science fiction, 122

Scotland, 4, 74

Seattle World Trade Organization protests (1999), 95

self, 20, 21, 37, 49, 64, 80, 93, 99, 132; abolishing part of, 85, 90–91, 119, 136, 152, 154; blame of, 52, 84, 162n2; punishment, 16, 90; sacrifice of, 94–95

self-interest, 69, 101; of Klein, 99; moral

television shows, 140
terrorism, terrorists, 120, 121, 122, 123, 129,
    130; September 11, 2001, 20–21, 59, 99
Terry, Fiona, *Condemned to Repeat?*
    (2002), 29
Third World, 2, 16–17, 41, 42, 51, 141;
    antisweatshop movement and, 96–101;
    producers in, 10, 103, 108; Third World-
    ism and, 42, 49
time and temporality, 142
tobacco, 90, 163n7
toleration, moral, 134
Tolstoy, Leo, 134
Toronto, 98
totalitarianism, 90
tourism, tourists, 100–101, 203
Townsend, Lucy, 58
Trump, Donald, 2, 13
truth, as unhandleable, 139–40, 143
Tsipras, Alexis, 7
tsunami of 2004, 95
Turkey, 120
Tusk, Donald, 121
Twain, Mark, 152
2,000-Watt Society, 91

unemployment, 22, 34, 45, 80, 123, 146,
    161n6
United Nations (UN), 8, 112
United States, 16, 30, 36, 45, 79, 105, 106,
    129, 137, 149, 161n6; Abu Ghraib scandal
    and, 128–29; as beneficiary, 150–51; civil
    rights movement in, 59; class in, 40;
    consumer spending in, 160n16; elections
    in, 23, 103; financial disaster of 2008 in,
    26, 36, 95, 130, 159n12; as giant vacuum
    cleaner, 159n12; graduated income tax
    in, 137–38; invades Iraq, 95, 121; jobs
    shipped overseas from, 156n10; loss by,
    150–51; middle class in, 37; military in,
    139–40, 165n10; patriotism in, 124; poor
    in, 19, 111; refugees and, 120; remittances
    and, 113, 115, 146; starvation in, 16; State
    Department, 1–2; as 12,000 watt soci-
    ety, 91; world economic disparity and,
    1–3, 137; as world policeman, 141

"us" and "we," 109, 151; as beneficiaries,
    36, 37
utilitarianism, 10, 67, 93, 118, 124, 156n2;
    anti-, 21, 119
utopian, 68

vegetarianism, 29, 72, 158n13
Vernon, James, 16; *Hunger: A Modern His-
    tory* (2007), 28, 30
victimization, victims, 29, 30, 61, 67, 76,
    82, 99, 103, 135, 145, 167n4; in United
    States, 145–46, 148
Victorians, 80, 81
Vietnam, 77; U.S. war in, 157n4, 167n2
violence: beneficiaries of past, 143–44,
    156n11; drug, 146; founding, 145, 147;
    leveling in world's resources by, 137–38;
    military, 13, 140; nation-states and, 147;
    political, 76, 77; refugees from, 120–21;
    slavery and, 48; at Standing Rock, 148;
    terrorism and, 122; Tolstoy and, 134
vitalism, of Nietzsche, 125
Volcker shock, 103

wages, 97, 114, 158n13
Wallerstein, Immanuel, 11, 41, 42, 47–48,
    63, 158–59n4, 159n11; world system of,
    40, 48, 62
Wall Street, 24, 26, 130
war, 92, 106, 121; sacrifice during, 106, 112,
    163n9; shifting priorities in, 91–92;
    U.S.-Iraq, 121, 129; Vietnam, 157n4,
    167n2. *See also* World War II
waste, 66, 67, 125
Weber, Max, 20, 168n6
welfare state, 80, 133, 162n2; emergence
    of, 11–12; origins of, 81–82; postwar,
    89–90
West, the, 48, 101, 136; affluent consump-
    tion in, 18–19, 111; position of disparity
    of, 2, 3
West, William John, 88, 163n5, 163n6
white privilege, 13, 145
Williams, Bernard, 12, 21, 124, 125, 135, 153;
    Moral Luck (1981), 95–96; on slavery,
    28–29

women, 67; as garment workers, 98, 99; luxuries and, 56, 57–58, 63, 64; sugar boycott by, 98–99

Woolf, Virginia, 9, 11; on London docks, 64–68

work, 133; Orwell on, 130–31

"Workers of the world, unite!," 33, 41

working class, workers, 41, 97, 114, 141; British, 35, 52, 87; at metropolitan core, 40, 114; migrants as, 112, 113

world, 18, 44; intolerability of, 125–26

World Bank, 42, 110, 112

world-systems theory, 40, 41, 42, 48, 62, 113, 158–59n4, 159n5

world trade, 64, 66, 90

World War II, 90, 91, 92, 89, 106; Orwell and, 35, 82, 87–89, 90, 106; rationing in, 12, 43–44, 87–89, 91, 104, 105–6, 107, 119

yahoos, in *Gulliver's Travels*, 56–57

"you," 11, 18, 36; aggressive, 38, 151, 167n2; relations to distant places of, 38–39

zero-sum economics, 49, 159–60n16; of Orwell, 44, 50

Zionism: expulsion and, 142–43

zombies, 122, 129–30